An introduction to branding

Melissa Davis

With a theoretical commentary by Jonathan Baldwin

ava | **Academia**
the environment of learning

IMPRINT

An AVA Book
Published by AVA Publishing SA
Rue des Fontenailles 16
Case postale
1000 Lausanne 6
Switzerland
Tel: +41 786 005 109
Email: enquiries@avabooks.ch

Distributed by Thames & Hudson (ex-North America)
181a High Holborn
London WC1V 7QX
United Kingdom
Tel: +44 20 7845 5000
Fax: +44 20 7845 5055
Email: sales@thameshudson.co.uk
www.thamesandhudson.com

English Language Support Office
AVA Publishing (UK) Ltd.
Tel: +44 1903 204 455
Email: enquiries@avabooks.co.uk

ISBN 2-940373-00-0

10 9 8 7 6 5 4 3 2 1

Design and chapter photography:
www.barkdesign.net

Production and separations by AVA Book Production Pte. Ltd., Singapore
Tel: +65 6334 8173
Fax: +65 6334 0752
Email: production@avabooks.com.sg

Index by Indexing Specialists (UK) Ltd.

More Than a Name

An introduction to branding

AVA Publishing SA
Switzerland

CONTENTS

MARKETING THEORY CONTENTS

INTERVIEW CONTENTS

HOW TO USE THIS BOOK

THEORY   PAGE / 42

See 'The Vision Thing'

INTERVIEW   PAGE / 67

See Karen Rice Gardiner

Theory Indicator
The theory sections are particularly relevant to specific places in the chapters they introduce – look for these Theory Indicators to see where. Refer back to the theory when you see these indicators to gain a fuller, more rounded understanding of the point being explained.

Interview Indicator
The interviews are particularly relevant to specific sections in the chapters they conclude – look for these Interview Indicators to see where. Read the interviews alongside the page featuring the Interview Indicator to gain a first-hand account of the point being explained in the text.

MORE THAN A NAME   CHAPTER 02 / HOW BRANDS ARE MADE

THEORY CHAPTER 02 /

The Vision Thing

Brands don't just arrive out of nowhere. They are the product of a company 'vision'. Although making lots of money is a vision of sorts, it is not exactly specific. Any successful brand needs to be part of a clearly defined set of objectives. Good objectives are often described as 'SMART':

Specific – What exactly do we want to achieve? Increased sales? Improved shareholder dividend? Greater market share?

Measurable – To what extent do we want to achieve these things? Objectives need targets that can be measured so a success is registered, or so that people involved can see early on that the plan isn't working. What increased revenue would be seen as a success? How much more of the market should be captured? What would shareholders see as acceptable when the company reports its profits?

Achievable – All objectives cost, whether in terms of money or human resources. There is no point setting out on a plan if the skills are not available, or if you depend on another company for components, but know there is a worldwide shortage at the moment. Companies can actually be too successful, and while running out of a product may increase its desirability it also hits its income and profits, so setting an achievable objective is vital; don't be too ambitious!

Realistic – Is it really likely that you will capture 100 per cent of the available market, make all your shareholders millionaires overnight or triple your profits in one year? Nobody ever got rich by being too timid and lacking ambition, but setting targets that are completely unrealistic is likely to result in failure.

Timed – When do you want to achieve the objective? Again, be realistic, but don't plan too far ahead either. Five-year visions tend to have lots of 12–18 month plans within them, and those plans in turn have 'milestone' events built-in where progress is checked. An objective can be achieved in a few days if it is small enough ('inform all stakeholders of our plans for a new product launch' could be done via a press release and email), but these tend to be part of a bigger objective (e.g. 'launch a new product'). Never set an objective as 'ongoing' – it will never be achieved.

A SMART objective might read something like: 'Increase revenue by eight per cent over the next 12 months by raising sales of our core product to the currently under-represented male 18–25 consumer group.'

Objectives like this allow everyone to stay focused on what is required, and develop a strategy that will help it be achieved. The brand will form part of this strategy somewhere along the line either as it is, or through modification, or even in the development of new brands. If the core product mentioned in the example above were a skin moisturiser, one possible strategy might involve launching a new, more masculine branded version of an existing product, which might be easier than trying to convince men that they should use a brand they associate with women. However, a product like a drink or snack item might be slightly repackaged, or promoted differently without any major change to the brand's overall identity.

Before decisions like this can be made, other tools need to be used such as the Ansoff matrix (see page 126) and a SWOT analysis (see pages 40–41).

"Brands don't just arrive out of nowhere. They are the product of a company 'vision'"

Stakeholder: The broader audience that the brand affects, including investors, press, customers, employees and associations.

42

MIXED MESSAGES | INTERVIEW | KAREN GARDINER

interview 2

From the brand manager's perspective:
Karen Rice Gardiner, Director of Creative Services, National Geographic Society

You say you undertook the rebrand to provide some consistency of the brand work internationally. Were there any other reasons for the rebrand, such as extending your audience reach?

We wanted to foster a perception that we were more relevant and contemporary than perhaps some people thought we were. We are a 'legend' brand and that means we need to work especially hard at proving relevancy and a contemporary attitude.

Was any research undertaken and what was the outcome?

We undertook a large quantitative branding survey, which measured ourselves against competitors in the same media categories, to discover what consumers thought of us and wanted from us. This survey also identified what kind of consumer (and their lifestyle characteristics and demographics) would be most likely to want to interact with us. We developed four customer segments from this research – the top tier were the most interested in the content we have.

Did you create new brand identity themes, such as the theme of exploration?

They are not new, but we had not, up until this point, really brought them into sharp focus. Many of us would work off one or two of them, but few of us used all of them most of the time. It is like a six-cylinder car running only on four cylinders. The car doesn't go as fast or as far.

How have you stayed true to National Geographic's core values through your rebrand – such as your commitment to education, and the magazine?

The rebrand helped us focus on our core values. It did not change them.

Is there any flexibility in applying the guidelines, both in design and language? For example, if the designer is creating for media such as the mobile phone.

There is not a lot of leeway granted for the use of the National Geographic house-mark because we use it as the identifier of the source of the product or the communication. So we insist that it is clearly visible and not impeded by other design elements or messages. Small spaces, like mobile phone screens, definitely present the toughest design problems for us. That was part of the reason why we changed the typeface in the logo, because it was too hard to read at small sizes. With regard to language, different media groups here use different taglines. We tried to make a single tagline work, but had no success. I think it is because the different media types (e.g. TV, print and digital) make a very big difference in the way our content is applied.

What has the rebrand done to improve the National Geographic brand? Has it increased brand equity or reputation, improved your ranking as one of the most-recognised global brands, or helped to attract a younger audience?

We think that it is working in all of these areas. We know it is resonating in our ability to attract a younger audience. We have not done any specific surveying because we are confident that we needed to do this rebranding.

67

Theory
Most visual arts degrees demand 20–30 per cent written work and these sections are a study aid for students working on this part of their degrees.

The theory section at the beginning of each chapter explains the academic and professional marketing theories that are often used to hone branding techniques explained in that chapter.

These sections are written by academic, Jonathan Baldwin, who is a lecturer in cultural theory to graphic design students.

Glossary Reminder
In addition to the glossary at the front of the book, the branding terms are re-explained on the page where they feature, for ease of understanding.

Interviews
Each chapter contains at least one interview with an industry expert. These interviews offer first-hand accounts of working with brands, as well as commentary on branding as a discipline. Interviews are included with branding agencies, brand trends people, graphic designers and design leaders from some of the world's largest brands.

Navigation
The navigation at the top of the page helps you gauge where you are within the book. It lists the chapter and the chapter heading at the top of the left-hand page, and the top of the right-hand page highlights the current section while also giving the title of the section before and the section after.

Headings
Each chapter is divided into headings and subheadings to signal what the text is discussing – this way, you can dip in and out of the book depending on what you are looking for. The table of contents lists all the book's main headings, and there are further contents details at the start of each chapter.

Pull quote
Quotes appear throughout the book to emphasise key points on the page. Like the headings, these work as signposts to the page's contents. Some of these quotes give a voice to industry leaders who have commented on the point being discussed, and where this happens, the quote is attributed beneath.

Caption heading and caption text
The captions support the images and explain the visual examples of the ideas and concepts discussed in the main text. The heading gives the factual details of the image, and where the design was not created by the brand team, the design companies are credited. Not all images show best practice within branding, but all are there to provide examples and offer ideas. The numbering beside the caption corresponds to the number beside the image or group of images.

Footnote
Where another publication is referenced within the main text or captions, a footnote gives the necessary information for you to research that publication further. A small number after the reference corresponds with the number on the footnote.

Main text
These subheaded essays fully explain the study of modern branding in all its complexity. Read this for a thorough understanding of branding, for fascinating examples and arguments, and to learn how to successfully brand a product or service yourself.

Tips for designers
There are tips placed throughout the book that can help graphic designers understand and focus on the job ahead. The tips appear within white boxes on the page.

INTRODUCTION

Brands and branding have always been hugely influenced by graphic designers. The visual interpretation and translation of brands to an audience is a fundamental element of branding. It is the emotional cornerstone for both the organisation and the product being sold. Design connects the audience to the brand.

Graphic designers often view their role in branding as logo creation, starting and ending with the brand mark, yet the graphic designer's role is much more extensive and requires knowledge beyond that of how to make an attractive identity. Branding is about understanding the brand values and positioning, and developing an expression across the various media. Failure to understand this role will ultimately undersell the brand. A good brand will tell a good story about the product or service and the organisation behind it, and the designer is part of the translation process – they are the artist and narrator of ideas.

The graphic designer invites people to re-examine their perceptions, to encapsulate a direction and create an emotional connection between the brand and its audience. It is no exaggeration to say that branding can change people's lives both as customers and employees. Empathetic brand expression can encourage success, adventure, exploration and risk-taking in small ways (like changing one brand of computer to another, unfamiliar one), to major life-changing events (like charity engagement or career changes). Good design will integrate what the brand says and does, and it requires creative involvement in the brand development process from the outset to completion.

This book explores the brand creation process and its impact on the designer. It aims to give designers a broader understanding of the business behind the brand, so that they can take a more informed role and realise their value within the branding process and the value of design as an asset to a brand. The aim is to encourage an integrated brand development process that results in a strong creative execution relevant to the brand audience.

The role of graphic design is changing as the brand environment changes. Brands are constantly seeking new ways of expressing ideas and communicating with audiences; they are continually seeking new and creative ways of promoting themselves to stand out from the rest. This has extended the role of the graphic designer into new areas of brand expression – to bring the brand to life through brand experiences and sensory connections, and then move beyond the experience by creating emotional connections.

The role of design in branding has also become more influential with a shift from a product-driven to an experience-led approach. The remit of the graphic designer is broader, because the expression of the brand experience can now be so broad. The graphic designer may play a much more influential role at the outset of projects offering ideas and knowledge of the practical brand application.

The graphic designer may be involved in designing retail spaces, services for brands, or new ways of interacting with different forms of media. The graphic designer may be part of a much wider team that feeds into the brand creation process to develop new ways of experiencing a brand: the designer may work with anthropologists and psychologists to analyse people's behaviour; with architects or interior designers to create spaces; with technology specialists in presentation or with writers to develop the narrative behind the brand. This progression means that graphic designers and creative directors can play much more pivotal roles within creative agencies and within companies.

The shift in branding is being driven by the brand's audience: our expectation of brands is becoming more sophisticated, more informed and more discerning and brands need to stand out to win our attention. We expect more from brands and are influenced by changes in society, like globalisation, travel, media proliferation and coverage of brands, and wider and greater

"GRAPHIC DESIGN IS A TRANSACTION. YOU ARE EMOTIONALLY TRANSACTING BY TRYING TO TRIGGER A REACTION. THE POINT OF COMMUNICATION IS A TRANSACTION AND THE DESIGNER NEEDS TO RESPECT AND VALUE THAT"

Ralph Ardill, Experiential Consultant

"Design is the visual articulator of the brand's expression. Brands often do the same thing and compete in the same field. What makes the difference between one company and the other is how they do it. Design is what translates this into the tangible – the interaction, the function, how it works. Design is how the brand proves itself"

Stefano Marzano, Philips Design

individual spending power. The strong anti-brand movement – best expressed in Naomi Klein's *No Logo* – a deeper analysis of brand behaviour among the public, and the high-profile collapse of Enron, has forced a shift in the way brands and their owners behave.

Brands, which have so often communicated to, rather than with, us are now seeking a 'dialogue' with their audiences. This dialogue involves an open communication with representatives of groups that the brands affect; community leaders, NGOs (Non-Governmental Organisations) and employees, for example. It may be extended to consumers participating in the brand creation process (for example, by voting for brands). This approach helps the brand manage its relevance, reputation and consumer perceptions, and gives the audience an opportunity to express their views. It is within this emerging brand environment that the contemporary designer is working.

As brands try to stand out by being more creative, and seek to level with their audiences, the make-up of the teams managing brands is likely to change. Marketeers with business backgrounds currently drive the brand direction, just as financial teams drive a company's fiscal policy. Often branding is under-represented at the board level of companies, yet it is as important to the survival of a company as product development, the financials, and its people. Every part of a marketing communications mix impacts the brand: advertising, design, market research, public relations, investor relations and social responsibility. Brand creates value within a company and, to make it work, the branding remit needs to be acknowledged and driven from the top of the company, with the processes and structures in place to sustain the brand. Emotion and creative expression are now becoming fundamental drivers for all consumers and this needs to be brought into the business approach. It makes sense that people who come from a creative background, such as design, should represent the brand view at the upper structures within companies. This offers huge opportunities for the graphic designer if they are proactive.

As branding has evolved as a discipline, so it has developed its own language. Branding is a melding of marketing and design, and this crossover between business and creative has generated its own lexicon. The brand language makes concepts easier to explain and is a way of bridging the gap between business expression and creative description in order to describe both the process and the inputs to that process. The language of branding aims to make sense of complex ideas, such as the notion of 'experiencing the brand'. A designer at ease with the language of branding can visually express brand concepts and ideas.

The challenge for the graphic designer who wishes to play a more significant role in the branding process, is to see and understand the whole picture: the business aspects of the brand, the trends in the branding, the way brands function, the corporate objectives and the relationship between the designer and the brand owner. With this fuller picture, the designer is able to challenge branding assumptions and influence the higher levels of the organisation. Designers are an urgent and energetic force in brand development, crafting the interface between the brand and the consumer into an effective communication vehicle.

MARKETING THEORY

More Than a Name is a book which looks at the fundamentals, the feel and the future of branding. Its content is based on interviews with branding experts within agencies, people who work on brand teams within companies, and with people who interact with brands.

Brand building and brand strategy are also based on marketing techniques and models. These are discussed and reviewed in each chapter by Jonathan Baldwin, a senior lecturer in graphic design at the University of Brighton, East Sussex, UK. These models detail the analysis behind the brand and techniques that can be applied at different phases in a brand's life. They will help the graphic designer understand the brand positioning and strategy behind the brand.

Communications: In the context of branding, the communications is the work that supports the brand campaign to inform people both within the company and outside the company of the messages.

GLOSSARY

This glossary describes words that are used throughout the text and sometimes used in branding as part of its own language.

3G: Third-generation mobile technology with broad multimedia applications such as video and cameras.

Acquisition: When one company acquires another. The brands may be integrated into the dominant company, remaining the same, or their trading might be ceased.

Agencies: Companies that offer brand expertise to service clients. These are often branding agencies, digital agencies, design agencies or public relations agencies.

Auditing exercise: An 'audit' in the branding context often means an early assessment into what branding collateral exists.

Best practice: A piece of work that is recognised by the industry as representing the best way to apply the brand.

Brand: The public face, usually carefully constructed, of a marketable product, service or even person. The image of a commodity is often supported by a brand identity.

Brand architecture: How an organisation structures and names the brands within its portfolio, either under the corporate brand name used on all products or service, through sub-brands linked to the corporate brand, or as individually branded product or service brands targeted for different markets.

Brand mark: The 'mark' or 'marque' that identifies the brand. Also known as the logo and can include a strapline.

Brand perception: How a brand is viewed by its audience.

Brand producer: The person who holds a brand project together; the central coordinator.

Brand spend: The amount of money spent on marketing a brand.

Brand values: The characteristics of a brand.

Channel: The medium or media format used in marketing the brand, e.g. television, radio, billboard, press.

Co-branding: When two or more brands appear together in marketing communications (see also p174).

Communications: In the context of branding, this is the work that supports the brand campaign to inform people both within the company and outside the company of the brand messages.

Concessions: A store within a store. Brands often use this tactic to enter into new markets or to be positively associated with a larger brand.

Consumer: The person that invests financially in the brand, normally by buying it.

Consumer-facing brands: Brands that sell products to a consumer market rather than a business market.

Corporate branding: Refers to corporate identity projects that involve the creation, rebranding or use of the corporate name. The corporate brand represents the company and may (or may not) be used to support sub-brands.

Creative of the brand: An expression often used to refer to the 'creative' output of the branding process, including the design and words.

10

Demerger: When a brand is split from another to stand alone. This often involves a name change and new identity for the new brand (see also p90).

Equity: The value of a brand and its worth. Brand equity is based on the sum of all distinguishing qualities of a brand, drawn from all relevant stakeholders (brand audiences). It is what makes the brand valued and valuable.

Fixturing: The interior fixtures of a retail store, such as shelving.

Flagship store: The main store which best represents the brand.

Franchises: Where the company controls the brand, but the store owner is responsible for the day-to-day running of the retail outlet.

Global/local: An expression used in marketing meaning that a global brand will be implemented with a local approach and flavour in individual countries (see also p182).

Hits: The number of imprints on a website created by a mouse, to determine which pages people are visiting and how many visitors there are.

Human factors: Those specialists who look at human behaviour as part of the design, engineering or brand creation process. These people are often trained in anthropology or psychology.

Hybrid identity: When two logos are used to create one identity.

Intranet: A closed internal internet used within a company by its employees (see also p179).

Journey: The audience journey or 'user journey', often used in relation to the website experience. This is how the audience progressively experiences the brand.

Licensees: Someone (or a company) that has bought the right to market the brand, or an element of the brand, under its own name. For example, HP will produce the iPod under the Hewlett Packard brand.

Loss leader: A product sold at a loss to encourage spending elsewhere in-store, e.g. stores sell best-selling books at a loss, gambling on customers buying other, more expensive titles once their attention has been engaged.

Marketing collateral: Marketing materials used for promotional means, such as websites, brochures and direct mail.

Marketplace: The brand's sector or market in which it exists.

Mindshare: The positive emotional response from the brand's targeted audience.

Narrative: A story that supports the brand.

NGOs: An acronym for a Non-Governmental Organisation. An organisation that is not part of the government (either local, state or federal), for example, Greenpeace and Amnesty International.

Parent brand: The main brand owner or holding company (see also p52).

Product: A tangible, marketable item that is often the basis for the brand.

Prospects: Potential new customers.

Reposition: When the brand deliberately moves its place in its market, usually to attract a new audience. Also referred to as 'shifting in the market' (see also p62).

Roll-out: The time it takes to launch the product, often runs from pre-launch through to post-launch phase.

Silos: A linear structure within a company that keeps different parts of the business in different divisions. For example, Marketing and Research & Development may be in different silo structures.

SMS: To send a text message using a mobile phone.

Spin off: When a brand is launched on its own, after it has been developed within another company.

Stake: When a company buys part of another company.

Stakeholder: The broad audience that the brand affects, including investors, press, customers, employees and associations.

Strapline (or 'tagline'): The supporting words or phrase that accompany a brand's logo, or are part of an advertising campaign. This is sometimes referred to as the 'sign-off'.

Strategy: An overused and often misinterpreted word. Usually means the overriding thinking and marketing theory behind the brand (for example, where it should be positioned in its market to attract its desired audience).

Sub-brand: A brand within a brand, for example, the Sony PlayStation is a sub-brand of Sony.

The proposition: The way a brand projects itself or what it says about itself.

The positioning: Where a brand sits in relation to its competitors.

Umbrella branding: The overall brand, which holds a number or sub-brands within its remit. The umbrella brand may have a completely separate brand identity to the sub-brands.

CHAPTER

01

DEFINING
BRANDING

INTRODUCTION

This is the chapter that makes sense of branding from a theoretical, historical and current standpoint.

Many people view branding as simply creating an identity for a company composed of a logo, a name and an identifiable style. Yet branding is much more than this. It encompasses both the visual and tangible elements of the brand, as well as the emotional and intangible pieces that create a connection between the brand and the consumer. This makes branding an exciting area to work in for the graphic designer, whose role is to translate and communicate ideas into reality.

The theory section helps to delineate brands from products and services, and looks at the way companies position brands.

The content of the chapter delves into the history and meaning of branding, addressing some of the basic questions in branding: What is branding? And why is it important?

At the end of the chapter is an interview with John Williamson, a director at one of the world's leading branding agencies, Wolff Olins, who talks about branding and the graphic designer's role within brand structures.

Chapter 1 Contents:

THEORY CHAPTER 01 /

++

The Anatomy of Consumer Goods

Which came first: Brand or product?

Modern branding can be something of a chicken and egg situation. Decisions to launch new products are often tied up with decisions about brands, and the two terms are used interchangeably – often wrongly.

So what is the difference between a product and a brand? Basically, a product (or service) is the thing that you buy and use. The brand is the promise of something. That something is intangible; it could be a guarantee of quality, a sense of prestige, or of heritage. Brands also offer a differentiating factor that makes it easier to choose between the many competing product variants. To give a few examples, running shoes are a product, as is shampoo. Coffee, cars, digital music players, hotels and insurance are all products too.

Faced with a dozen or more types of coffee on a supermarket shelf, how do you make a choice? If you are a connoisseur of coffee, you may know what blends to look for and make a rational, reasoned choice. But if you are a busy individual trying to get your shopping done as quickly as possible you will probably buy a recognisable brand. It's like going to a party and feeling a little lost until you spot a familiar face in the crowd.

The recognition factor is important to brand owners because it often takes precedence over factors such as price. This is known as the 'price elasticity of demand' and suggests that small changes in price (up or down) will not adversely affect sales. If the brand recognition is high, the price elasticity is high too – which can be extremely valuable if the company wants to run a price promotion or increase profits.

Often, there is confusion in the mind of the consumer between brand and product, most famously in the use of the word 'hoover' to mean vacuum cleaner. Hoover is in fact the name of a manufacturer of electrical goods, but this became so well known that the brand became synonymous with vacuum cleaners, to such an extent that the word has entered the English dictionary and people might say 'I'm doing the hoovering', for example. So when people talk of their 'hoover', they may not actually mean a Hoover vacuum cleaner. Compare this situation, however, with Dyson vacuums. People who own Dysons often refer to it as 'their Dyson', and it can't be confused with other cleaners in the way that Hoovers can. Similarly, 'Walkman' became a word used to mean any personal stereo, and 'IBM Compatible' came to mean virtually any personal computer that wasn't a Mac. IBM's own share of the PC market declined because of this.

Although in the case of Hoover and Sony's Walkman it could be argued that the misperception did more harm than good (and in IBM's case, it was disastrous), such things sometimes work in the brand owners' favour. Many people believe that AOL is the Internet rather than just an ISP. And people will regularly ask for a 'Coke' rather than a cola. Brands can spend a great deal of money setting up such linkages or 'mindshares', and competitors have a hard time shaking the misperception.

A company entering a crowded market place with a new product may rely on their existing brand to help it succeed. However, some products and brands are often interlinked at launch. Kellogg's is a good example of this. It has a range of breakfast cereals all under the Kellogg's brand umbrella. Each product has its own marketing budget and often competes for a similar audience (Rice Krispics, Frosties and Coco Pops in the UK all chase after a similar market, for example). Over time each of these products became a brand in its own right, each with something of a following – in 1999 when Kellogg's changed the name of Coco Pops to Choco Krispies to tie in with the Rice Krispies brand and the European market, consumers rebelled to such an extent that within months the name changed back. In this case the brand was the product; change the brand and you are perceived to have changed the product. Each of these Kellogg's brands has taken on a life of its own to such an extent that they have been extended into the growing breakfast snack bar market.

Kellogg's is a successful brand in its own right (in October 1997 a Henley Centre report was published in the UK in which people were asked how far did they believe something to be honest and fair: family doctors scored 85%, and Kellogg's 83%), but it also invests heavily in the idea that a product should be a brand too. For new launches the Kellogg's name offers a guarantee of quality, but once the product has taken off its own name becomes the brand. This is often referred to as 'multiple product branding'. Few companies appear to be able to work like this (or need to) and for most it is the umbrella or parent brand that offers the guarantee in a crowded market – known as 'corporate branding'.

The table on the right shows how some companies such as Nestlé, Apple and Kellogg's adopt a multiple-product brand strategy, while others prefer a corporate branding strategy. Apple's example is interesting because it exists in a world that is dominated by model numbers rather than names. For example, a Sony DVP-NS355, a Philips DVDR70 and a Toshiba SD24VB are, at the time of writing, all DVD players in the UK market. Hardly memorable, but in such a fast-changing world it is easier for manufacturers and retailers to use model numbers for identification and rely on the corporate brand to do the hard work.

Mindshare: Winning over people at the emotional level.

Corporate branding: A branding product or service aimed at a market of companies or corporations. Also known as 'B2B', or business-to-business branding.

PRODUCT/SERVICE	CORPORATE BRANDS	PRODUCT BRANDS
Running shoes	Nike Adidas	Nike product brands: Air Zoom Vapour Plus, Shox 2:45 Mayfly, Air Pegasus II
TVs / DVD players	Sony Ferguson LG Philips Toshiba	Sony Ferguson LG Philips Toshiba
Personal computers	Apple Sony Dell	Apple product brands: Apple iMac Apple G5 Apple Xserve Apple iBook Apple Powerbook
Digital music players	Apple Creative iRiver	iPod iPod mini iPod photo iPod shuffle
Coffee	Nestlé Kraft	Nestlé product brands: Nescafé Original Nescafé Original Decaf Nescafé Gold Blend Nescafé Blend 37 Nescafé Cap Colombie Nescafé Alta Rica Nescafé Kenjara Nescafé Espresso Nescafé Fine Blend Nescafé Gold Blend Decaffeinated Nescafé Cappuccino Coffee-mate
Vacuum cleaners	Hoover Dyson	Dyson product brands: DC03, DC04, DC07, DC14, DC15, DC05, DC08
Breakfast cereals	Kellogg's Quaker Nestlé	Kellogg's brands in the UK: All Bran, Banana Bubbles, Bran Buds, Bran Flakes, Coco Pops, Common Sense Oat Bran, Corn Flakes, Corn Pops, Country Store, Crunchy Nut Corn Flakes, Frosted Wheats, Frosties, Fruit'n'Fibre, Golden Crackles, Golden Crisp, Honey Nut Loops, Multi-Grain Start, Nut Feast, Raisin Splitz, Rice Crispies, Ricicles, Special K, Sultana Bran Nestlé brands in the UK: Shredded Wheat, Honey Nut Cheerios, Shredded Wheat Bitesize, Nesquik Cereal, Honey Nut Shredded Wheat, Clusters, Fruitful, Golden Nuggets, Shreddies, Golden Grahams, Coco Shreddies, Cinnamon Grahams, Frosted Shreddies, Triple Berry Cheerios, Strawberry Cheerios, Fitnesse and Fruit, Triple Berry Shredded Wheat, Cheerios, Force Flakes, Cookie Crisp, Fitnesse

BRAND HISTORY

The word 'brand' is derived from the Norse word 'brands', meaning 'to burn'. Branding, in this form, has been used for thousands of years to denote ownership or origin. It was originally applied to farmed animals and human slaves for some 4,000 years and there are branding scenes recorded on Egyptian tombs dating back to 2000 BC. Branding was also used as a symbol of shame on fugitives, galley slaves, gypsies, vagabonds, thieves and religious zealots up until the early 19th century in the USA. Branding is also applied as decoration to show tribal affiliations in various parts of the world to this day. The original concept of brand registration or copyright emerged with cattle brands in the USA where each rancher would uniquely brand cattle to aid identification during 'droves' involving cattle from many ranches.

The world of branding as we know it probably started at the end of the 19th century with the industrial revolution. The emergence of the department store radically changed the way in which people shopped and made a much wider range of products available to ordinary people, introducing competition between suppliers as more than one product became available for a given purpose. Branding helped to identify origin for the first time and attempted to affect buyer loyalty. Mass production of consumer goods went hand-in-hand with technological inventions and by the early 20th century people became defined by what they bought. The new consumer shopped in their newly-found leisure time, read newspapers and listened to the radio. By the 1920s the concept of mass marketing and public relations (PR) had been introduced into the American market, helped by the birth of the tabloid paper and the work of Edward Bernays, nephew of Sigmund Freud, who is credited as the father of PR.

Some of today's largest companies have been around since the 1800s. Procter & Gamble was established in 1837 originally as a soap and candle maker, later becoming a driving force behind branding as a discipline, as they fought to assert themselves in a local market that already boasted 12 candle makers. Philips started trading in 1891 and Ford in 1903. In those days, it was not unusual for companies to build entire towns to house their workers or build schools for their employees' children. People, literally, lived the brand.

Managing brands had become a complex undertaking as early as the 1920s when companies started to manufacture a range of products. Henry Ford, whose Model T accounted for 60 per cent of the market in 1920, introduced specialisation on the production line, believing that different departments did not need to know what each other were doing. This structure of departments, or silos, is common in corporations today. In the 1980s contemporary manufacturing organisations pushed back against the Ford model by introducing a cell structure of multi-disciplinary functions working together to perform multiple tasks. This made manufacturing and the creative process flow more freely.

Ford had originally been convinced that 'the company's future lay in the production of affordable cars for a mass market'[1]. However, it was General Motors (GM) that understood that people wanted choice, when the head of General Motors, Alfred Sloan, announced a product strategy of 'a car for every purse and purpose'[2] in the company's 1924 Annual Report. Sloan merged Ford's use of common components with unique styling to generate a range of cars sharing the same common underpinnings – choice at a low price. In the same year Procter & Gamble became one of the first companies to set up a market research department to study consumer preferences and buying habits, and a Research & Development department to turn need into product. Ford, meanwhile, was the first company to have a dedicated in-house design department – called a 'style' department – which was created in 1933 by Edsel Ford, Henry's son.

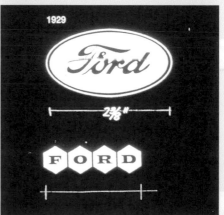

1. Ford website, www.ford.com
2. General Motors website, www.gm.com

1

3

1: FORD HERITAGE PROMOTION
2: FORD LOGO DEVELOPMENT
3: FORD MODEL A, 1903
4–7: FORD VINTAGE POSTERS: The vintage posters show The Ford Times (Canada) 1915 (4), a Model T advertisement (6), a Ford Consul advertisement for the MK11 (5) and an early Ford V8 advertisement circa 1933 (7).

When Ford Motor Company was founded in 1903, there were already 88 car manufacturers in the USA. In 1908, the Model T was introduced. By 1920 it accounted for 60 per cent of the market and 1.5 million Model Ts were sold by 1927. Ford introduced automotive classics like the Lincoln in the 1930s at the luxury end of the market, and the Thunderbird in the 1950s. It now owns a family of automotive brands including Ford, Lincoln, Mercury, Mazda, Jaguar, Land Rover, Aston Martin, and Volvo, yet its actual brand identity has changed little over the decades.

4

6

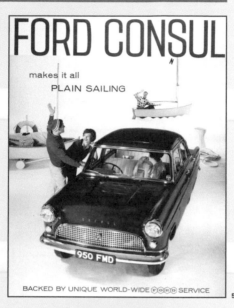

5

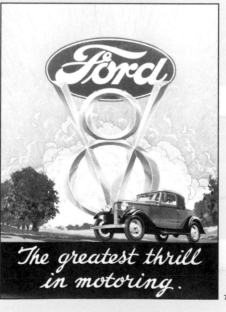

7

Consumer: The person or people that 'consume' the brand – that buy it.

Silos: A linear structure within a company that keeps different parts of the business in different divisions. For example, Marketing and Research & Development may be in silo structures.

"By the 1950s brands were becoming ubiquitous, helped by an economic boom and the advent of television advertising"

"Look, Mom—no cavities!"

Crest Toothpaste stops soft spots from turning into cavities— means far less decay for grownups and children.

1

2

1–3: VINTAGE ADVERTISING FROM PROCTER & GAMBLE

The concept of brand management was first introduced in 1931. Brand management meant having one person or entity in control of the brand. In this year, Procter & Gamble, now a huge consumer goods company and owner of dozens of household brands, created a marketing organisation under Neil McElroy, the company's promotion department manager, based on competing brands managed by dedicated groups of people. The system provided more specialised marketing strategies for each brand and Procter & Gamble's brand management system was born. McElroy also invented the soap opera by introducing sponsorship for radio plays.

By the 1950s, brands were becoming common, helped by an economic boom and the advent of television advertising. 'By 1967', according to Crainer and Dearlove, authors of *The Ultimate Book of Business Brands*, '84 per cent of large manufacturers of consumer packaged goods in the US had brand managers.' The 1980s advertising boom, driven by agencies like Saatchi & Saatchi, brought brands to the forefront of our lives. The emergence of service businesses in the 1990s – partly a result of deregulation and an increase in technology – widened the landscape of branding as these businesses used branding to differentiate themselves

when product or service offerings were similar. As Wally Olins, a brand expert and co-founder of branding agency Wolff Olins points out, 'There were 178 phone companies in Britain in 2000 compared with one in 1980.'[3] The amount of product choice had the potential to confuse consumers, so branding became the means of differentiation between highly-similar products.

The 1990s saw the rise of huge brands like Microsoft, which used aggressive branding and publicity techniques in a sector that was mostly unbranded at the time. Technology was not considered exciting by marketeers in the late 1980s and early 1990s; companies like Microsoft and Apple proved it otherwise.

By the mid-1990s branding was ubiquitous and crossed into untraditionally branded areas like politics and charities: the UK's Labour party was rebranded as 'New Labour' before the 1997 election to present a new face to the nation – it was a successful rebrand at the time. The late 1990s and the dot-com hype was often a case of over branding, where the value of technology companies was over inflated by promises rather than substance.

In the 21st century, brands now play to people of every generation, social class

"In the 21st century, brands now play to people of every generation, social class and culture"

3. Wally Olins *On Brand*, Thames & Hudson Ltd. UK, 2004

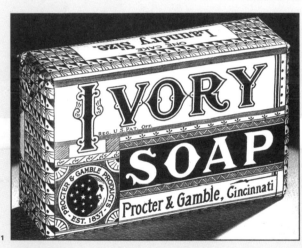

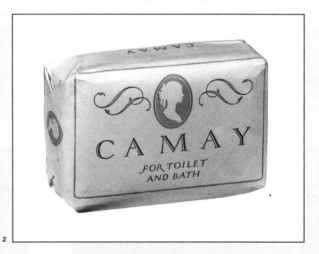

and culture. A product or service is no longer a necessity at the core of the brand. Brands can be based around a nebulous concept: Britain's New Labour launched the now defunct 'Cool Britannia', to promote the country as innovative, artistic and 'cool'. The US government successfully created its 'War on Terror' after 9/11 to create a real feeling of fear, supported by its own brand identity (familiar to CNN viewers) and reinforcing the backbone of US foreign policy.

Brand structure and brand management have helped build businesses, market products and services, and manage reputation. Behind the brand is careful business management controlling the way the brand expresses itself. Branding is now no longer a practice restricted to the expertise of those within companies and branding agencies; it is something that is becoming a necessity in most sectors, simply to stand out and survive.

1–3: HERITAGE BRANDS IVORY SOAP, CAMAY AND TIDE FROM PROCTER & GAMBLE

P&G is one of the biggest brand owners in the world. It is the holding company behind many household products, including Ariel, Tide, and Ivory, with over 12 billion dollars' worth of brands in its portfolio. A candle and soap maker, William Procter and James Gamble, started the company in 1837. By 1859, 22 years after the partnership was formed, its sales had reached $US1 million.

P&G was one of the pioneers of brand management. In 1924 it introduced a market research department to study consumer preferences and buying habits – one of the first in the world. By the late 1920s a brand management system was in place where competing brands were managed by different departments – a structure which was revolutionary at the time and unquestioned today.

The company still remains a force in the world of branding and in early 2005, signed a deal to acquire The Gillette Company for $US57 billion, making it the largest acquisition in P&G history.

"Behind the brand is careful business management controlling the way the brand expresses itself"

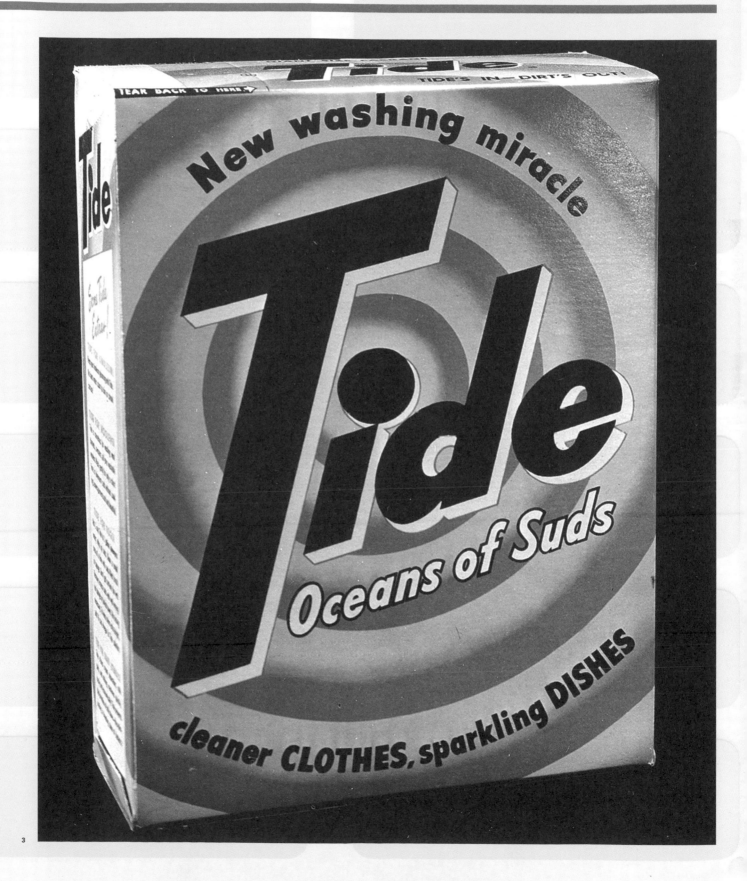

1922–1947

"Good branding is about pushing the creative boundaries within the context of the business of the brand. It is about understanding business. It is about creating stories"

Iain Ellwood, Interbrand

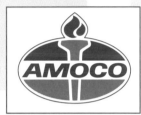

1989–2000

1930–1947

2000–

1947–1958

bp

2000–

1958–1989

Images © BP P.L.C. 2000–2005

BP BRAND MARK PROGRESSION

Oil and gas company BP took root in 1901 when its founder, William Knox D'Arcy, was given a concession to explore for oil in Persia (now Iran). In 1905 he sought additional funding from the Burmah Oil Company before oil was struck in 1908 – the first commercial oil discovery in the Middle East. In 1909, the Anglo-Persian Oil Company – as BP was first called – was formed to develop the oil field, with Burmah Oil owning 97 per cent of the shares.

Throughout most of its history, BP has been perceived as a distinctly British brand with colonial overtones. Its distinctive green and yellow colours helped make it one of the world's most recognised brands. For a century, the logo went through minor reiterations until a high-profile rebrand in 2000 repositioned BP. The new logo was an innovative and radical move, and has marked a transformation in BP's marketing and communications, to (in their words) 'demonstrate environmental leadership'.

The Helios, BP in shield and the BP letters are all trademarks of BP P.L.C. The AMOCO torch and Oval Device is a trademark of BP Products North America Inc.

1971

1978

1985

1988

NIKE 'SWOOSH' BRAND MARK PROGRESSION

The famous Nike 'swoosh' was created for Phil Knight, head of Nike by a graphic design student, Carolyn Davidson, back in 1971. Then, Nike was just a fledging company and Davidson a keen design graduate needing work. Knight needed a design for a shoe stripe and briefed Davidson to create something that represented movement.

Nike lore states that when Davidson presented the designs to Knight, he wasn't overly impressed, saying, "I don't love it, but it will grow on me". He needed to get shoes printed, so he ran with the 'swoosh', and Davidson invoiced him for $US35. Davidson went on to set up her own design agency, boosted by Nike as her founding client. She was fully compensated by Knight in 1983 with an envelope containing Nike stock.

The 'swoosh' is now one of the most recognised and imitated brand marks in the world. Nike's 'Just Do It' slogan, from a 1988 ad campaign, is a brilliant piece of aspirational copywriting that is often associated with the brand mark.

"Brand structure and brand management have helped build businesses, market products and services, and manage reputation"

Reposition: When the brand deliberately moves its place in its market, usually to attract a new audience. Also referred to as "shifting in the market".

Communications: In the context of branding, the communications is the work that supports the brand campaign to inform people both within the company and outside the company of the messages.

Brand mark: The 'mark' or 'marque' that identifies the brand. Also known as the logo.

"Over time, brands have become important as they set an expectation of quality or price"

DEFINING BRANDING

Many people associate brands and branding with multinational corporations, but brands exist wherever there is a competitive marketplace. They help us select one product or service over another in a complex world of increased choice, especially where the differentiation between products is slim or difficult to evaluate. Many products now have a broad range of standards and similar features or, in other cases, the service or product may have become a commodity competing on price and quality. Some fundamentals have not changed – people can choose simply on price, availability and location – but where competition and choice exists, the brand matters. More than a century ago most manufacturers were local with little competition, but as imports became established and industrial efficiency improved capacity, manufacturers dispersed their markets in order to feed capacity and reduce costs. Over time, brands have become important as they set an expectation of quality or price.

Brands today represent more than a product, service or brand identity (the name and logo, design and voice of the brand). A brand is synonymous with the business and the style behind the product or service; it encompasses the people working for the company and a philosophy and spirit that sustains it. Brands offer a set of values, a vision and an attitude. Organisations establish a brand position to project a consistent public and internal image. This brand position sets perimeters to help respond to opportunities and challenges and also gives context to those who work for the company.

Once a brand has established itself in the market, it must continue to prove its effectiveness to stay in the market through ongoing brand activity. The purpose of brand campaigns may not be solely focused on selling a product or service, but to also build awareness, improve a reputation or to affirm or change perceptions. The brand identity itself does not have to be visible – brands can be associated with events or viral campaigns, which are promoted by word-of-mouth rather than visible trademarks or logos. Companies can spend millions on creating a brand and millions more on maintaining and sustaining a brand, but equity in the brand can be lost more quickly if a brand consistently fails to engage its audience, or if its behaviour is inconsistent with its messages and values.

At the heart of every brand is its audience. The consumer is no longer simply the person buying the product or service, but a broad spectrum of 'stakeholders' who include customers through to employees to external agencies and local communities. Each stakeholder may experience the brand in a different way, but there should be consistency in brand behaviour. The relationship between the brand and the consumer is two-way – what the consumer thinks of the brand matters as much as how the brand projects itself to the consumer. This two-way interaction is at the heart of managing the brand perception. This is where branding happens: it is the dialogue that helps create and sustain a relationship between the organisation and its audience. And good branding, according to the experts, must engage.

1900

1904

1909

1930

1948

THE SHELL PECTEN BRAND MARK PROGRESSION

Shell has one of the most recognised brand marks in the world. The word 'Shell' first appeared in 1891 as the trademark for kerosene that was shipped to the Far East, presumably because the tankers shipping the kerosene had been named after a different seashell.

The Shell 'pecten' or scallop shell was first introduced in 1904. The reasons for the choice of the particular Pecten symbol are thought to have related to the coat of arms of one of Shell's customers, Mr Graham, who imported the kerosene into India. The Graham family had adopted the St James Shell after their ancestors made the pilgrimage to Santiago de Compostela in Spain (throughout history, a scallop shell has identified pilgrims walking the Road to Santiago).

The logo has always remained true to its origins through its ten iterations. The current emblem reflects a trend towards simplicity in graphic design. Like most global brands with a lot of equity in the appearance of the brand mark, the mark is scrupulously guarded to ensure that its appearance is not altered or misrepresented in any way.

The Shell emblems and images are used with permission from Shell Brand's International AG.

1955

1961

1971

1995

1999

Marketplace: The brand's sector or market in which it exists.

Stakeholder: The broader audience that the brand affects, including investors, press, customers, employees and associations.

Brand perception: How a brand is viewed by its audience.

THEORY   PAGE /16
See 'The Anatomy of Consumer Goods'

"THE IDEA THAT BRANDS ARE A NECESSARY EVIL IS CHANGING"

The Helios is a trademark of BP P.L.C. © BP P.L.C. 2000–2005

1–16: The brand marks of footballer David Beckham (1), BP (2), Virgin (3), Ford (4), Innocent Drinks (5), Mini Cooper (6), KLM Airlines (7), Philips (8), Burt's Bees (9), Procter & Gamble (10), Ikea (11), National Geographic (12), Orange (13), Nike (14), Topshop (15), and Shell (16).

First there were trademarks, which helped to differentiate one product from another, now there are brands. Brands enable an audience to identify not only with just a trademark, but the quality and value of what they are getting. In a commoditised world, the brand creates commercial success and shareholder value. Logos, or brand marks, are used as brand identifiers with those of the world's top brands being worth billions in their own right, the brand alone accounting for more than one third of shareholder value.

An annual study by brand consultants, Interbrand and JP Morgan, ranked Coca-Cola as the world's most valuable brand in 2004 with a brand value of $US67.3 billion, down 4 per cent from the previous year. In 2002 the Coca-Cola brand was worth $US69.6 billion and the brand alone accounted for 51 per cent of its stock market value. Microsoft, IBM, GE and Intel remain in the top five most valuable brands. McDonald's was ranked seventh in 2004 with a brand value of $US25 billion. This had decreased from its value in 2002 of $US29.3 billion with its brand worth 71 per cent of shareholder value.[4]

4. Rita Clifton and John Simmons, *Brands and Branding*, BBC Television, 2003

9 BURT'S BEES
10 P&G
11 IKEA
12 NATIONAL GEOGRAPHIC
13 orange™
14 Nike
15 TOPSHOP
16 Shell

"Brands used to be impenetrable forces; there used to be a magic and a mystery to how things happened and where they came from, most people didn't care then, but now they do. They care because they've got the time and the money to care. We're going through sustained economic growth – we're better off and better educated and corporate bashing is entertaining. The smart brands realise that they can't address all these questions so opt for the alternative: to try and engage people to take the brand with them"

Ralph Ardill, Experiential Consultant

Brand: The representation of a product, service or even an intangible. The brand is the persona of what sits behind it.

DEFINING EFFECTIVE BRANDING

Ralph Ardill, formerly a brand strategist from brand experience agency Imagination, says that companies must engage their audience if they are to be effective: "Most communication that companies invest in is redundant. It is not asked for or particularly effective. When you look at the total communication investment that a brand has, it is hundreds of millions of dollars each year and no one has any idea how effective it is."

Many brands may succeed in communicating to an audience, but fail to engage. Engagement happens by identifying and exploiting the magic in a brand: the insight or idea that connects to the audience. It can be an intuitive process and requires a mix of strategic business thinking and creative ideas. The thinking and creative process must never stop.

Brands fail to engage when their impact is measured by the quantity rather than the quality of their communication, such as the amount of direct mail distributed, the number of 'hits' on a website, or the number of people on a database. If good branding is about triggering an emotional connection – how else does someone choose from 35,000 trademarked products in a supermarket?[5] – then emotional effectiveness needs to be measured. Brand engagement is best measured through recognition and surveys that analyse the value of the brand and the effectiveness of the message – does the audience know the brand and what does it represent to them? These surveys create a more powerful view of brand impact than response numbers and can identify branding issues much earlier than sales promotion campaigns. Managing a brand also requires measuring the reputation of that brand both within the organisation and externally, as well as managing and protecting the brand identity to prevent dilution or inconsistency. Those responsible for the brand need to be fully aware of the brand perception, the marketplace, the competition, wider trends and social influences, and the ever-changing relationship with the consumer and other audiences.

In the 21st century, it seems that no area of society is immune to branding. Deregulation and privatisation, along with effective reduction in government funding for basic public services such as health and education, mean that schools, hospitals and universities need to find other ways of funding to survive and differentiate themselves from similar services. Branding offers that opportunity – when two things exist in the same area, branding defines their differentiation. In this context anything can be branded: funeral parlours, universities, political parties, countries, towns – even you. But good branding is more than applying a name or a logo: it must seek to reflect the values of the subject and match behaviour with values. In doing so it must connect with something deeper in the audience. It must be authentic. Authenticity means that the brand is made to consistently execute its values. Branding is the long haul; it is what makes businesses sustainable. It marks the future of the product and service and is the mirror of its success or failure.

WHAT IS BRANDING?

"Bridging the gap between brand strategy and design is creative magic. You need someone to conceptualise and come up with those ideas"

Iain Ellwood, Interbrand

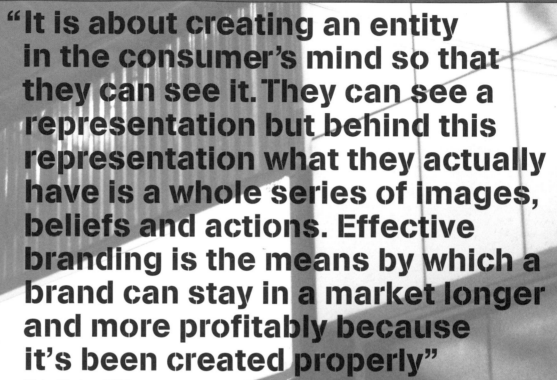

"It is about creating an entity in the consumer's mind so that they can see it. They can see a representation but behind this representation what they actually have is a whole series of images, beliefs and actions. Effective branding is the means by which a brand can stay in a market longer and more profitably because it's been created properly"

Michael Hockney, D&AD

5. Figures sourced from Kevin Roberts, *Lovemarks: The Future beyond Marks*, PowerHouse Cultural Entertainment Books, USA, 2004

Hits: The number of imprints on a website created by a mouse, to determine the pages people are visiting and how many visitors there are.

Brand perception: How a brand is viewed by its audience.

"A brand makes value visible: value in the product or service and value in the corporation"

Steve Everhard, Multos (a division of Mastercard)

WHY IS BRANDING IMPORTANT?

Branding is important because of its relationship and impact on the world we live in. Brands affect people's lives simply because they are part of our daily choices and decisions. In today's world, with broad competition for virtually all products and services – including charities and the not-for-profit sector – there seems to be little that has been left untouched by branding. Basic services and industries, like academia and healthcare, have developed into increasingly competitive environments and branding will help individual institutions differentiate themselves.

The combined value of the world's biggest brands is fundamental to the global economy – brands are now one of the most powerful tools in the western world and account for one-third of the world's wealth. A brand is, according to Rita Clifton, head of Interbrand, 'the most important single corporate asset'[6]. Some of the largest companies behind the brands are worth more than some countries' total income. Statistically, the annual income of the five largest business corporations is more than double the combined GNPs (Gross National Product) of the 500 poorest countries. It is therefore not surprising that brands have the influence and power to change society.

Branding is important because of the way the company behind the brand behaves. Its creation or demise can affect government policy, social and industry trends, the global economy, as well as the stakeholders who have an interest in the brand (including investors, employees, customers and the press). The collapse of US energy company Enron in 2001, involving widespread executive fraud and mismanagement, led to new regulations, with stiff penalties for companies and senior individuals that fail to comply. The reverberations of the bankrupt company were felt from governments to suppliers and individuals. While Enron's public-facing brand had been strong, it was an effective facade for severe mismanagement. Enron's collapse damaged stakeholder confidence in corporations and emphasised the need for corporations to be more transparent, accountable and responsible, with 'good governance' policies in place.

The sheer power and wealth of the big multinational brands and their comparable power to governments has persuaded many that the companies behind the brands have a role to play in society. Brands and branding will not disappear, but are likely to become more ubiquitous across industries and as a global presence. Companies use branding as a way of increasing wealth, sustaining their business and improving their reputation. They also want to improve the living conditions and earnings of individuals in order to improve the individual's spending power. The benefits, therefore, can be mutual.

Yet the idea that branding will become a necessity in traditionally 'unbranded' sectors like the not-for-profit sector and in education horrifies many individuals involved. The up-side is that branding makes the entity accountable to its audience. Any brand analysis forces a company or institution to look inwards and review the way it operates. It must analyse its impact on its stakeholders and review how it delivers its service and how it is perceived, in order to work out a way to differentiate itself. It must question its values and ensure that it behaves in line with those values. If a brand or brand owner fails to follow through on its proposition to the market, then it will lose integrity and credibility – the essential properties needed for a good brand. Inward reflection can lead to an improvement in the way a brand is delivered.

People are passionate about brands whether they support them or not. While some brands inevitably carry a financial status and equity that can make them powerful, they are ultimately accountable to their audience. It is this audience that has the power to change and influence the direction of branding; to determine what is important to their future and, as a consequence, to the future of branding.

NGOs: An acronym for a Non-Governmental Organisation. This is an organisation that is not part of the government (either local, state or federal), for example, Greenpeace and Amnesty International.

6. The Economist, Rita Clifton and John Simmons, *Brands and Branding*, Economist Books, UK, 2003

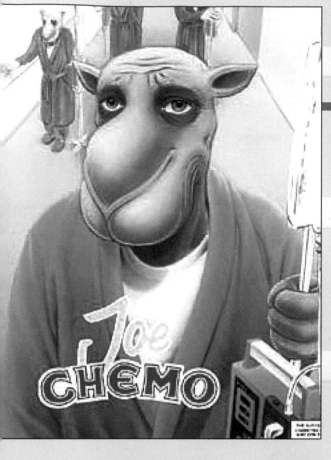

1, 2: ANTI-BRANDING PROPAGANDA FROM ADBUSTERS.ORG

Adbusters is a Canadian organisation that is the current bastion of culture jamming and the anti-corporate movement, with the intention to 'topple existing power structures and forge a major shift in the way we will live in the 21st century'. It is a magazine, website and an advocacy advertising agency – the magazine has 120,000 in circulation, most of it USA-based.

Adbusters anti-brand activism highlights the negative behaviour and impact of brands through spoof ads and campaigns. Most corporations still view the anti-corporate movement as extremist, but are aware of its influence and consequently keep up-to-date with what is being said on websites such as adbusters.org and corporatewatch.org. Although there may not be direct dialogue between the culture-jamming organisations and the corporations that they attack, the views of the culture-jammers often eventually move into the mainstream and are articulated by influential NGOs and consumers.

Images by Shari Swan, Streative Branding

3, 4: FUNERAL PARLOUR, MONTREAL, CANADA

It seemed possible that some sectors of society and industry – like funeral services – might be left untarnished by the branding wand. But now there's a competitive market for the dead. This funeral parlour in Montreal has created a competitive brand edge. Suitable for servicing the deceased of any denomination (just replace the crucifix with the Koran), it also has a bar, restaurant, gallery and 'spiritual library', all adorned with designer furniture. The local celebrities are already requesting a slot.

The burial industry also seems to be flourishing with new ideas, and adopting an increasingly popular environmentally friendly agenda. There's a range of natural burial sites available, organic biodegradable coffins, 'eco-caskets' and even a bamboo coffin on the market (awarded the winner of the Best Coffin Manufacturer in the UK 2004 by the *Natural Death Handbook*). There are also various organic techniques available for treating the recently deceased. As the world's population continues to grow and people become more concerned about the environment, there's no doubt that the green approach to death is a growth industry – and possibly a 'branded' industry in time.

interview

John Williamson, Board Director, Wolff Olins

How would you describe branding?

Powerful brands have at their centre an idea that is big enough for you to want to be a part of it. The idea is big, unique, simple and true, and the branding agency brings the idea to life.

The brands that are going somewhere have a powerful idea. The idea behind our work with Orange was 'optimism'. It is an abstract idea and a human thing – a social, cultural idea, rather than a product. So we came up with 'The future's bright the future's Orange'. Nike has 'Just do it': it spoke to the masses, saying you can be someone if you just do it – you don't have to go to Harvard.

Good brands are like novels that you can't put down – they are the highest form of art and they have to tell a fantastic story.

What is the role of the designer in branding?

Graphic design is the one route into branding – to take an idea, a view of the world, and then translate that into a reality. Design is both of the world and of your imagination and is the part that makes things tangible.

We live in a visual medium and so visuals have more power, whereas words are not so immediate.

Do you believe that brands need to be authentic – to deliver on their promise, for example?

What is authenticity? People say that the Beatles were authentic but the Spice Girls were not, but I don't think it matters. I don't think it's about authenticity, but about truth. Truth is whether people believe what the brand says to you.

Does good branding have to have a good product or service behind it?

Brand is the totality, and product is a part of the branding. Branding starts with a big idea. Nike designs good shoes, but are they better than other sports shoes? It is more about the brand, than the shoes.

On the other hand, Apple has created an icon – an object of desire – with the iPod. It has reinvented the music world with the iPod. It could be that the iPod is the Bauhaus of product design, the pure aesthetic, but it is really a piece of tribalism. They have successfully built a community around the iPod as people can tell by the design of the earphones whether you have one – whether you are 'in' or 'out'. It is a cult, and cults are now inclusive.

What do you believe is the core issue of brands today?

The relationship between the consumer and the brand is the key issue in the future.

In the latter part of the 20th century, brands had an imperial nature – IBM was the Titan and it ruled the world. Now the new leaders in branding are pathfinders – they are more equal and engaging; they are more interactive. It is more than creating a dialogue with their audience – how you interact and research has to be part of the relationship.

Look at the music industry. Consumers find it more interesting to find stars than have them pushed on them, and shows like 'Popstars' help create stars. It is about consumer participation rather than consumption. The music business is trying to change the way it works and other industries will follow.

> "The brands that are going somewhere have a powerful idea"

How do you convince the people at the top of a company that branding is the way forward?

Branding is about creating wealth through ideas and engagement. It is a testament to the strength of ideas that leads to commercial success.

Branding is a way of rewriting the rules for business. It is the only long-term sustainable business. Branding distinguishes things and that makes money.

The only way to make real money is to do things differently. Yet, most people are content with making the same money as everyone else. The difficulty is in choosing what to invest in and the argument is the return on investment. There is no magic formula.

Do brands have a role to play in being more responsible?

Responsibility is a key part of the brand. Brands are a vehicle for liberating the world. They give consumers real choice and people a chance to have a higher standard of living. It is the way in which people vote – they are voting on a set of values and ideals.

Brands will increasingly seek to have responsible consumers. They want to attract the right kind of consumer and so they must act responsibly. This will be a two-way thing – to be more selective about their consumer, brands also need to be more aware of the social issues.

> "Branding is about creating wealth through ideas and engagement"

02

HOW BRANDS ARE MADE

INTRODUCTION

Every brand project will have a history and it's important that the designer understands a brand's origin. It could be created from an acquisition, a merger, the result of a rebrand or a new addition to a family of brands. This chapter investigates the different business scenarios that may affect a brand from the graphic designer's point of view.

The theory discussed in the chapter's opening describes the 'SWOT analysis', which shows how the brand is performing and where it sits in the marketplace. 'The Vision Thing' addresses the underlying brand strategy while 'Brand Families' shows how many well-known brands may have the same owner.

The main body of the chapter highlights things that may affect design when a brand is acquired, mergered or rebranded, for example.

Parent and sub-brand structures are detailed, as well as those brands that have been successfully driven by a dominant personality (like Virgin's Richard Branson). There's also an example of a new trend where a parent company builds its profile to carry an overall responsible message for the brand family.

At the end of the chapter there is an interview with the global brand team from National Geographic, discussing a rebrand which took five years to complete. The interview is in two sections, offering the perspective from the internal brand team and the design agency.

Chapter 2 Contents:

THEORY CHAPTER 02 /

+++

Swotting Up

Companies need to take a good look around them in order to decide what sort of strategy is required – are they riding high at the moment, or is there a threat around the corner that needs to be dealt with urgently? Are they strong in some areas but weak in others? Should weaknesses be addressed, or can they be ignored safely?

A SWOT analysis identifies strengths, weaknesses, opportunities and threats and can be used in many different situations – for example, project teams can use it to identify whether they have the skills they need to be successful, and football managers can use it to decide what tactics to play or if they need to buy new players.

In branding, a SWOT analysis can be used before a strategy is developed, or to help decide how to support an ageing brand. Anything listed in the analysis should be supported by evidence. Opinions are not allowed unless the facts support them – and this can make a SWOT analysis difficult to do, but helpful at the same time as it forces a level of objectivity.

STRENGTHS	Things we are doing well. Play to these strengths; don't risk losing sight of them.
WEAKNESSES	Things we are not doing so well. We either need to correct them (by raising/lowering price, improving quality, updating design etc.) or avoid them (by positioning ourselves differently).
OPPORTUNITIES	Are our competitors weak in a particular area? Are new markets developing? Is there a new trend? Have we developed a new technology or manufacturing technique? Is the government about to change the law in our area? Attack these opportunities – take advantage with a price promotion, with an advertising campaign, by sending review products to journalists, by holding a press event, by investing in a new factory etc.
THREATS	Are competitors developing new products? Are customers getting tired of what we have to offer? Has technology left us behind? Are changes in the law going to affect us? Is it necessary to defend against these threats by investing in research and development, lobbying the government, launching a PR offensive etc.?

"In branding, a SWOT analysis can be used before a strategy is developed, or to help decide how to support an ageing brand"

THEORY CHAPTER 02 /

++

The Vision Thing

Brands don't just arrive out of nowhere. They are the product of a company 'vision'. Although making lots of money is a vision of sorts, it is not exactly specific. Any successful brand needs to be part of a clearly defined set of objectives. Good objectives are often described as 'SMART':

Specific – What exactly do we want to achieve? Increased sales? Improved shareholder dividend? Greater market share?

Measurable – To what extent do we want to achieve these things? Objectives need targets that can be measured so a success is registered, or so that people involved can see early on that the plan isn't working. What increased revenue would be seen as a success? How much more of the market should be captured? What would shareholders see as acceptable when the company reports its profits?

Achievable – All objectives cost, whether in terms of money or human resources. There is no point setting out on a plan if the skills are not available, or if you depend on another company for components, but know there is a worldwide shortage at the moment. Companies can actually be too successful, and while running out of a product may increase its desirability it also hits income and profits, so setting an achievable objective is vital; don't be too ambitious!

Realistic – Is it really likely that you will capture 100 per cent of the available market, make all your shareholders millionaires overnight or triple your profits in one year? Nobody ever got rich by being too timid and lacking ambition, but setting targets that are completely unrealistic is likely to result in failure.

Timed – When do you want to achieve the objective? Again, be realistic, but don't plan too far ahead either. Five-year visions tend to have lots of 12–18 month plans within them, and those plans in turn have 'milestone' events built-in where progress is checked. An objective can be achieved in a few days if it is small enough ('inform all stakeholders of our plans for a new product launch' could be done via a press release and email), but these tend to be part of a bigger objective (e.g. 'launch a new product'). Never set an objective as 'ongoing' – it will never be achieved.

A SMART objective might read something like: 'Increase revenue by eight per cent over the next 12 months by raising sales of our core product to the currently under-represented male 18–25 consumer group.'

Objectives like this allow everyone to stay focused on what is required, and develop a strategy that will help it be achieved. The brand will form part of this strategy somewhere along the line either as it is, or through modification, or even in the development of new brands. If the core product mentioned in the example above were a skin moisturiser, one possible strategy might involve launching a new, more masculine branded version of an existing product, which might be easier than trying to convince men that they should use a brand they associate with women. However, a product like a drink or snack item might be slightly repackaged, or promoted differently without any major change to the brand's overall identity.

Before decisions like this can be made, other tools need to be used such as the Ansoff matrix (see page 126) and a SWOT analysis (see pages 40–41).

"Brands don't just arrive out of nowhere. They are the product of a company 'vision'"

Stakeholder: The broader audience that the brand affects, including investors, press, customers, employees and associations.

"Any successful brand needs to be part of a clearly defined set of objectives"

THEORY CHAPTER 02 /

++

Brand Families

Many of the leading brands we see around us are actually owned by a few companies. Owning several brands allows a company to sell successfully to different consumer groups without damaging its reputation with those groups. For example, a company can sell chocolate at a premium to its upmarket audiences, and sell virtually the same product in cheaper-looking packaging to an entirely different group. If it did not do this, it would only be able to sell to one group, leaving the other as fair game to competitors.

Arcadia is one of the UK's most successful fashion retail companies, but it only trades on the stock market under the Arcadia name. Its high street brands manage to operate without cannibalising each other's sales.

Kraft Foods are famous in many countries for, amongst other things, Kraft Philadelphia cream cheese. But being well-known in one area makes it difficult for a brand to extend into others – would you trust Heinz coffee, or Nissan crisps for example? For the same reason, Kraft also owns other brands such as those to the right – but this is only a small sample of the hundreds it owns.

> "Many of the leading brands we see around us are actually owned by only a few companies"

HIGH STREET BRAND	THE KEY DIFFERENTIALS
ARCADIA	
Topshop	Trading on its newly regained cool image, Topshop features regularly in popular fashion magazines as 'the place to shop' and promotes well-known and new design talent.
Topman	The male equivalent of Topshop (often found in the same store). It is more trendy with a younger feel than its stable-mate, Burtons.
Evans	Targeting larger women (16+ UK dress size) in the 25–55 age range, Evans is known for ensuring that women in this group – often ignored by other chains, including Arcadia's own – are not condemned to wearing unstylish clothes.
Dorothy Perkins	With a wide customer base of 20–50 year-old women, the average Dorothy Perkins customer is in her mid-30s. It is known as being affordable and up-to-the-minute in terms of fashion and boasts stores in most UK towns.
Burtons	Over 100 years old, Burtons targets 25–34 year-old men, selling everything from leisurewear to suits.
Miss Selfridge	Established in 1966 Miss Selfridge relaunches itself every few years. It now has stores worldwide and is particularly strong in the young female customer base.
Wallis	A boutique brand launched in 1923, Wallis boasts an in-house team of five designers who produce ten looks each year. The brand is seen as a fashion leader.
Outfit	This is a comparatively new store that is found in out-of-town retail parks and acts as an outlet for big-name branded clothes left over from Arcadia's other stores at the end of the season. Customers are attracted by bargains.

PRODUCT	BRAND	INTERNATIONAL REACH INCLUDES:
Coffee	Maxwell House	Instant coffee popular in USA, China, France, Germany, Hong Kong, Ireland, Poland, Russia, Taiwan, South Korea and UK.
	Carte Noir	One of the fastest growing brands in the UK basing its product on a long tradition of coffee-making. Popular in Ireland and the UK.
	Kenco	Super premium coffee brand in Belgium, France, Ireland and UK.
	Kaffee HAG	The world's first decaffeinated brand of coffee and popular in Austria, Germany and Italy.
Drinks	Capri-Sun	Sold in the USA.
	Kool Aid	Sold in the USA.
Cheese	Philadelphia	More than US$1 billion in sales around the world including North America, Australia, Austria, Belgium, Germany, Holland, Hong Kong, Ireland, Italy, Japan, Philippines, Saudi Arabia, Scandinavia, Singapore, UK and Venezuela.
	Dairylea	Processed cheese slices aimed at children in Ireland and the UK.
	Dairylea Lunchables	Convenience snacks aimed at the kids' lunchbox market.
	Kraft Singles	Processed cheese slices aimed at the sandwich market in Australia, Hong Kong, Indonesia, Malaysia, Singapore, South Korea, Spain, Philippines and UK.
	El Caserio	The number one processed cheese slice in Spain.
	Cheez Whiz	Spreadable, real-cheese brand created for children in Philippines and Venezuela.
Chocolate and confectionery	Lifesavers	Sold in the USA.
	Toblerone	Launched in Switzerland in 1908, popular in over 100 countries.
	Marabou	Sold in Denmark, Finland and Sweden.
	Freia	Sold in Norway.
	Suchard	Popular in Austria, France, Germany, Spain, Switzerland and the UK.
	Daim	Sold in Denmark, Finland, France, Germany, Norway, Sweden and the UK – where it is known as 'Dime'.
	Bis	Sold in Argentina and Brazil.
	Terry's	Sold in the UK.
Biscuits	Ritz cheese crackers	Sold in Central America, China, Ecuador, Hong Kong, Indonesia, Peru, Taiwan, Thailand, Venezuela and the UK.
Desserts	Bird's Custard	Powdered custard popular in Ireland and the UK.
	Bird's Angel Delight	Powdered dessert popular in Ireland and the UK.
Food	Vegemite	Sold in Australia and New Zealand and also exported globally.
	Taco Bell food kits	Sold in the USA and Europe.
	Oscar Mayer bacon	Sold in the USA.
	Shake 'n' Bake	Sold in the USA.
	Oven Fry	Sold in the USA, Thailand, Venezuela and the UK.
	Nabisco	Sold globally.
	Jello	Sold in the USA.

KRAFT

UNDERSTANDING THE PROCESS

Brands are created for various reasons: it may be to capture a new audience, to reposition a company or existing brand, or to offer something new. Every product or service that operates in a competitive environment needs to be supported by branding and communication to explain to its audience why it exists or why it has changed.

It is important for the designer to understand the context of the brand they are working with and why it exists. To understand what's behind a brand, you need to take a look at its history, its maturity, its market positioning and its environment. This helps the designer develop the appropriate design communications.

The designer may have a part in the brand creation decision – for example, helping to decide whether to rebrand or create a new brand, but usually the designer will come on board once these decisions have been made. Ideally, the designer will also be involved creating the communications that will support any changes to the brand and identity. As experiential consultant Ralph Ardill says: "It is not just about the logo; it's about the first six months. A lot of corporate identity projects fail because they are not set up properly."

THEORY   PAGE / 42

See 'The Vision Thing'

"It is not just about the logo; it's about the first six months. A lot of corporate identity projects fail because they are not set up properly"

Ralph Ardill, Experiential Consultant

INTERVIEW   PAGE / 66

See Tom Geismar

INTERVIEW   PAGE / 67

See Karen Rice Gardiner

BRAND CREATION SCENARIOS

There are a variety of brand creation scenarios that may involve the designer, each with its own threats and opportunities that the designer should be aware of. Some of these scenarios are as follows:

Rebrands

Rebrands are changes to an identity, signifying to an audience that something has changed. For the designer, a rebrand is a delicate operation and also one that can be very rewarding. A full understanding of the brand and its direction is needed to determine how far the identity should change and the designer is often fully involved in this process. Rebrands also need to be supported by clear communications explaining the change and its impact on its audience.

Threats:
The core brand values may be compromised, driving away those loyal to the brand. Or the change may create a disconnection in the mind of the audience, giving competitors an opportunity to step in.

Opportunity:
The brand is enlivened and updated, occupies a more contemporary position and appeals to a more extensive or new audience.

Mergers and Buy-outs

Mergers occur when two or more companies combine efforts to, as is common in business, create a bigger market share. The companies will usually have equal management control with board positions being shared out among existing members. A buy-out or takeover may
be more fraught behind the scenes – depending on whether it was an aggressive merger or not – although a designer would not be involved until the outcome is clear. Often a merger or buy-out will result in the creation of a new identity, but this can be a tentative and time-consuming process as decisions are vulnerable to change further down the line. In the short term, designers may be asked to produce a hybrid identity combining two logos, or an existing logo with an additional strapline.

If there is a new identity, the emerging identity should reflect an integrated set of brand values (for a merger) and be supported by a clear message of how this will benefit the customer and other audiences, including employees. Mergers or buy-outs can result in the new company owning unwanted brands, which may later be sold off; in turn, companies can buy these 'spare' brands instead of entire companies. A key consideration in any

merger or buy-out is staff morale. There can be months of uncertainty and a company is faced with the task of integrating a workforce in flux. Clear brand direction can help consolidate a workforce behind a new strategic direction for the business.

In 1998, a new company called 'Citigroup' was formed following one of the biggest mergers in the financial world. Two companies, Citicorp and Travelers Group, merged to become Citigroup Inc., with 275,000 employees in more than a hundred countries and territories. The emphasis of the merger was to have a huge global presence and the new company instantly became the largest provider of financial services. The new Citigroup identity used the trademark Travelers' red umbrella as its logo.

Threats:
The resultant conglomerate may alienate both brands' traditional audience if they no longer understand what the brand represents.

Opportunities:
The support provided by each brand for the other can promote a more capable and dynamic organisation, opening up opportunities to offer services around a broader range of needs.

Stake: When a company buys part of another company.

"A full understanding of the brand and its direction is needed to determine how far the identity should change. The designer is often fully involved in this process"

1

1: KLM AND AIR FRANCE MERGER

Two national carriers, Air France and the Dutch-owned KLM merged in 2003 to create the obviously named group 'Air France-KLM', in an unprecedented move in the European airline industry. Although Air France holds 10 per cent of the 'voting rights' and 96.33 per cent of economic rights over KLM, the combination of the two brands has been positioned as an equal partnering or 'joining forces'.
The communications behind the new merger emphasise that customers now get more from the integration of two major national air carriers – such as more destination choice and more opportunity for Air Miles – and that the merger will 'capitalise on two well-known brands'. Time will tell whether both brands will retain their individual identities or whether KLM, which has a lesser stake, will become part of Air France.

Image courtesy of Capital Photos (for KLM ©)

"A brand acquisition may have little visible impact on the customer"

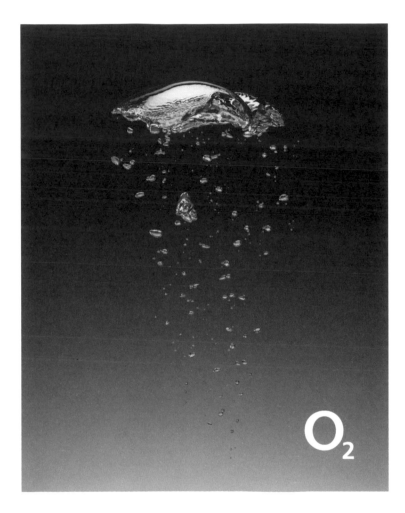

1

Demergers and Spin-offs

A demerger happens when two brands separate and can be the result of a legal instruction or a decision to separate a brand. Management buy-outs or a decision to divest of unwanted businesses may also create a demerger. A company that de-merges tends to start afresh with a new identity. This can be supported by a lot of marketing to let people know that the company is now trading as something new. The designer may be restricted by legal deadlines, which require that no trace of the former company name must exist by a certain date.

Brands may also be separated from a parent brand for an opportunity to enter a new market and offer a new service that is beyond the brand owner's core business. Spin-off brands may be 'incubated' within a parent company, with financial and technological backing, until they are ready to stand alone in the marketplace. Or they may simply be sold off if they are no longer relevant to the core business. This often gives the designer an opportunity to create a new identity.

Threats:
The new brand may appear weak and directionless without the support of the other.

Opportunities:
There is a chance to establish a new, and perhaps more radical or adventurous, market position.

1: O_2 DEMERGER FROM BT
LAMBIE NAIRN

In November 2001, UK telecom giant, BT, demerged its mobile businesses and a new holding company, mmO_2 plc, was created. In May 2002, the company launched its consumer brand, O_2, which united its businesses in the UK, Germany, Ireland and the Netherlands under a single brand.

Branding agency, Lambie Nairn, used the core concept of mobile communications as being 'essential for living' as the backbone to the identity. The challenge for branding agencies is to ensure that the identities can work across different regions as well as various media platforms. Oxygen is essential for life, and the symbol O_2 symbolises the ubiquity of the product. The identity of the bubbles represents oxygen underwater.

THEORY   PAGE / 40
See 'Swotting Up'

"A company that de-merges tends to start afresh with a new identity"

Acquisitions

If a company wants to grow in a crowded market or expand without having to launch a new brand, it could acquire one that already exists. Companies often sell brands when they wish to consolidate their business interests; to simplify their 'brand portfolio'; to sell off a brand that is surplus to requirements as it is dormant or no longer fits the portfolio; or simply to raise some cash.

A brand acquisition may have little visible impact on the customer. Many brands are purchased and continue as if nothing has happened, leaving the identity unchanged. The acquired brand may enhance the buyer's brand portfolio and altering it may not be in the interests of the buyer or the customer. If an acquired brand is to remain the same, the challenge for the designer is to ensure that it remains true to its original philosophies and principles – that is, the qualities that make it worth buying in the first place. It is often down to the skill of the acquirer to integrate existing brand values into the new corporate structure, and this needs to be identified at the outset. But be aware that while things may initially stay the same, they could change over the long term.

Threats:
The strengths of the brand may not be developed by the acquirer or are altered to create something that does not adhere to the original brand.

Opportunities:
Acquisition can increase the appeal and accessibility to the market for the brand. A larger company, which acquires a brand is often able to invest in that brand and expand its presence and range. For example, the production of the Aston Martin has risen from 60 cars to 4,000 a year since Ford acquired the brand.

2: BEN & JERRY'S ICE CREAM

Ice cream brand, Ben & Jerry's, went through some rocky times after it was acquired by giant consumer goods company, Unilever, in 2000. The acquisition by a global multinational was a far cry from the brand's roots and values.

Ben & Jerry's was originally started out of a petrol station by school-friends Ben Cohen and Jerry Greenfield in Vermont in 1978. It had a loyal following due to the quality of the ice cream and the strong social values behind the brand. For a brand that stood by anti-corporate values, it seemed unusual that the two founders would sell the company to one of the world's biggest corporations for $43.6 a share (the ice-cream had reached sales of US$237 million). On announcement of the acquisition, Unilever stated that it was 'determined to nurture [the brand's] commitment to community values' and has continued to support local community initiatives. At first, Unilever rapidly expanded the product range and caused confusion among consumers. They later reigned in the product lines, and the existing brand plays on its original creativity and humour.

3: STARBUCKS

Starbucks bought the Seattle Coffee Company, a chain of coffee shops in the UK, to gain a foothold into the UK coffee market. Seattle Coffee Company was, at the time, a popular coffee chain. By rebranding the stores as Starbucks, including changing the interiors to the Starbucks style, the US coffee company was immediately able to establish a street presence. It has continued to acquire other coffee stores to spread its presence – sometimes opening two stores in the same street.

The Starbucks chain continues to expand at a massive rate around the world: within nine months in 2004 it opened 1,344 new spaces. By early 2005 it had 8,569 stores in more than 30 countries. According to its newsletter, Starbucks intends to expand to 15,000 US stores and 15,000 international stores.

BRAND FAMILIES

Parent Brands and Sub-brands

The majority of parent brands are low-profile holding companies, with an audience of investors and the press. There is currently debate as to whether the 'parent' should have a separate brand identity from its sub-brands. The role of the parent company today is changing because they are no longer simply answerable to investors and the press, but to a much wider audience. This audience can include employees, customers, government and any other interested parties. Some parent brands are creating their own identity to 'speak' to this wider audience, particularly in relation to ethical issues.

Brands can be structured into families with the parent brand as the 'umbrella brand' owning a number of sub-brands. The sub-brands can come in different contexts:

The sub-brands may each have separate identities, which bear little resemblance to each other, and may even compete across audiences (for example, the brands owned by consumer goods holding companies, Unilever or Procter & Gamble). In this scenario, the parent brands generally keep a low profile, while the sub-brands have the external identity roles.

Sub-brands can be the products of a company and the 'parent' – the maker and owner of the products – will also be a brand. The behaviour and reputation of the parent and sub-brands will affect each other. This structure can also be applied to other brand scenarios such as countries: the European Community is a parent brand, while its member countries are each sub-brands and the behaviour of the sub-brand directly affects the reputation and perception of the parent brand.

The sub-brands may be a family of brands, which is closely associated with a personality behind the parent brand – the personality is usually its founder. In this scenario, the personality of the parent brand is fundamental to the brand's success, as it gives an overriding identity and set of values to the sub-brands.

Sub-brands can have identities that are stronger than the identity of the parent brand. It is not always necessary for sub-brands to have coherent identities among themselves or with their parent. A new sub-brand can offer an opportunity to breakaway from the perception of the parent brand to attract a different audience. For example, some financial institutions have set up an internet-only bank with a distinct identity that is not associated with the parent brand. A sub-brand can also offer an opportunity to promote products or services at a different price range than that of the parent.

Sub-brands can be launched as new primary brands, supported by huge campaigns to raise awareness of the brand and communicate its positioning – often an expensive undertaking.

Parent brands are also becoming more prominent by promoting their 'own brand' products as brand extensions. Tescos, a UK supermarket chain, was one of the first own-brands in the UK to introduce a range of its own products not commonly associated with supermarkets, such as financial services. Woolworths extended its brand under its own name years ago with its supermarkets in New Zealand, by offering a range of 'plain pack' goods at a lower price.

NATIONAL GEOGRAPHIC™

NATIONAL GEOGRAPHIC
CHANNEL

NATIONAL
GEOGRAPHIC
.COM

1

National Geographic brand families

The extension of a parent brand through sub-brands can help reposition or reinforce the parent's identity. National Geographic expanded its media formats beyond its established National Geographic magazine to include TV channels and a major website. "The magazine is still the mainstay of the National Geographic Society – it is the diary of the planet," says Charlie Graves from National Geographic's licensing division. "Over the past decade, National Geographic has branched out and started to do things beyond the magazine – with TV channels, books and varied partnerships. We wanted to use the name in an appropriate way." The key for a brand like National Geographic is to use the core positive messages of the parent brand and adapt these to the sub-brands – in National Geographic's case, these messages are the themes of exploration and education, targeting people who are curious about the world, even if they prefer to travel from their armchair while watching a TV channel.

THEORY   PAGE / 44

See 'Brand Families'

"Parent brands are also becoming more prominent by promoting their 'own brand' products as brand extension"

easyCruise.com
holidays at sea

easyHotel.com

easyInternetcafé
the cheapest way to get online

easyJet.com
the web's favourite airline

easyMoney.com
the credit card you design to suit your needs

easyPizza.com

easyBus.co.uk
low cost intercity travel

easyValue.com
comparisons for online shopping

2

3

4

3, 4: BRAND PERSONALITIES: STELIOS HAJI-IOANNOU AND RICHARD BRANSON

Some parent brands have succeeded by basing their product and service offerings around a strong charismatic founder. Richard Branson's Virgin carries the personality of its owner and the Virgin values – a commitment to service, a way of doing things differently, a chance to give the customer a better deal – and his media profile is as large as the company's. Another high-profile personality brand is US domestic doyenne, Martha Stewart, America's guardian of stylish living. Her brand has a stable of products and media, including a magazine, books, TV show, website, syndicated newspaper column, national radio show and a mail-order catalogue.

For personality brands, the brand is not only identified with its founder, but by consistent creative execution across the brand portfolio, which helps promote the parent brand. Yet a brand that is intrinsically linked to a personality can also expose it – no brand likes bad publicity. When Martha Stewart was indicted in June 2003 for lying to investigators about a stock sale, she was forced to resign as chief executive and chairwoman of Martha Stewart Living Omnimedia. The company's stock decreased, advertising sales slumped and the company lost US$19.3 million in three months prior to her conviction. But on conviction, in mid-2004, the price of her stock surged and a sense of her being wronged may, in the end, boost her appeal. On conviction she was already preparing for a comeback with her own TV series.

2: THE easyGroup BRAND FAMILY

easyGroup was set up by Greek magnate and 'serial entrepreneur', Stelios Haji-Ioannou. It is a series of brands offering mass services, like car rental, an airline and internet cafes, at a low cost with differential pricing based on demand. While the 'easy' brand carries strong brand associations, easyGroup is the private holding company of Stelios, acting as a business incubator rather than a brand in its own right. It is the product brands, or sub-brands, which carry the tangible brand experience. The easyGroup brands have a distinctive style in look, feel and attitude, which stems from the brand characteristics based around its founder. The brand offers no-frills better deals with a sense of fun rather than first class service. Some of the sub-brands currently exist without much content – they are, instead, portal sites offering cheap deals.

1

"Brands can be structured into families with the parent brand as the 'umbrella brand' owning a number of sub-brands"

"Sub-brands can have identities that are stronger than the identity of the parent brand"

1: APPLE'S SUB-BRANDING

The Apple iPod is an incredibly successful sub-brand, which has created a new market of customers beyond loyal Apple product users. The music player has successfully taken Apple out of its realm as a niche computer manufacturer, and moved it into space previously dominated by companies like Sony. It has also given the company the ability to win over PC-users to buy other Apple products.

The design and quality of the product is distinctly recognisable as Apple, even without the Apple brand mark on the front. The company has also licensed the iPod to Hewlett Packard to create its own version of the product. Before the iPod was introduced the MP3 music player market was stagnating and prices were dropping. The iPod has regenerated the entire market.

Umbrella branding: The overall brand that holds a number of sub-brands within its remit. The umbrella brand may have a completely separate brand identity to the sub-brands.

BRAND ORIGINATORS

A graphic designer working on a new brand must be absolutely clear on why the brand exists, its positioning and what message it gives to its audience. Building a new brand is a process of building awareness and reputation among the audience, establishing credibility and setting expectations. The brand communication must be authentic and true to the product or service that is being offered. Even then, it takes time to make an impact – and this impact is often dependent on the budget behind the noise and the ability to deliver the product or service.

New brands can seemingly emerge from nowhere and do well. The reality is that good new brands will have started small – the quality of the product or service being refined before making a splash (companies often 'pilot' brands to test whether to take them further). The key to success is an emotional link between the brand and its audience – and a great idea. The brand should offer differentiation, based on an understanding of what the audience wants, and a passion and belief in the product or service.

The words 'brand', 'product' and 'service' are becoming increasingly interchangeable, as a well-developed example of each demands a clear vision of what it might offer in terms of the other two. As client support and services increasingly become a differentiator between competing brands, and the sum product of the brand is seen as more than the actual goods sold, these terms will become synonymous.

It can be easier to establish a new brand if there is a history of product or service experience that has already earned trust and credibility. A new product or service brand can trade on the past successes of the organisation. Sony Corporation, for example, established credibility with the creation of the Walkman. Apple Computer's fortunes and reputation changed with the introduction of the iMac and, later, the iPod. However, these brands (or the products behind them) are the exception in that they have achieved iconic status. Most new brands need to be worked harder to establish an entry-level of credibility.

Another emerging area for companies creating original start-up brands are those that have worked behind the scenes as a supplier or under the name of the big brands. Market and product knowledge can make it easier to set up as a new brand.

1

1: BRAND ORIGINATOR INNOCENT DRINKS

Innocent Drinks creates fresh juice smoothies in a bottle. Its differentiator from the outset was to make drinks from pure unadulterated fruit, without the preservatives – even when they were told it couldn't be done. Innocent has employed 'nature' as its theme – a theme now much imitated by other food brands as health awareness moves into the mainstream.

"Innocent is about naturalness, purity and nature," says Dan Germain, the creator of the Innocent labels. "We don't mess around with it. 95 per cent of brand and marketing is in the bottle." Like any good brand, Innocent has a good start-up story: the founders first made their smoothies at a music festival back in 1998 and put up a sign asking whether their smoothies were good enough for them to quit their jobs and start a business. The 'Yes' bin was over-flowing. The next day they resigned.

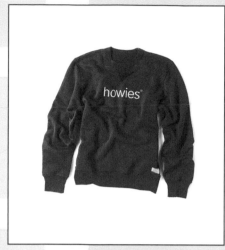

2: BRAND ORIGINATOR HOWIES

Howies is a clothing business with a message: "a desire to make people think about the world we live in". The husband and wife team worked on the idea of building a clothing brand for years before creating a company.

The outdoor wear they create is perfectly supported by a brand style that promotes the outdoors and all the good stuff that comes with it – freedom, nature, sports, friends. The character of the brand has a youthful feel and their main philosophy is to design quality clothes that last longer rather than following fashion fads. The quality of creative execution across the brand, from the photography to the clothes, has helped build Howies' reputation and success so far.

Many marketing strategies have been developed over the years on how to successfully create a brand. A more recent debate is raging over whether the key to successful branding is more heart-felt and emotional than that of business-school strategies – branding is, after all, the packaging of emotion. Whichever method is applied, any brand message must be authentic and true in its expression, and that is the starting point of the graphic design.

Many brands that are currently emerging as successful, original brands have a common theme: purity. Whether the products are food, clothes or beauty products, some of the upcoming brands stand by the formula of caring for the quality of their brand with no preservatives, no additives and no hidden surprises – you get what they promise. Although these brands seem to appear out of nowhere, most have been years in the making – Green & Black's organic chocolate, now ubiquitous, is over ten years old; Innocent Drinks reached its fifth birthday before becoming a mainstream brand, and surf-brand Howies was in the making for seven years before its owners decided to dedicate a full-time business to it.

"**The brand communication must be authentic and true to the product or service that is being offered**"

57

1: BRAND ORIGINATOR AUSTRALIAN HOMEMADE

Australian Homemade is, surprisingly, a Dutch brand. They sell chocolates and ice-cream with a distinctive Australian Aboriginal theme. Each chocolate is beautifully crafted with symbols of Aboriginal art and the ice-cream is made on the premises. Like other brand originators that are currently gaining mindshare, Australian Homemade focuses on the naturalness and quality of its products: they promote the brand as 'absolutely pure'.

The brand has so far expanded across the European continent, and in Asia Pacific through a franchising model, with strict brand rules on presentation, product and service, from shops that look more like they'd sell surfwear than confectionery. "The success is firstly down to the quality of the product. You can have a flashy brand, but if the product is bad, no one will buy it," says Jeroen Bruins Slot who heads up the company. "Then there is the appeal of the brand – what it stands for, what it radiates and how people perceive it – this is the marketing part. The design of the brand is also very important – it can make your brand or break it. The design has to reflect your brand, not bury it."

"It can be easier to establish a new brand if there is a history of product or service experience which has already earned trust and credibility"

"The reality is that good new brands will have started small"

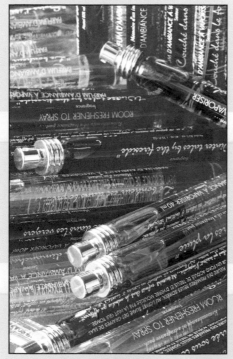

2

2: BRAND ORIGINATOR TERRE D'OC

Terre d'Oc is a fragrance brand founded by French perfumers, Valerie Roubaud and Patrick Lions, who have created perfumes for the large French fashion houses. Based in Provence, the brand is already well-established in France and launched in the UK in 2004, positioning itself in exclusive shopping areas.

The brand story plays on traditional perfume manufacturing: everything is handmade, and the scent is created from traditional know-how with expertise from Grasse, long renowned as the perfume capital of Europe. Products are based around anything that carries a fragrance: candles, incense, oils and room sprays.

This is the first time that Terre d'Oc has set up independent retail stores – and it's a risky move. Many other brands choose to get a foothold in a new market by selling through 'concessions' such as a range within a store rather than own-branded retail outlets. Concessions can offer a safer route, but less brand profile or exposure.

Mindshare: Winning over people at the emotional level.

59

A CHANGE IN IDENTITY

1

**1: THE REBRANDING EVOLUTION
OF BP'S HELIOS LOGO DESIGN**

BP's rebrand was a bold and risky move
in 2000. It created its new brand mark,
called the 'helios', supported by the message
'Beyond Petroleum'. It immediately positioned
the major oil company as concerned about
reducing environmental damage, opening it to
criticism by a cynical press, NGOs and
consumer audience, who saw it as style over
substance. Despite the cynicism, about 40 per
cent of BP's business was in natural gas at
the time of the rebrand, and its solar
business was one of the world's largest. Five
years on, the company has improved its
communications behind the rebrand and is
perceived as being committed to change for
the better.

All images © BP P.L.C. 2000–2005. The
Helios, BP in shield and the BP letters are
all trademarks of BP P.L.C.

Rebrands

People often associate rebranding as a
name and identity change, but it can be
more subtle than this; a rebrand can be
just a slight alteration to an identity. For
example, Heinz's iconic baked bean tin
rebranded a few years ago with just a
small change in its logo typeface. The
letters were slightly thickened to give the
brand a more modern appearance, without
detracting from the years of value
accumulated by the original.

An organisation will rebrand when it is
seeking to change consumer and business
perceptions about its product, service or
company: the brand may be outdated;
it may wish to leave its historical legacy
behind; it may desire to enter a different
market or to augment its current audience;
or it may wish to refocus in order to appear
more contemporary and audience-aware.
A rebrand signifies a direct call to the
audience to tell them something has
changed, and encourages them to take
another look.

Rebrands can take the form of a new
brand identity. However, a change in the
name or colour palette is not a necessity,
particularly if there is a strong emotional
connection and credibility associated
with the existing identity. The degree of
change to a rebrand will depend on how
dramatically the company wants to change
and reposition itself. Refreshing a brand or
fundamentally changing the brand can be
risky, and those implemented by high-
profile companies regularly attract bad
press. British Airways and the Post Office
were condemned for the apparent waste
of money when rebranding their product .

Any rebrand will inevitably have a
significant impact on the value of
the brand. The rebrand must be
communicated well to all audiences

– failure to explain the rebrand can
threaten the effectiveness of the move.
Explaining the rebrand to employees is
particularly important as they are the best
publicists of a rebrand, so a failure
to communicate or involve them in the
process is an opportunity missed.

Some brands change identity to have
consistent international product names,
recognising the global nature of their
audience and the increasingly travelled
consumer. A name change for cleaning
product Jif to Cif; beauty brand Oil of Ulay
to Oil of Olay and chocolate bar Marathon
to its US name, Snickers, has also
probably saved money on long-term
production costs by using consistent
international packaging.

There can be a temptation to rebrand
a business as aspiring to values and
behaviours that stretch beyond its
capabilities. While there is room for
aspiration – where the brand may be
promising something it does not yet
deliver – any rebrand must be authentic.
The designer should challenge and stretch
the client, but the stretch must be within
the context of the business. There have
been some high-profile disasters where
millions have been spent on rebranding,
only to alienate an existing audience
and be lambasted by the press and
consumers. There must be a clear and
defensible connection between the new
brand, the behaviour of the brand and
the products, services and people
behind the brand.

Accenture was created in 2001 from
a demerger, which prompted a name
change from Andersen Consulting to
Accenture. The decision to change was
a legal one, which required that the
company severe ties to its former links
(the Arthur Andersen firms and AWSC).
This meant that a deadline was set to

remove the name 'Andersen Consulting'
from every piece of marketing material,
including any websites, which mentioned
the company on its client list. The result
was a massive rebrand operation carried
out on a global scale. Teams were set up
around the world to ensure that every
piece of communication that was still
needed was renamed Accenture, and any
old material destroyed. This also included
contacting partners, suppliers, or clients
who had the old name on their website
or marketing materials to request the
removal of the name. The scale of the
task ensured that Accenture was launched
into the market with a huge impact and
high awareness.

Demerger: When a brand is split from another to stand on its own.
This often involves a name change and new identity for the new brand.

2: KALL KWIK'S REBRAND

Kall Kwik is a print and design retailer that rebranded after ten years. The company was set up as a high-street printing service in the UK, aimed at small businesses and individuals. It expanded through a franchise model. As the printing market has developed, the business shifted from a printing shop to a design and printing outlet that was managing bigger business customers, but its brand mark remained the same. The issue with a franchise model like Kall Kwik's is that each outlet is a separate business and it is the owner's choice to implement the rebrand. While head office offers support and materials, they are unable to dictate change. Consequently, the new brand can have less impact if all the shops do not conform.

"The degree of change to a rebrand will depend on how dramatically the company wants to reposition"

FRENCH CONNECTION | fcuk®

3: FRENCH CONNECTION UK REBRAND

UK clothing retailer, French Connection, transformed itself from just another high street store, to a trendy, eye-catching, brand by renaming itself FCUK in 1997. The brand was relaunched with campaigns like 'FCUK Fashion' – at the time it was irreverent, controversial and hugely popular.

Seven years later, in 2004, the company made a loss that has prompted talk that its once revered rebrand has now had its day. *The Guardian* newspaper wrote: "The 18–30 year olds which are the company's target market and were once proud to sport 'FCUK like a bunny" and "FCUK for England" on their chests are now spurning FCUK fashion and taking their spending power elsewhere."[1]

"We wanted to foster a perception that we were more relevant and contemporary than perhaps some people thought we were. 'Iconic' brands need to work especially hard at proving relevancy and a contemporary attitude"

Karen Rice Gardiner, National Geographic Society

1. 'Oh FCUK, where have our customers gone?'
The Guardian newspaper, UK, 17/11/04

"A brand may reposition to target a new audience or to change its market altogether – such as shifting from an upmarket position to a lower one"

Repositioning

A repositioning is when a brand shifts its positioning in its market without making any overt changes to its physical identity. Although in appearances a repositioning may seem softer than a rebrand, it can have just as much impact. A repositioning can be a difficult tactic for a brand – while it may open the brand up to a new audience, it may also alienate its existing one.

A brand may reposition to target a new audience or to change its market altogether – such as shifting from an upmarket position to a lower one. A brand may also reposition if it has suffered negative publicity; it may be an attempt to revive a failing brand; or to adapt to new market developments like new technology. Any shift in positioning of a brand must be communicated through PR and advertising, as there is no obvious visual identity change. It is the message that counts. Repositioning can work well for brands that have become outdated through defunct technology or overtaken by new technology.

Many of the major oil companies have repositioned themselves to be viewed as more environmentally caring, and as offering a more sustainable and cleaner means of powering the world, by selling products such as renewable energy and clean fuels. This major reposition was first adopted by Shell in the mid-1990s in a move to manage its brand and reputation after damaging publicity in 1995 prompted by a Greenpeace campaign after Shell proposed sinking a defunct oil platform, the Brent Spar. The company was also in the press in the same year for its operations in Nigeria involving allegations of associations with human rights abuses. Its consequent repositioning has included an active dialogue with Non-Governmental Organisations (NGOs), the publishing of strict guidelines on the way Shell does business, and anti-corruption work, which has resulted in a marked improvement of image and reputation.

BP followed suit by adopting an environmental agenda with its rebrand and supporting line, 'Beyond Petroleum'. The latest, and perhaps most surprising, turn around is energy company, Exxon (also trading under ExxonMobil) which, after refusing to address the environment as an issue because of lack of scientific proof, has now been promoting a friendlier stance on climate change and emission reduction – including giving around US$26 million to Stanford University in the USA for research on greenhouse gas reduction. The reposition seems to have been timed with a change of leadership at the top of the company in late 2004.

Strapline (or 'tagline'): The supporting words of a logo, or part of an advertising campaign. This is sometimes referred to as the 'sign-off'.

"A repositioning can be a difficult tactic for a brand – while it may open the brand up to a new audience, it may also alienate its existing one"

The car manufacturer, Skoda, was always the laughing stock of the car world. It successfully repositioned itself by holding its former negative image up to ridicule, before demonstrating that its new cars were different. It teased people into considering that assumptions can be misleading and encouraged them to take another look.

MasterCard is a global brand providing a credit and debit scheme for payment through partnering banks and financial institutions across the world. It is very similar to its competitor VISA. In 1995 MasterCard launched a global campaign that explicitly acknowledged there are some priceless things you just can't buy, while at the same time reminding their audience that for everything else there is MasterCard. The identification of priceless elements in individuals' lives was localised in many languages and cultures with success for the recognition of the brand. The campaign used a globally consistent concept executed in dozens of languages. Up to this point many payment schemes had a common positioning of acquiring a payment card because of what it might allow the holder to achieve in the future. MasterCard repositioned the brand away from a competitor positioning of future opportunity and right into a recognition of what is important in the cardholder's life, while leaving the brand mark unchanged.

Apple now releases some of the most innovative and well-designed products in the market today, but made a disastrous decision to reposition in the mid-1990s in an effort to increase its customers by targeting the PC audience. The prompt was that Microsoft was about to introduce Windows 95 in the midst of much hype and publicity. In an attempt to pretend it was like everyone else, Apple alienated its existing and incredibly loyal user base by trying to appeal to PC users instead. The company was in danger of losing its creative edge, it was in financial difficulty, and its loyal customers were upset. Ironically, Microsoft financially propped up the ailing company. It wasn't until Steve Jobs came back as CEO that Apple refocused on what it was – a computer company for creative people and for those who like to 'think different' (as Apple's strapline said).

MIXED MESSAGES

The idea that a parent company is the quiet, financial-facing owner of the brand is changing. Some parent brands are now creating their own identity to take a clear stance on responsible behaviour and create an open discussion with their audiences.

Diageo – the owner of nearly 70 alcohol brands around the world – actively promotes a sensible drinking policy; Ford Motor Company, the owner of many brands such as Ford, Jaguar and Land Rover, takes on 'issues' such as road and vehicle safety; and Unilever, which owns numerous global food and domestic brands has 'rebranded' its parent Unilever logo, to be identified with ethical food sourcing and sustainable development.

This tactic of sending out positive messages from the parent brand is becoming more popular as customers become more aware of the issues associated with brands. By tackling issues such as child-labour for fashion brands, the destruction of the environment for transport and oil companies, the addictions and accidents associated with drinking for alcohol brands, health and sourcing issues for food brands, and the possible health issues for

mobile phone brands, parent companies can use their own brands as a proactive means to avoid negative publicity or costly lawsuits. Common to all brands is the issue of selling to children and young teenagers, as well as supply chain issues, such as ensuring that a company's suppliers adhere to good standards of business practice.

Diageo's sensible drinking policy is common among drinks brands in response to government concern over alcohol advertising. Companies are anxious not to have their advertising banned in the same way as cigarette companies did in the 1980s, and so are implementing their own voluntary code of good behaviour.

Injecting an ethical message into the parent brand also carries inherent risks. Any negative action or negative perception of the parent brand is likely to affect its sub-brands. This may be a risk for the brand, but for the consumer, it is a step forward: if the parent brand is promoting responsibility then they must uphold it if its reputation is to be maintained.

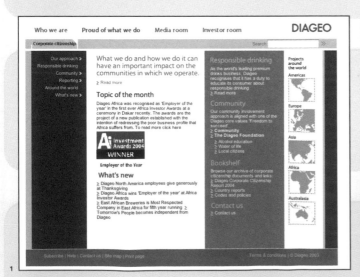

1

1: BRAND ORIGINATOR DIAGEO

Dutch brand, Diageo, is the owner of over 70 alcohol brands. It now uses the parent brand to promote a key message of responsible drinking.

This approach of associating a parent brand with social responsibility is part of a growing trend among brand owners, and there is good reason for it. Alcohol brands are concerned about future legal implications if they do not acknowledge the issues around drinking or continue to promote drinking without making people aware of the risks. Some of the large buyers, like university bars, insist that alcohol companies promote safe drinking. Using the parent brand to carry the responsible message addresses the responsible agenda, without necessarily impacting on the individual brands.

"Any negative action or negative perception of the parent brand is likely to affect its sub-brands"

Sub-brand: A brand within a brand, for example, the Sony PlayStation.

Parent brand: The main brand owner or holding company.

interview 1

From the designer's perspective: Tom Geismar from New York design agency Chermayeff & Geismar

The National Geographic rebrand took five years, starting in 1999. While visually the shift for the brand is not radical – the yellow border of the brand is the prominent feature of the identity – the rebrand was a massive auditing exercise for a global brand that has been around for decades.

National Geographic is a non-profit organisation run by the National Geographic Society. It is best known for its magazine, which is published all over the world, and the National Geographic TV channel. It also distributes content in other formats like the web, and through licensing deals – from clothing to furniture. National Geographic's major themes are about exploration and education.

How did the rebrand come about?

The impetus for the rebrand came from National Geographic's employees, particularly the designers who were working with the identity across different media on a day-to-day basis. They were the ones who had to convince the leaders to change.

What was the process for the rebrand within Chermayeff & Geismar?

When we first started the National Geographic rebrand we did a situation analysis which took one year. No design was done at this stage. Our analysis looked at where the company was. We also interviewed people within the company and reviewed how the National Geographic Society distinguished itself from the rest of the organisations.

The audit also involved reviewing their existing materials, including names and signatures. We then did research which analysed the meaning of the name and the colours, as well as how National Geographic Society was viewed in relationship to the National Geographic product.

The rebrand is a slight visual shift from the old National Geographic identity. What was the thinking behind this?

We decided to make the rebrand a subtle change because both old and new material are still around. National Geographic is an entrenched identity – the name has such respect and brand equity tied up in it.

From a design perspective we made minor revisions. We changed the lettering so that it is easier to use across different technologies. We also created a relationship between the box (which is the National Geographic logo) and the lettering. People associate National Geographic with photography and with its yellow colour, so we wanted to make more use of that – the result is a cleaner, more contemporary look. We have isolated the logo against a clear dark background so that it stands out.

Is there any flexibility for countries to apply the brand in different ways within their own region?

The basic design principles have some flexibility – the company is so diverse that you have to be flexible. We have given people design principles to follow, such as before and after shots and details on how to use photography well. But people are encouraged to do creative, inventive things with the design when they use photography and/or create new products.

interview 2

From the visual identity manager's perspective: Karen Rice Gardiner, Director of Creative Services, National Geographic Society

You say you undertook the rebrand to provide some consistency of the brand mark internationally. Were there any other reasons for the rebrand, such as extending your audience reach?

We wanted to foster a perception that we were more relevant and contemporary than perhaps some people thought we were. We are an 'iconic' brand and that means we need to work especially hard at proving relevancy and a contemporary attitude.

Was any research undertaken and what was the outcome?

We undertook a large quantitative branding survey, which measured ourselves against competitors in the same media categories, to discover what consumers thought of and wanted from us. This survey also identified what kind of consumer (including lifestyle characteristics and demographics) would be most likely to want to interact with us. We developed four customer segments from this research – the top tiers were the most interested in the content we have.

Did you create new brand identity themes, such as the theme of exploration?

They are not new, but we had not, up until this point, really brought them into sharp focus. Many of us would work off one or two of them, but few of us used all of them most of the time. It is like a six-cylinder car running only on four cylinders. The car doesn't go as fast or as far.

How have you stayed true to National Geographic's core values through your rebrand – such as your commitment to education, and the magazine?

The rebrand helped us focus on our core values. It did not change them.

Is there any flexibility in applying the guidelines, both in design and language? For example, if the designer is creating for media such as the mobile phone.

There is not a lot of leeway granted for the use of the National Geographic house-mark because we use it as the identifier of the source of the product or the communication. So we insist that it is clearly visible and not impeded by other design elements or messages. Small spaces, like mobile phone screens, definitely present the toughest design problems for us. That was part of the reason why we changed the typeface in the logo, because it was too hard to read at small sizes. With regard to language, different media groups here use different taglines. We tried to make a single tagline work, but had no success. I think it is because the different media types (e.g. TV, print and digital) make a very big difference in the way our content is applied.

What has the rebrand done to improve the National Geographic brand? Has it increased brand equity or reputation, improved your ranking as one of the most-recognised global brands, or helped to attract a younger audience?

We think that it is working in all of these areas. We believe it is resonating in our ability to attract a younger audience. We have not done any specific surveying because we are confident that we needed to do this rebranding.

03

BRAND ANATOMY: CONTEXT, TONE, STYLE

INTRODUCTION

Similar brands can be distinguished in subtle ways by the
way they present themselves to an audience through their style
and tone. The graphic designer is often the architect of these
subtle differences.

Before the creative process starts, there is a strategic piece that
often sits behind the brand. The start of this chapter shows the
PEST method of analysing a brand's make-up.

The main body of this chapter looks at context, narrative, style,
tone and naming – all are fundamental elements of the creative
process. A designer must understand the environment in
which the brand exists, from the global context to its immediate
environment and channel of communication. A narrative can
then be formed around the brand to help communicate and
contextualise the brand for its audience and for the designers.
Style and tone cover how the brand projects itself in a verbal,
visual and emotional way. Finally, the chapter looks at one of
the most contentious areas of branding – the name.

Imagery from some of the world's leading brands and graphic
designers is used to demonstrate points. There is also an interview
with design company, IDEO, which approaches design in a
different way. Its method of watching and analysing human
behaviour has made it one of the leading design companies
in the world.

Chapter 3 Contents:

THEORY CHAPTER 03 /

++

PEST Control

No brand exists in a vacuum, and a PEST analysis helps a company determine the political, economic, social and technological environment the brand will live in.

The list below is a sample of considerations for the environment into which the brand will be launched.

POLITICAL	Environmental policy Taxation (on the company, on consumers) Competition regulation (Can we take over a competitor? Do we risk monopoly investigation?) Consumer protection (What are our responsibilities?)
ECONOMIC	Economic growth Interest rates Exchange rates (What effects will they have on demand by overseas customers? What effect on the cost of imported components?) Inflation Consumer spending
SOCIAL DEMOGRAPHICS	(Social and economic make-up of consumers) Lifestyle changes (e.g. home workers, single households, first-time house buyers) Leisure time Fashions and fads
TECHNOLOGICAL	Spending on research New discoveries and development Speed of technology transfer Rates of technological obsolescence Changes in material sciences

There is no point launching a premium-priced product if it is likely that interest rates will rise soon and reduce consumer spending. Equally, if government policy is turning against particular products (sugar, salt) then launching a highly sweetened or salted snack would backfire. But if social tastes are turning towards quality of life and leisure time, then family cars, sports equipment and games consoles may be areas to become involved with.

"No brand exists in a vacuum, and a PEST analysis helps a company determine the political, economic, social and technological environment the brand will live in"

BRAND 'RULES'

Branding is a marketing discipline and the basics of branding are common to all areas of marketing: define your audience, know your market, differentiate yourself, choose a route to market and then make your brand stand out. Brand building starts with a clear set of rules – a brand must define its positioning (where it sits in the market) and offer a clear proposition (how it presents itself) to its audience. This is supported by brand values that form the backbone of the character and behaviour of the brand.

As our lives become more complex and full of choice, branding is starting to change business by making the intangible, tangible. It offers more than a frill around a product or service – when people are passionate about particular brands there is an emotional connection that goes beyond the appreciation of the product or service. The attachment could be triggered for a number of reasons: there may be a status associated with the brand; the person may be attracted by design or form; it may give a brilliant service, or a simple, functional, practical use that makes the person connect with the brand. While emotional connections with brands are not new – most successful brands have always

understood that emotion is key – the difference today is that emotion is becoming a basis for branding. Brands need to have a deeper connection with their consumers if they are to thrive and prosper. Some brand experts refer to this as connecting with the 'spirit' of the brand; others call it a 'sixth sense'. Applying the traditional brand 'rules' makes it difficult to capture this nebulous spirit. Spirit must be captured in the creative execution.

To trigger an emotional response or connection is difficult for brands that have offered, until now, a simple product or service. Many brands still remain product-based and driven on sales, and don't know how to connect. Others simply add key emotional verbs to their straplines ('love' is common) and assume that this is enough to make us, the consumers, buy into the brand. But emotional connections are created through the behaviour of the brand, by its style, by the way it 'speaks' to us, and the quality and nature of the product or service. This chapter explores these elements of brand anatomy – the make-up of the brand that helps to create a connection with the audience.

"A marketing- or brand-dominated business depends for its survival on its customers' goodwill"

Wally Olins, *On Brand* [1]

1. Wally Olins, *On Brand*, Thames & Hudson Ltd., UK, 2004

BRAND NARRATIVE

Brands start with a great idea that tells a good story. Everybody understands a story – stories cross borders, and they connect generations, class and cultures. Stories are created for their audience and this is what makes them powerful. The story – or narrative – behind a brand is its backbone.

Brands often struggle with trying to be all things to all people. One simple story will help focus the aims of the brand or the brand project and create a single goal. Stories help create simplicity out of complexity by defining a single route through a maze of possibilities, and it is the designer who must translate the story into the visual element and execution.

Stories can be used at any stage of brand ideas generation. The creation of a brand must start with a story: 'The future's bright, the future's Orange' was the main strapline for mobile phone operator Orange's launch created around the idea of optimism; Nike's 'Just do it' – one of the most successful straplines in branding – is about self-realisation. From the main story, chapters can be created in the form of campaigns. Stories can be used to

create a scenario describing how people will interact with the brand in a particular environment, or used to understand a different audience. Think in terms of the one central idea that you are trying to tell people, then the one key message and how this can be communicated, and work within the boundaries of the values of the brand. The story behind a brand campaign will help the designer visualise the brand execution.

Every brand has a story about how it came to exist. Brands, like countries, have a history that can make people proud – yet many brands hide their stories because it may make them look dated or expose them to criticism. Old or new, brand stories make a brand seem more real – helping people contextualise the brand's existence.

1

"Great brands are like novels that you can't put down"

John Williamson, Wolff Olins

2

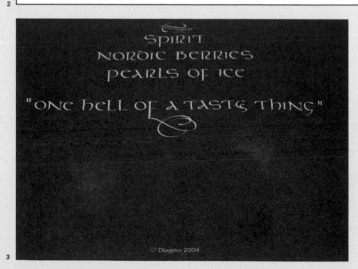

3

1–3: NORSK VODKA PROMOTION
CRUSH DESIGN

The fairy tale *The Norsk Tales: The Town That Night Forgot* was created for the launch of Smirnoff's Norsk vodka and copies were mailed to journalists and press outlets. Although the story concerns the discovery of a new magical spirit to be drunk, nowhere in the book was the Smirnoff brand referred to by name. The only traditional branding on the publication was that of parent company Diageo, discretely tucked out of the way at the back.

1

1–4: GUINNESS STOREHOUSE, DUBLIN
IMAGINATION LTD.

Old brands can tell a good story – it's just that sometimes the story can fade over the years. Guinness is a 240-year-old brand that reinvented itself to remind the world of why it was special. The brand director hired John Simmons from Interbrand to create some of the stories that went to the heart of Guinness as a legend brand with the idea of uniting the brand's past with its future. A series of stories were created, playing on the brand's 'inner strength' message.

Guinness also hired brand experience and design agency, Imagination Ltd., in 1998, to create an experience of the brand by building a new home for Guinness, which would replace the existing 'Guinness Hopstore' exhibition. Built within the heart of Dublin, the key to the design of the new experiential home, entitled the 'Guinness Storehouse', was to make it a focal point for people in Dublin – not just tourists, but the Irish community in which Guinness' roots lie. With bars, galleries, exhibition spaces and an events space, the venue uses words and narrative around it to tell the Guinness story.

2

"Brands start with a great idea that tells a good story"

BRAND CONTEXT

No brand exists in a vacuum. Brands operate in the context of an audience and their environment affects the audience. The environment sets a 'context' for the brand – everything from global events and trends, to politics, street trends and fashion. Context includes our existing perception and knowledge of the brand, to the immediate context, or medium, in which we encounter the brand. Mistakes are made when context is narrowed to simply looking at the brand's immediate competition; instead, context must be in the framework of a brand's audience so that it is relevant to the audience, rather than reacting to its competitors.

The graphic designer needs to be aware of both the broad and immediate context of the audience and brand in order to offer valuable insight and direction for the brand. The designer should consider how changes in context will impact the brand and how the brand can lead rather than follow.

Brands are influenced and affected by global context, such as politics, economic factors and cultural trends. A buoyant or depressed economy will affect consumer buying behaviour and financial investment in the brand. World events change brands: after the events of 9/11 and the creation and publicity of a 'War on Terror', fear and insecurity have reigned as dominant emotions within many populations. This atmosphere changes people's behaviour – the travel industry having probably borne the brunt of people's fear. This emotional environment also affects people's choice of governments and their leaders and, in turn, policies and international affairs. A USA-lead invasion of another country impacts on how brands are perceived in other parts of the world. Since the war in Iraq, sales of some of the biggest US brands have declined in countries outside of the USA: Coca-Cola, Marlboro and McDonald's have all taken a slump[2], while new alternative brands like Mecca Cola – the Islamic response to Coca-Cola – have emerged, complete with anti-corporate and anti-imperialist sentiment.

Globalisation has probably been the most dominant force to impact on brands and brand behaviour in the past decade. There is brand uniformity at opposite ends of the world, from coffee to food to cleaning products to clothes. Globalisation has changed people's outlook of brands and prompted a vocal anti-globalisation movement. It has also sped up the development and increased consumer spending power within those nations that were once considered 'developing': Brazil, Russia, India and China (coined the 'BRIC' nations) are now being keenly eyed by brands as huge new growth markets. Within this context it is possible, in the longer term, that there will be a shift in brand spend by global companies from the West to these emerging nations – they represent a huge, mostly untapped, middle-class population with money and an open attitude to brands.

1

1: SAMSUNG FLAGSHIP STORE IN MOSCOW IMAGINATION (US) INC.

In 1988 Samsung restructured with the mission of becoming one of the top five electronics companies. It is now a dominant player in the electronics market.

When Samsung launched in Russia it was viewed as an elite brand. Design and communications company, Imagination (US) Inc., was commissioned to create the Samsung brand showcase space in the centre of Moscow. Brands in Russia, particularly elite brands, allow people to view but not touch. Imagination turned this concept on its head to offer something new – an experience of the brand where people are able to demonstrate, touch and feel the products.

2. 'A deeper reason why Europe is rejecting US brands' *The Financial Times* newspaper, UK, 5/11/2004

"Street trends reflect buying habits, attitudes and behaviours, and can be great influencers for the direction of brands"

Globalisation has affected those working with brands on a day-to-day basis. Most brands now have an international context simply because of their global reach. Hence, cultural context must be considered in brand executions – what works in the UK may not work in the US or Japan. This is why some brands leave local campaign implementation in the hands of the local marketing people.

Within the framework of global context, it is still the immediate environment that, arguably, has the most influence on people's behaviour. One of the best ways to gauge the immediate context is to look at the street. Street trends reflect buying habits, attitudes and behaviours, and can be great influencers for the direction of brands. A scan around the restaurants, clubs, shops, art, architecture, interior design, services and fashion in some of the world's biggest cities can offer an insight – and inspiration – for branding ideas. For example, there's a 'street art' or graffiti movement that has emerged on the streets of some of the major European and US cities (Amsterdam, London, Paris, New York) with artists using graffiti as a means of reclaiming open spaces. Brands looking for cultural validity at street level are already approaching these artists to help design products for them.

Audiences might also contextualise a brand by its history, including their previous contact. The designer needs to be aware of the historical context of the brand (for example, if the brand is trying to reinvent itself). History can be an advantage as it can give a brand meaning – in the current climate it is said that people are turning back to the old heritage brands as they offer familiarity, trust and credibility.

Finally, the immediate context should be viewed from the experience of the brand. It is important to understand how the audience will interact with a brand within its media – an audience in a retail space will have very different needs from those experiencing a brand online. The simplest way to understand how people react to brands in their immediate environment is to develop a story from the point of view of the audience within that environment.

2: PANDA THUG SKATEBOARD
CAT THUG DESIGN FOR SKATEBOARD
BLACKIE FOR CREME

Graffiti and street art can lend kudos to brands aimed at the youth market. UK graffiti artist and musician Blackie helped skate label Creme brand their boards by developing the animal thug series.

Brand spend: The amount of money spent on marketing a brand.

THEORY   PAGE / 72
See 'PEST Control'

BRAND STYLE

Like someone choosing to dress in a particular way, brand style can be a surface appearance or reflect a greater depth. Brand style must capture the 'spirit' of the brand – the emotive element that makes us like or dislike a brand, or be indifferent to it. Style is shown in the way the brand projects itself in form, function and service. It can project an attitude we either empathise with or dismiss.

Brand style comes from the core – that is, the values of the brand. Brand values are the belief systems behind the brand. They are usually described as succinct adjectives that are often associated with archetypal characteristics: fun, rebellious, winning or inventive, for example. The designer must integrate the values into any brand communication, and their creative ideas should work around these.

Memorable brands have a distinctive visual style that cuts across language barriers. Italian clothing label, Diesel, for example, has highly creative imagery that often contains a political or social message, with rebellious but trendy values behind it. Spanish fashion brands Zara and Mango offer a particular style, not just in the clothes, but in their attitude and approach (both do very little advertising). A brand's style can be recognised solely by its characteristics rather than a logo.

A dominant personality behind the brand can also create a style for the brand by projecting a certain character and values on the brand. This can be done through a highly visible founder with charisma or through an inanimate character or a person associated with the brand. Paul Newman's salad dressing, for example, is seen as a glamourous, yet butch and hard-working brand, partly due to the film-star personality of its founder. Elle MacPherson's underwear range is daring and sexy – a style associated with its supermodel endorser. EasyGroup's founder Stelios Haji-Ioannou has a cheeky style that challenges the dominant global brands in areas like the airline industry, with his brand EasyJet.

Brand style should be played with, rather than restricted to one particular look and feel. Consistency comes from applying the brand character and spirit to the different brand audiences.

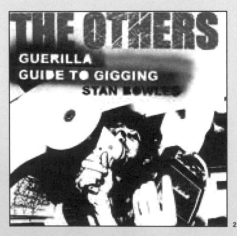

**1–3: A GUERRILLA GIG ON LONDON'S UNDERGROUND
THE OTHERS' WEBSITE STYLING, DVD SINGLE
SAM BANNISTER / ANDREW KENDALL**

Dispossessed UK teen band 'The Others' specialises in 'guerrilla gigs'. Contacting their technology-savvy audience via their website and mobile phones, they have played impromptu gigs at the BBC in response to being asked to discuss the phenomena, and most famously, on London Underground's Bakerloo line. By subverting the normal marketing channels, the band has built a loyal fan base which is absolutely committed to the product offered. Is this branding? For the record company profiting from their sales it is, although the band themselves might beg to differ.

4

4: LANCÔME ADVERTORIAL
ME COMPANY

The advertising campaign for Lancôme features the added celebrity glamour of Mick Jagger's daughter, Liz, to promote Lancôme's summer products. This campaign was designed in 2003 to run in Spring/Summer 2004.

5

5, 6: KENZO CLOTHING
ME COMPANY

Me Company is a world-renowned design agency, known for its highly-rendered 3D images created from stories and characters. Its digital style gives the images a depth and magical quality that many have tried to imitate. The blonde model featured in this Kenzo ad, An Oust, has had her image digitally manipulated to create an imaginary brother for the campaign. The campaign ran globally as press, posters and billboards.

6

1: NATURE ADVERTISING CAMPAIGN FOR DIESEL CLOTHING

Clothing brand, Diesel, has a very distinct advertising style, using the brand as a
vehicle to poke fun at topical issues or carry more political messages about issues such
as the environment. This 'Nature: Love it while it lasts' campaign is a jibe at the
destruction of our environment and also uses lascivious imagery and characters to
attract attention. The clothes seem secondary to the message.

2: ADIDAS CAMPAIGNS
180/TBWA

Adidas advertising has a particular storytelling style that plays on the personalities of sports
stars and the nature of sport as competition. No campaign looks the same as each has
a distinct creative execution (unlike Diesel, for example, which has a recognisable style of
imagery and character of ads).

A Napoleonic-scale battle scene with 50 of the world's top football players was used to promote
a new Adidas football boot during the UEFA competition in 2004. The image uses iconic
references to portray the ferocity of the competition rather than using an overt image of the
football boot.

3

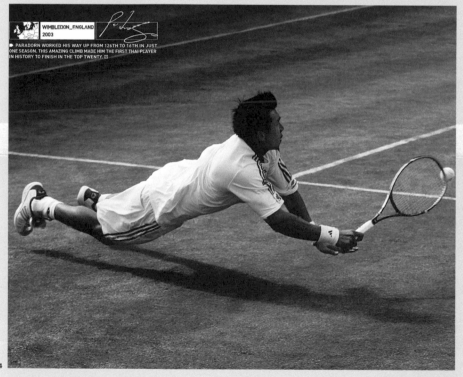

4

3–5: ADIDAS CAMPAIGN
180/TBWA

Each Adidas campaign currently plays on the ability of a particular sports-person in a unique creative style using different stories and creative direction to highlight the achievements of the athletes.

For example, some All Blacks' players were covered in acrylic paint for a travelling art exhibition titled 'Impact: The Art of Rugby', which coincided with the Rugby World Cup in 2003.

5

BRAND TONE

Brand tone is the pitch at which the brand communicates to its audience. First impressions count for a lot – the way somebody speaks, the way they look, the people they associate with and their tone of voice, can create an impression that is hard to shake. It's the same with brands. Tone comes through in both design and language and a brand's tone can differentiate one brand from another when they're in the same market.

It is possible to judge the tone of a brand by its design, who it is associated with (other brands or the people that endorse the brand), the language used and the services offered. Its price also affects its pitch. The doughnut brand, Krispy Kreme, is widely available throughout the USA but currently only available in the UK at one of the most exclusive department stores in the world, Harrods. Its exclusive associations and limited accessibility tells us something about the product even if we haven't tasted it. A brand speaks to us in a huge range of tones that reflect its persona: for example, warm and friendly (Apple), aloof and exclusive (The Ritz), deliberately pretentious (Chanel), hectic and energetic (Red Bull), or humourous (Innocent Drinks). The tone must be authentic and consistent, otherwise it could be open to misinterpretation.

The tone of a brand may change as the brand develops; it may speak differently to different audiences, but the character and values will remain consistent. A car manufacturer will 'speak' differently to its audience for different models. A clothing brand will have one tone for its adult range, compared to the kid's range. Brands change tone when they want to attract a new market. HP and BMW have always had a strong business bias, but both brands have cleverly adapted a new tone through associations with the creative industry and noticeable, creative advertising.

Tone reflects the brand's attitude so it is crucial to speak at the right pitch, otherwise an audience can feel alienated. Market researcher Kristen Davis says many brand-owners fail to look at how the brand 'speaks' to its audience: "This means brands may end up targeting the wrong audience. Analysing the way the brand 'speaks' to its audience is important – the brand may be patronising its market or pitching itself at the wrong level."

Tone can mature or reinvent itself as the brand develops, just as our own voice and appearance change as we grow older. And as we might occasionally reinvent ourselves to stay looking young, an aging brand may go in for a little cosmetic surgery.

"The tone of a brand may change as the brand develops. It may speak differently to different audiences, but the character and values will remain consistent"

1

1: INNOCENT DRINKS

Innocent entered a market to do things differently. It wanted to introduce drinks that were 'made from nature' with no preservatives or additives, just pure fruit. The brand was one of the first food brands in the UK to use clever, cheeky labels as a substitute to advertising. "You have someone's attention for a few seconds while they're holding the bottle, so why not use it?" says Dan Germain, creator of the labels. Every label tells a different story, always returning to the essence of the drink – made by nature. Its tone is humorous, honest and simple.

1–3: MAHARISHI CAMOUFLAGE PRINTS

Clothing label, Maharishi, has a distinctive style, which is identified by global influences and motifs in the product. Despite its international popularity, it remains a small, arts-inspired brand.

In 2004 Maharishi launched the DPM (Disruptive Pattern Material) brand, including an encyclopaedic art book of the same name by the company's Founder, Hardy Blechman. The book explores the nature of camouflage and its changing associations – from its roots in the natural world, to its adoption by the military, and its current popularity in areas of civilian culture, such as art, fashion and music. There is a strong anti-war sentiment throughout the book and associated products, which seeks to remind people of the natural origins and aesthetic beauty of camouflage.

All images taken from DPM (Disruptive Pattern Material), an encyclopaedia of camouflage published by DPM Ltd. (www.dpmhi.com).

Photo: Neil Davenport, concept: Karolyn Cohen-Solal

2

1

3

88

4: BLISS BODY CARE PRODUCTS

The packaging, labelling and tone of the Bliss products, along with the entire Bliss experience, have been carefully crafted to appeal to an upmarket audience with a sense of humour – they call it 'tongue-in-chic'. The company started in New York as a spa and has since opened in London with a supporting range of beauty products. The spas are bright, funky and ultra hip, created by Marcia Kilgore, who shows a keen understanding of branding.

5–7: BURT'S BEES PERSONAL CARE PRODUCTS

The cosmetics industry has spawned dozens of individual brands, each with a distinctive style and look. US brand, Burt's Bees, uses its founder's story to promote its products and brand character. The brand was created by Burt Shavitz and Roxanne Quimby – Roxanne came up with the notion of the company and made candles (their first product) from Burt's stockpile of beeswax that he had amassed over the years. The style of the product oozes 'naturalness' (perhaps because of bearded beekeeper Burt present on many of the labels) and has some interesting naming and contents – Poison Ivy soap, for example.

"Brands need names that work in a multi-channel world as well as across different countries"

BRAND NAMING

Naming can be an emotional part of the brand creation process. People tend to either love or hate names and new brand names have often been blamed for the failure of a product or company. "At least as many expensive rebranding exercises meet with derision or disaster as renewed enthusiasm from customers and investors", says the UK's *Observer* newspaper, which tracked the share prices over five years of companies that had changed their names.[3]

The naming process can be expensive for many brands. It can include paying for the creative development of the name, buying the rights to the name and changing all materials to include the new name and identity. Companies change their brand names for various reasons: to make themselves sound friendlier and approachable; to sound less dated; or to indicate to an audience that the brand has changed. The most important point behind naming is that the company understands why it wants to change, and where it is heading. This direction, along with the values and beliefs of the brand, must be translated into the naming and brand identity process. While names are often created by copywriters and logos created by designers, the specialisms should work in tandem on naming projects, beside the brand strategists.

Brands need names that work in a multi-channel world as well as across different countries. A brand name should ideally reflect the values of the brand, and not necessarily the personal taste of the brand owners. It is best to think of names in a practical context – if you were working for that brand, would you feel comfortable answering the phone with the name? Is it memorable and easy to pronounce? Does it work in an international environment or does it need to be renamed for different markets (the latter is an expensive undertaking)? If the name is completely made up, it will need publicity to support its birth.

Particular naming styles tend to go in trends. For a while, the names of Greek and Roman gods and goddesses were popular – they're now all registered. Another trend was to use a Latin word as the root word that had some meaning, and add an extra vowel or two. Two high profile examples in the UK were 'Consignia' for the Post Office Group (based on the verb, to consign) and 'Arriva' for the main London bus company (seemingly connected to the verb 'to arrive', which sets a high bar for a brand promise). The former failed. During the dot-com era there were many names prefixed with an 'e' to signify a technology or website company or product. Another more recent naming tactic is to combine two names to describe the brand (along the lines of 'PlayStation').

With any naming process, the brand needs to plan the follow-up. There needs to be a lot of noise to make people aware of the new name and to explain, in a simple way, why it has been done and its significance. Accenture – the name for one of the world's leading management consultancies – is not necessarily the catchiest name, but it was launched with a full fanfare and it has since stuck. When the UK's Post Office Group renamed to Consignia, the results were disastrous, yet there was nothing wrong with the name itself. Consignia is an attractive name for a mail and logistics company, and a little trendier and more dynamic than its wider

market competitors, DHL, TNT and Deutsche Post. However, the communications behind the name were too complex; people thought the long-standing British institution, the Post Office, was changing, while in reality it was a name change for the holding group of the Post Office, not the customer-facing side. After an uproar in the press, Consignia was consigned to the graveyard of names, and the Post Office Group now remains as it was.

Companies can spend millions changing a name for a brand. They must buy all the rights to that name and then create or change all marketing collateral (letterheads, etc.). If that name fails millions can be lost. In 2002, PwC Consulting, part of PricewaterhouseCoopers, briefly renamed itself to 'Monday', the new name was 'concise, recognisable and global'[4] according to the chief executive of PwC Consulting. The press and PwC's peers jeered. The rebrand was estimated to cost £75 million and came to an end less than two months later when IBM bought the business, and replaced 'Monday' with its original birth name – plain old PwC Consulting.

Whether renaming works is continuously debated and it is unclear if companies truly measure the cost of the exercise. While the logistical costs of naming can reach the millions, a good name can help inspire a workforce, create pride in the brand and company, and change perceptions for the better. These intangibles must be weighed against the tangible costs. The challenge is to get the name right.

1: OCADO LOGO AND NAME

Ocado is the name of a home delivery online supermarket. The name was created from scratch and reinforced by prominent advertising and imagery at launch. The logo appears to be derived from tribal influences; the name sounds like an exotic fruit, but in reality, both are the brain children of a branding agency: "Everyone asks us what it stands for," says Martyn Allen, in charge of branding at Ocado. "We just liked the sound of it."

fcuk®

french connection someone

fcuk®

2, 3: FRENCH CONNECTION NAME CHANGE TO FCUK

Possibly one of the most noticeable name changes in the 1990s was the renaming of French Connection UK to FCUK. Provocative, taunting and controversial, the name change successfully moved the brand from being just another high-street retailer to a trendy label. The company claims the name was inspired by the shorthand used on faxes, but it was a very deliberate rebrand strategy. Its cleverness was also in its adaptability, supporting campaigns like 'FCUK for England' during the football championships, and slogans like 'FCUK Fashion'. Yet such a bold name is bound to have a sell-by date – FCUK seems to be losing its 'cool' status after seven years, judging by its falling sales.

"A good name can help inspire a workforce, create pride in the brand and company, and change perceptions for the better"

3. 'New name – but is there a new game?' the *Observer* newspaper, UK, 23/09/2004
4. 'Everyday is Monday for PwC' the *Guardian* newspaper, UK, 10/6/2002

Marketing collateral: Marketing materials used for promotional means, such as websites, brochures and direct mail.

interview

Ingelise Nielsen, Head of Communications, IDEO

IDEO calls itself a 'design and innovation company'. The company, which started in Silicon Valley, is known for its unorthodox approach to design. They use multi-disciplinary teams of designers, engineers, psychologists and anthropologists to create products – whether that product is a toothbrush, a website, or a 'smart space' (an improved, more efficient design space).

The key to IDEO's success lies in its approach to design, one which is purely driven by the person using the product. Part of this approach is to get to the tangibles as soon as possible and give the client something to play with. This may take the form of a prototype made from plastic, or a retail space made from cardboard.

What is the design process at IDEO and how do you apply this?

A market and human focus is at the core of our expertise.

We discover new things by observing people and looking at their behaviour. It is this observation which helps us understand the problem, the limitations, the market and the competitors.

When we observe people we select those who are at the extremes – the experienced users and the novices – and by testing these extremes we end up with the medium. It is our insights that lead to innovation.

The observations can be cross-cultural, such as looking at the way washing machines are used in different cultures – to come up with a good product design. Different behaviours are based on cultural differences as well as factors like space restrictions. In Japan, for example, they would never throw their washing on the floor like people do in the UK. This will affect the way the product is designed. Or if we're redesigning a school environment, we'll observe teaching methods and also look at how the students use the space.

Once we're through the observation phase, we brainstorm with the client and visualise the key ideas. The next phase is to test ideas and make the first prototype, which could be made from plastic and cardboard. We move into experience prototyping quickly after that.

How do you translate the brand into the design of a product?

Transmitting the brand is to do with the experience so we go to lengths to demonstrate the product or experience from the customer's standpoint. The brand is the DNA of the company and it must come through the product.

What is the relationship between the client and yourselves? Do they tend to understand design?

When we work with clients, we rely on their expertise. But it's important that the designer understands their client and ensures that the functions of the design support their business values.

The best projects are the ones where the client has a committed team in place – so you have a client champion.

People in branding often refer to the 'savvy consumer' – someone that is difficult to please and less loyal. Does this make design more difficult?

Consumers are more discerning now and people are careful about where they spend their money. You need to understand the depth and intelligence of the user to create something knowledgeable and new.

We design 'appropriate technology' that has design thinking behind it. But something that is appropriate does not always have to be totally intuitive – if the benefit the person gets from using the technology is greater without being intuitive, then you can bend the rules a bit.

"Transmitting the brand is to do with the experience so we go to lengths to demonstrate the product or experience from the customer's standpoint"

CHAPTER

04

BRAND
AUDIENCE

INTRODUCTION

The audience is the most important and relevant person for a brand. It is crucial that the graphic designer understands it.

This chapter analyses the changing nature of audience behaviour in today's over-branded environments, looking at how people are responding to brands.

The theory at the start of the chapter discusses the difference between customers and consumers, and how they are important to the brand. It also looks at the lifecycle of brands, and the necessity of capturing a small minority early who can take the brand to a majority.

The main content of the chapter covers new consumer attitudes and the new approach of brands that want to engage in 'dialogue' with their audience. It discusses business brands, internal brand audiences (employees) and how to work with brand values and product brands. It draws on examples to compare different audience approaches, such as UK clothing store Topshop compared with Marks & Spencer. It also offers tips for designers.

The interview at the end of the chapter is with Michael Hockney of the D&AD, an established global design body and educational charity. Hockney compares the old ways of branding to today's approach.

Chapter 4 Contents:

THEORY CHAPTER 04 /

++

The Pareto Principle

About 80 per cent of the time you probably only wear 20 percent of the clothes you own. And 80 per cent of the time you probably only listen to 20 per cent of your CDs. This '80:20 rule' – more properly known as The Pareto Principle after the mathematician who devised it – can be applied to all sorts of areas of life and the generalisation can be uncannily accurate.

When businesses rank customers by sales value the 80:20 rule becomes an important reality: 80 per cent of business is often done with only 20 per cent of customers. The implication is clear: focus on a few customers, as they are the key to your survival. Dell, HP and other computer manufacturers break their business up into segments of which business and education are far more lucrative than individual consumers. Many branding decisions are based on what the 'big' customers want as losing those sales will dent profits considerably.

But is this relevant to brands such as Coca-Cola or Nike? After all, they sell to millions of individuals so surely they are all equally valuable? It is important to understand that the people who ultimately buy the product, the consumers, are not the original customers. From a brand's point of view there is a big difference between customers and consumers. For example, the biggest bulk purchasers of Coke are supermarkets, fast food chains and cinemas, while Nike see their important customers as sports stores like JJB Sports in the UK and Footlocker in the USA. If one of those customers decides to stop selling a brand (or 'de-list' as it is known), it will be in trouble because they form an important part of the supply chain. Most brands are highly dependent on just a few major outlets.

The US-based supermarket chain Wal-Mart has come under scrutiny recently for its virtual monopoly power in deciding which products succeed and which ones fail. On the face of it, Wal-Mart can argue it is acting in consumers' interests by using its power to squeeze prices. But this power has an effect – some recording artists and film studios have to produce 'family friendly' versions of their CDs and DVDs, while in October 2004 Wal-Mart withdrew copies of comedian Jon Stewart's book *America*, which contained a fake photo of naked US supreme court justices because, according to Wal-Mart spokeswoman Karen Burk, "we felt that the majority of our customers would not be comfortable with it". Decisions like this have led to accusations that companies with too much

"Companies with too much power in the supply chain can impede free trade and even free speech"

power in the supply chain can impede free trade and even free speech. In the UK farmers are concerned that profit margins are being squeezed so low by the monopoly of a few supermarket chains that they can no longer make a living. Meanwhile consumer groups believe the choice and quality of food is compromised by the quest for lower prices combined with greater profits. Although awareness of these practices is high there is little motive to make changes: in the USA, Wal-Mart contributed four per cent of the economy's growth between 1995–99, while downward pressure on prices helped keep inflation low.

Brand managers need to keep these major customers onside. Andrew Marshall, chief operating officer of SFT, a company that sells equipment to food producers, told foodproductiondaily.com: "If three out of the five major multiples (in the UK) got together to de-list any one brand name, they could do so. In other words, they could break that brand. Over 80 per cent of food sold in the UK is done through the big five supermarkets [now the big four following Safeway's takeover by Morrisons]. It is essentially a monopolistic situation." Consequently, many retail customers can ask brands to fund costly promotions (such as two for the price of one), or charge large fees for premium shelf space – the shelves at eye level and at the ends of aisles are particularly sought after. Refusing to fund promotions and store loyalty cards is not an option, and smaller customers such as corner shops (who account for 80 per cent of the total number of customers, but only 20 per cent of total sales) are forced to sell at full price – or more, if a brand is to recoup some of the costs of big-store promotions.

The 80:20 rule continues down the chain – 80 per cent of a store's business may be done with 20 per cent of the local population, for example. This also determines what brands they stock – in poor neighbourhoods or areas with large student populations, supermarkets stock more dried pasta and rice, and more tinned products with their own, cheaper, branded products getting more shelf space than well-known but expensive brands.

It is worth bearing in mind the power of the retail outlet in branding decisions, and applying the Pareto Principle when considering who the most important customers really are.

"Many branding decisions are based on what the 'big' customers want as losing those sales will dent profits considerably"

THEORY CHAPTER 04 /

++

The Product Life Cycle (PLC)

Some products and services are easy to develop while others take time. Some take off quickly while others are slow burners, building up a momentum over time. Some stay around a long time, while others are just fads and soon die. This is known as the product life cycle (PLC).

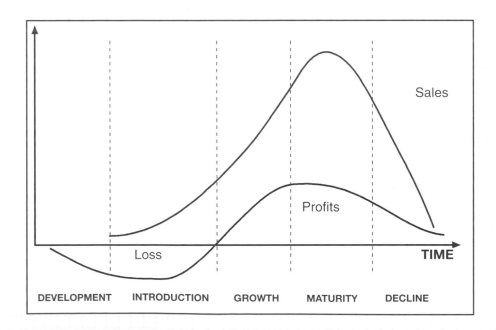

No product or service launches without development, but this process costs money. In deciding whether to go ahead with a new product some maths is needed: can sales recoup costs? Will the product have to be so expensive it will damage sales? Will sales decline before a profit is made? Can declining sales be arrested by modifying the product? Can modifications be made cheaply? Can the company survive while it is losing money or will our money run out before a profit is made?

Most companies have a rolling programme of development so as one product is growing a replacement is being developed, ready to launch as the old one enters the final phase of its life.

Where brands fit in the PLC		
PRODUCT CLASS	Soap Cars Television	These tend to have longest life cycles
PRODUCT FORM	Soap powder/tablets/liquid/liquid tablets Family cars, SUVs, compacts, vans Compact TV, LCD, widescreen, portable, pocket	These tend to have longest life cycles
BRAND	Persil Automatic, Persil Non-Bio, Ford Ka Sony Wega	Ability to change quickly due to competitors' initiatives and consumer tastes
STYLE	Off-road vehicles, town cars	A mode of expression
FASHION	'Rocket' styling on '50s cars, metallic paints, wood veneer-effect TVs, black plastic TVs, silver TVs, environmentally friendly products	Popular style in a particular field
FADS	'Make your own soap flake' kits, clear plastic exposing inside electronics, motorised scooters, fluffy dice and nodding dogs	Enters quickly, is adopted quickly, declines just as quickly

THEORY CHAPTER 04 /

++

Consumers and the PLC

Companies often label consumers based on where in the product life cycle (PLC) they are likely to buy the product. This is known as the 'Consumer Life Cycle' (or CLC). The different types of consumer (with rough percentages) are:

INNOVATORS	Quick to purchase new products out of curiosity or other social need – not always based on ability to pay higher costs. 2–5% of potential consumers.
EARLY ADOPTERS	Tend to be more deliberate, but base decisions on experience of innovators. 10–15% of consumers.
EARLY MAJORITY ADOPTER	Even more deliberate, but less conservative than early adopters. Account for around a third of purchases.
LATE MAJORITY	Conservative group, very slow to buy, but account for another third of purchases. Laggards (last of all to buy). Account for 5–10% of consumers.

Although it might be tempting to go for the majority adopters who together form up to 70 per cent of potential consumers, the innovators and early adopters are vital as they are the people who will engage in the most essential type of viral marketing: word of mouth.

Recently several new product classes have depended on innovators and early adopters. In the UK, digital terrestrial television (DTT) and digital audio broadcasting (DAB) were initially slow to take off as their benefits were difficult to understand, and the equipment needed was expensive. As innovators and early adopters grew the cost of producing the equipment fell, and people communicated the benefits to friends and colleagues. These are what Malcolm Gladwell calls 'mavens' in his book *The Tipping Point* and their unbiased, but enthusiastic advice triggers the next group to buy.

"Although it might be tempting to go for the majority adopters who together form up to 70 per cent of potential consumers, the innovators and early adopters are vital as they are the people who will engage in the most essential type of viral marketing: word of mouth"

THE AUDIENCE CHALLENGE

Today's brand audience is elusive and fickle. We earn more and borrow more than our parents or grandparents ever did. We have high expectations, and demand more choices. We are brand-savvy, ever more discerning, less loyal and more informed than any audience before us. We know when we are being targeted. We pose a difficult, but irresistible challenge for brand-owners who want to win our attention, our money and even our love.

We live in a complex world. Demographics used to offer a simple way to market brands – it was possible to define whole sections of the population based on the colour of their shirt collar, and by the wages they took home. The 'housewife' chose the laundry detergent and shopped for food for the kids. Choices were limited. Now definitions of target audiences are more detailed than ever before. Most traditional structures, like the extended family, no longer exist for the majority. We are more globally aware, more exposed to media, broader in our views and wider in our tastes, than ever before. As an audience, we appear more cosmopolitan, multicultural, and essentially more diverse than ever before. This is the dilemma for many brands; how to find an empathetic dialogue on a common ground that is increasingly hard to locate.

1, 2: PLAYSTATION ADVERTISING

If the elusive market made up of 18–35 year-old males is not watching TV anymore, then advertising on games is mooted as the best way to reach it. Sony PlayStation offers 'in-game' advertising on their games where companies can advertise their brands as part of the 3D setting. PlayStation calls this a co-branding opportunity and it is a revenue booster.

While the gaming community offers a huge potential youth market for advertisers, it is still early days and minimal marketing spend compared with well-established TV advertising.

"Today's youth are used to sponsorship. If a kid went to a concert and there wasn't merchandise to buy, he'd probably go out of his mind"

John Roberts, organiser of Woodstock '94 music festival[1]

1. Naomi Klein, *No Logo*, Flamingo, UK, 2001

THEORY   PAGE / 98
See 'The Pareto Principle'

CONSUMER ATTITUDES

We are, in branding speak, a 'fragmented' audience and so brand-owners seek to categorise us in order to understand us. But rather than using the traditional demographic categorisation techniques – that placed us in groups based on our age, earnings and marital status – the clever brands now communicate to us in line with our behaviours and attitude. This is because people now cross demographic divides – we marry later, go clubbing at 40, or could be a high earner at 25.

Brands, therefore, attempt to communicate to us on a number of levels, cutting across professional status, gender, sexual preference and culture. There are other commonalities that an audience buys into, even though that audience may include different ages, earnings and social class. These commonalities are a brand's traits or character, and the way a brand projects itself. In other words, its attitude.

"An attitudinal approach means that brands are saying, 'this is what we are about. If you are too, come in'" says Kristen Davis, market researcher and director of Affinity; "To analyse this, brands need to understand why the consumer behaves in a certain way. People either share the values of the brand, which is why they buy into it, or they aspire to the values of the brand." If we are buying into brand values, then we are responding to the way the brand speaks to us – how it projects itself and how it behaves. This is a deeper sense of the brand than that of its product or service.

This attitudinal model works well as a substitute for the demographic model. Instead of using defined audience categories, many of those working in branding now simplify the audience under one key description: the 'savvy consumer'. This savvy consumer has a degree of marketing exposure, brand awareness and intelligence. The savvy consumer can be targeted according to their environment, their preferences and the context in which they receive the brand message. Above all they are open and receptive. This is a categorisation technique that is defined from the marketing position of the brand, and it helps to focus the brand message. However, the savvy consumer can present difficulties for marketers: the consumer believes they know the brand, but may be basing their attitude on out-of-date information or heritage prejudices, or they may steadfastly refuse the brand due to poor experience or the impact of influencers.

Once a brand's positioning is clear, it is then faced with the challenge of selecting the appropriate media to reach its audience and, most importantly, making that encounter memorable. A brand may succeed in getting your attention, but to be memorable it must 'engage' you.

The audience analysis will happen at the beginning of a brand's life; at the outset of a change to the brand or a new branding campaign. Market researchers play a key role in defining the brand audience and their needs. This will be fed into the creative process as part of the brief to the brand, advertising or design agencies, including media planners who decide what media to target. Without having an understanding of the audience, work on any aspect of the brand will be meaningless. From an initial analysis a segmentation will result that identifies the market to be addressed where the brand message should find resonance.

GENERAL TIPS FOR DESIGNERS

01 Be fully briefed on the brand's audience prior to working on any brand project

02 Decide on the most effective channels to reach your audience

03 Analyse how the brand speaks to its audience, not just what the audience thinks of the brand

04 Make sure that the graphic design reflects the character and values of the brand. Test the thesis: If you saw the design in isolation, how would you describe the brand's attitude?

05 Be as creative as you can – the campaign must be engaging and memorable

"An attitudinal approach means that brands are saying, 'this is what we're about. If you are too, come in'"

Kristen Davis, Affinity Coaching

CAPTURING THE AUDIENCE

For the latter half of the 20th century, television advertising was the mainstay of the brand – the guaranteed medium to hit its audience. In the 1960s there was only one commercial TV channel in the UK and a limited number of newspapers and magazines. If you wanted to speak to the nation's housewives you advertised during the TV programme, *Coronation Street*, or in the magazine, *Woman's Own*. In the USA, daytime soap operas had been in existence for more than ten years, sponsored and supported by consumer cleaning brands. Later, daytime talk-shows targeted the stay-at-home mums (and university students). Today however, the multi-channelled, multimedia home poses problems; families rarely sit together to watch TV and each family member has a magazine or a website aimed precisely at them.

In 2003 Coca-Cola's then-president said that its company would move away from TV as the 'anchor medium'. Procter & Gamble's global marketing officer later declared that "TV stopped working sometime around 1987". It seemed that TV advertising was being declared dead because it failed to attract the youth of today – a prime target for brands. This was a shock to a branding industry that had spent the best part of half a century pouring money into TV advertising. According to *Wired* magazine in the USA, the 18–34 year-old male is now reinventing advertising. The 'typical' male now multitasks at such a rate – surfing the web, watching TV, listening to music, and doing homework, in simultaneous motion – that he has developed the ability to 'filter out' brand messages. TV advertising can be blocked through technology like TiVo. Those in advertising, like Kevin Roberts CEO of Saatchi & Saatchi, argue that TV is not dead, it's just that most advertising on television is boring. A good ad will be talked about – but most fail to capture the imagination.[2]

With or without TV as the branding industry's advertising favourite, companies will be likely to diversify their advertising spend into other areas such as online advertising, advertising on games and ambient media; but these are currently the exception, not the rule. Many ad agencies set up online advertising divisions at the tail end of the 1990s, but it's hard to find a good online ad, and clever and creative viral marketing campaigns appear infrequently. There still isn't a compulsive enough reason for brands to pull away from their TV habits of half a century.

More desperate measures have been used by brand creators to capture 'youth' and the younger generation, and this is viewed by some as emotional bribery. Companies, particularly in the USA, have been criticised for branding that targets children of pre-teenage years and even toddlers. Although many companies have policies and guidelines that restrict youth targeting, some go to extensive lengths and tactics to win over extra names for their mailing lists. University students in the USA are paid to listen to ads, or are tempted by free give-aways: in September 2004 the BBC's *Newsnight* aired a programme about leading brands that gave away iPods or a flat-screen TVs to university students ('consumers aged 18 to 24') if they registered five friends on the brand's website[3]. Whether this is tantamount to emotional bribery or is simply brand business is debatable: the marketing agencies driving these campaigns simply want to meet their sign-up targets, the students want a free iPod, and the company behind the brand gets one more name on their mailing list, which is probably removed within a month. Such tactics are simply sophisticated direct marketing and fundamentally miss the point of good branding: no loyalty is encouraged or credibility established.

"If we don't watch the ads, it's like we're stealing TV"

Homer Simpson

1: THE BRANDING OF THE UK'S
MAIN POLITICAL PARTIES:
CONSERVATIVE AND LABOUR

"In late 2004, I participated in a market research group for an established brand that was battling with how to reach a 'young' (up to 35 years old), savvy, wired audience – we all had broadbrand at home. Halfway through the research they showed us some TV ads, hoping we would recognise their own expensive ads. Not only were their ads not familiar, but people claimed either not to watch TV or not have seen the ads: 'sorry I've been travelling'; 'sorry I've been living in a different country for the past year'; 'sorry I don't watch TV much anymore', were the responses. At which point the market researcher cried out: 'None of you should have got through our screening process if you don't watch TV!' But perhaps that's just the way things are now"

Kim Temple, Blacks Market Research Group

2. Kevin Roberts, Lovemarks: *The Future Beyond Brands,* PowerHouse Cultural Entertainment Books, USA, 2004
3. *Newsnight,* BBC TV, 22/09/2004

CONSUMER DIALOGUE

With such a complex, brand-aware and vocal audience, it is not surprising that brands now talk about entering into a 'dialogue' with their customers. Brands, and the companies that control them, are no longer perceived as untouchable entities. We expect them to be accountable, responsible and transparent. We want them to listen and, perhaps, to change their behaviour. If we're unhappy, we expect a range of channels to air our gripes as customers (websites, the media, an industry governing body or complaints department). The best way to get us onside is to talk.

Market researcher, Kristen Davis, describes the shift in consumer attitudes to brands: "On the one hand brands can offer a security that we don't have. On the other, we expect more from them and the corporations they represent – to be accountable and responsible. We have a lot more to choose from so we are less tolerant. There is a feeling that corporations have got away with being unaccountable for so long, brand-bashing has now become almost a hobby. All this means that brands, while more powerful than ever before, are also more vulnerable."

The 'customer' – always the person at the core of the brand – is now no longer simply the person buying the product or service. The brand customer is anyone who the brand affects or who has an interest in that brand: employees (and their families), investors, the government, the press, non-governmental organisations (NGOs), activists and local communities. These are the people brands categorise as their 'stakeholders' and understanding them is now an important part of managing the brand.

To understand what 'dialogue' is, think more in terms of community meetings rather than market research sessions. Good brands are actively seeking the opinions of every group of stakeholders and these are fed into the management of the brand and the changes to the business. The dialogue may be manifest in meetings with NGOs to understand the issues facing the corporation; it may be in direct communications from the CEO to his or her employees.

Effective dialogue is not simply a public relations exercise – it is a necessity for the survival of brands now faced with numerous audiences and audience views. It ensures that there are fewer surprises in managing the brand's external perception and reputation. If a brand suffers from negative publicity, a history of dialogue between stakeholders and the brand will limit the damage. This shows a shift in companies' approach to branding, from a 'command and control' stance, where many accepted what they said, into that of more open communication.

"A few companies are starting to build their brands more scientifically – and in doing so have pushed marketing to new frontiers. The key is combining a forward-looking market segmentation with a more precise understanding of the needs of customers and a brand's identity"
The McKinsey Quarterly[4]

A brand, in the long term, cannot afford to continue losing customers or employees, and it cannot afford continuous damaging publicity about its management, operations or working practices. Every brand is vulnerable because every industry has a potential hot-spot that can flare up to severely damage a brand or create expensive lawsuits – for example, issues around health and sourcing for food brands. You only have to look at McDonald's and its shift from being the most libellous corporation in the world to its recent stance in 2004 on supporting a movie called *Super Size Me*, which actively attacks its unhealthy food and selling techniques. McDonald's was able to harness the publicity of the movie to openly address issues that concerned its audience – the movie effectively offered a springboard for the brand to express and reinforce its position. Brands can use dialogue as a way to respond to issues with the aim, ultimately, of improving brand behaviour.

Stakeholder: The broader audience that the brand affects, including investors, press, customers, employees and associations.

4. Nora A. Aufreiter, David Elzing and Jonathan W. Gordon, *The McKinsey Quarterly*, No. 4, 2003

"The 18–24 youth market is wired, educated, cynical and irrational. They're into brand authenticity. They believe that companies should give back something to the world in which they operate"

Shari Swan, Streative Branding

1: MCDONALD'S 'SUPER SIZE ME' ADVERTISING CAMPAIGN

Companies, particularly the multinationals, are seeking to 'engage' their audiences through communication and dialogue to lead to better relations and less bad press. This engagement is usually behind closed doors (often referred to as 'stakeholder dialogue' sessions). McDonald's in the UK went a step further in response to a well-publicised film, *Super Size Me*, which targeted the fast-food chain's nutrition standards and quality of food. The film was based on one man eating McDonald's constantly for a month, resulting in a body so unhealthy that by week three, his doctor was begging him to stop.

McDonald's, which is known for its litigious actions, instead issued an advertisement in the press in response to the movie. The tone was temperate and reasonable, which acknowledged support for the movie, but pointed out that their average customer was not eating McDonald's three times a day.

"But what may surprise you is how much of the film we agree with...What we don't agree with is the idea that eating at McDonald's is bad for you" ending with an opportunity to plug the new healthy-look McDonald's and its products. The tone of the ad reflects a turn-around in McDonald's publicity and responsible branding stance.

1

> "Stop racing after every new fad and focus on making consistent, emotional connections with consumers. If you stand for nothing, you fall for everything"
>
> Kevin Roberts, Saatchi & Saatchi[5]

Women's Clothing Shops

Topshop is a store that changed its approach to marketing in the late 1990s. Before this, the shop was another standard retailer found on the main street across UK cities. Its clothes were mid-range market, its shops were mediocre. In 2005, Topshop is featured widely in the world press: every week, over 200,000 customers walk through its London Oxford Street doors. The shop manages to attract women of all ages, from celebrities to teenagers.

The change came about when the company decided to offer attitude, rather than simply clothes. The flagship London store had a make-over and installed an in-house DJ, a café, and reinvented its range of clothes. Now, Topshop has major fashion designers to create their ranges; they back student fashion awards and get the best to design mini collections; and they also stock clothes from innovative market stall sellers around London. The shop sells fashions that are cutting edge and, for the most part, cheap. Its clothes may not last, and the trends may go out of style, but the customer knows what they are getting – a constant turnover of the latest trends at a reasonable price: "Our philosophy is to have a point of differentiation – and that is we are always first. We're a democratic brand – we don't pitch to a certain age group. Our customers are savvy and demanding and we must provide what they want," Sameera Hassan, a senior press officer for the brand, explains.

In 2004, the brand introduced new concepts: Topshop To Go brings clothes to home or work for those without the time to go shopping, and a personal shopping service with stylists is now available for those seeking a new wardrobe or particular outfit. These services are not new to those with money, but Topshop, in following their 'democratic' approach, is the first to supply this to their demanding, savvy customers of the high street.

Compare Topshop with Marks & Spencer (M&S), a traditional English brand, which has been struggling to generate healthy sales of its women's-wear lines, despite great success in other areas of its business, such as its food halls. Marks & Spencer also offers ranges of well-made clothes – along with innovations such as bringing in leading designers to clothing ranges.

Yet its women's wear is not doing well. While the product may be good, the atmosphere and shopping experience is not. There is no fun in shopping for M&S women's wear. The atmosphere feels dowdy and outdated and the colours of the interiors are drained and drab. It seems that the company is afraid that change will alienate their 'average' size 14 female customer (once promoted in an M&S advertisement) and affect their reputation as a great place to buy sensible underwear. Yet its status quo of M&S women's wear is not working, and most women – size 14 or not – prefer a shopping experience that makes them feel good. M&S cannot and should not become a copy of Topshop; its problem is that its women's wear has no strong identity that engages a broader mass market. There are no attitude or values to buy into because there are none being projected from the brand itself.

5. Kevin Roberts, *Lovemarks: The Future Beyond Brands*, Powerhouse Cultural Entertainment Books, USA, 2004

YOUR M&S

TOPSHOP

1: MARKS & SPENCER RETAIL SPACE
2: TOPSHOP RETAIL SPACE

Marks & Spencer posted a loss in 2005
as compared to Topshop, which has gone
from strength to strength. Topshop's themed
interiors and high turnover of stock have
contributed to creating a more exciting
consumer experience.

THEORY   PAGE / 100
See 'The Product Lifecycle (PLC)'

THEORY   PAGE / 102
See 'Consumers and the PLC'

"Wider competition, increasing client expectations and a need to recruit the best people are just some of the factors driving a change in business communications"

BUSINESS BRANDS

Businesses can be reserved and many business brands seem to deliberately reinforce this stance. Businesses speaking to other businesses tend to be more conservative in their approach than consumer brands and creativity is often restricted by a fear of alienating an audience. Businesses may consider their audience to be more serious than someone on a weekend shopping trip, and there are undoubtedly bigger budgets at stake, but many fail to acknowledge that they are selling to people, not entities.

Market researcher Kristen Davis, says: "Business and consumer audiences should not be targeted differently. Instead, you need to analyse the relationship. Consumer brands may have more of an intimacy or heartfelt connection with the customer, such as someone who has a passion for Nike trainers. But a business brand has a different type of emotional connection – this could be aspirational or achievement-related to help people improve in their work. The relationship means getting that bit in the middle right – meeting expectations and maintaining the quality of the relationship. Fundamentally, however, people still buy into the basic, traditional values like security, reliability and honesty."

Service is the key seller for business and consequently it is the relationships between people that matter. Businesses selling products differentiate themselves by the after-sales care and support; by dedicated sales people who look after the client; and by an acknowledgement that maintaining the client relationship is important. Throughout the 1990s there

has also been an upheaval within the professional service industries as traditional manufacturing corporations have moved to knowledge-based product and service delivery (such as consultants offering specialists services). In professional services, it is the person bchind the business brand that matters, yet service should be a given in business – it is how that service is delivered by the people behind it that is key and this needs to be expressed in any communication.

Often, businesses that sell to other businesses (commonly referred to as B2B), adopt a verbal and visual language that is conservative and safe. Words expressing the importance of customer service are overused to the point where they have become meaningless – hundreds of businesses claim to 'add value', offer 'solutions' and 'respond to customer needs'. Particular sectors also resort to safe colours, using blues and blacks to signify reliability. The challenge for the designer is to stretch a business brand beyond safe territory. Just a slight shift away from the traditional can make a business brand stand out.

Business brands are changing, however. Plain language is becoming the norm in professional service sectors although many still have a long way to go. Wider competition, increasing client expectations and a need to recruit the best people are just some of the factors driving a change in business communications. Smaller, dynamic businesses are challenging the more traditional businesses, because they can deliver services with more flexibility and speed. Client expectations have also

increased: people expect a professional standard of service and a one-to-one relationship; extra basics, such as a good website, online facilities (like websites, or extranets, that service clients directly) and transparent billing procedures, are becoming standard practice.

This change is significant in traditional professional service industries such as law firms. Many firms grew their business through word-of-mouth, reputation and contacts. Now most have in-house marketing people responsible for raising the profile of the firm, developing websites and attracting the top university graduates.

Partnerships in business are also becoming more common to reach new markets or offer new or different services for a wider audience. For example, a mobile phone operator with a lead in the consumer sector, may team up with another business to offer tailored business services for their clients.

John Blyth, head of marketing at Kall Kwik UK, the country's biggest printing and design company, believes there needs to be more boldness in business branding: "Business brands often play it too safe because they are fearful of alienating people. But it is better to be bold and have people support you with strong feelings, at the risk of alienating a small minority, rather than have indifference." Kall Kwik rebranded its franchises throughout the UK to appeal to the B2B sector rather than the small business and consumer market.

1, 2: SOFTIMAGE | XSI
ME COMPANY

Softimage, a Canadian software company, commissioned London-based design agency, Me Company, to design new packaging for its product SOFTIMAGE | XSI. The product is aimed at a business audience, although predominantly in the creative industries. It offers a good example of how design can make a 'business-to-business' brand stand out without having to change the tone or style of the brand.

Images courtesy of Softimage Co. and Avid Technology Inc.

3, 4: THE REBRANDED KALL KWIK

Kall Kwik is the largest printing company in the UK. The company is prominent as a printing retail outlet, but as the design and print industry developed over the past ten years the brand became outdated. In 2004 the company rebranded both its logos and interiors to better cater for its business market.

INTERNAL BRAND AUDIENCES

Brand-building within companies for the benefit of their workforce has become a booming area. It can unify employees in a society where people constantly change jobs and careers. Here, it is also important for companies to stand by a consistent and clear set of values to help retain and attract employees. People are committed to a company when they identify with and believe in its values – values reflect a company's culture and the way it treats its employees.

An internal brand can be a connecting element within a company. The employee is as much the brand as the name and the logo. They are also the external spokespeople of a brand and a united and informed workforce is good for staff motivation, retention and recruitment. Corporations of any size now have disparate workforces caused by global working, outsourcing and people choosing to contract. There is a lack of loyalty between employer and employee, stemming from job insecurity and numerous 'restructuring' and redundancies that have been made across most industries; as companies merge, partner, demerge and acquire others. All this change can lead to an internal identity crisis. At the same time, many people now seek more 'meaning' from their work and employer – and they want to know that their commitment is rewarded both financially and emotionally.

Many companies are now differentiated by the service that they offer and that quality of service rests with employees. If many products in a sector are similar in function and price, then it is the support and service that will affect the decision-making process. An employee relationship with the customer can make or break a transaction or contract, and this makes internal branding even more important. People need to believe in the company they work for, if they are to support that company externally. Yet the shift to a service approach based around people, has required a huge change in mind-set for many big brands that have traditionally been product-based.

The growth of internal branding has been accompanied by a tendency to create 'internal brand values' that, in theory, define the characteristics of the people within the company. Words are written down like labels: 'professional', 'insightful' and 'fun' are common values. But strong brands have strong internal cultures that employees recognise simply because they experience them every day. "In highly effective organisations, brand values do not require writing down and dissemination. Words on their own are meaningless," says Ralph Ardill, Experiential Consultant. Behaviour is the best way to promote internal brand values and this comes from the top of the company. Internal brand values or 'business principles' within companies can set perimeters and guide people on how to respond in certain situations, but these are meaningless if not acted upon.

A designer is likely to encounter an internal branding project as part of a rebrand process or after a significant change, like a merger. When the company is changing its external perception it may also want to adjust its internal one. Internal branding requires some clever, tactical thinking but most of all it requires feedback and input from the employees. You may be dealing with an audience that has little interest in, or even hostility towards the 'brand', so your role will be to engage them with some clever unbranded tactics. The best starting point is to go back to the core of what makes the company great to work for or to inspire people about the new company. Changes to people's immediate environment tend to be more effective than attempting to change people's behaviour. As with all branding projects, communication is key – you need to explain the branding is taking place and what you hope to achieve. Internal branding should be supported by brand awareness programmes, such as those of training or induction. The next logical step is to work with human resources to help create and roll-out branding strategies for staff, although collaboration between human resources and brand teams is still a rare undertaking.

"Behaviour is the best way to promote internal brand values and this comes from the top of the company"

"With a product brand you can spend 75 per cent of your time, money and energy trying to influence customers and 25 per cent on everything else, while with a service brand you have to spend at least 50 per cent of your time and money influencing your own people. In order to get an effective service brand, people have to be taught to live the brand they work with"

Wally Olins, *On Brand*[6]

6. Wally Olins, *On Brand*, Thames & Hudson Ltd., UK, 2004

Roll-out: The time it takes to launch the product often from pre-launch through to post-launch phase.

Responsible Internal Brand Building

Brands that 'do good' are often doing it for their employees. One of the main drivers for undertaking 'corporate social responsibility' or ethics-related programmes is to improve the reputation of the company brand amongst its employees. In many cases, employees are demanding a commitment from their employers to areas such as human rights and the environment.

A partnership with a charity or international organisation, such as the United Nations, can make employees feel proud of the company and boost the reputation of the company externally. The aim of a partnership is often to involve employees and offer the company's expertise and talent to that partnership rather than pure funding. Some companies let employees volunteer in community programmes on work time where each employee's hours are collated and documented for inclusion in the company's 'Corporate Responsibility Reports'; other companies offer employees the opportunity to work abroad with their partner charity for a short time. This approach to internal brand building is now being adopted by many large multi-national brands and can have a significant positive impact on the brand, both internally and externally.

1

"One of the main drivers for undertaking 'corporate social responsibility' or ethics-related programmes is to improve the reputation of the company brand amongst its employees"

"The growth of internal branding has been accompanied by a tendency to create 'internal brand values' that, in theory, define the characteristics of the people within the company"

Can your company help us improve this supply chain?

We think so.

Thanks to TPG, the Dutch mail, express and logistics giant, the United Nations World Food Programme is already strengthening its lifeline to the hungry poor.

As the world's largest humanitarian organisation, WFP fed 110 million people in 2005. But with more than 800 million still in the grip of chronic hunger, it is slow for fresh thinking – yours.

Partner with WFP and leverage your firm's unique expertise and assets to build a better world, while motivating your employees, customers and shareholders.

"There is no end to our commitment to feed the hungry. Companies like TPG are helping WFP revolutionise the way we achieve our mission."
JAMES MORRIS, WFP EXECUTIVE DIRECTOR

WFP United Nations
World Food Programme

For more information on how your company can be involved, contact WFP's corporate partnerships division at WFP.CorporatePartnership@wfp.org or on (39).06.6513.3232

1

1: TNT PARTNERSHIP WITH WORLD FOOD PROGRAMME
2: TNT WALK THE WORLD EVENT TO RAISE MONEY FOR THE HUNGRY

Global provider of mail, express and logistics services, TNT, has used a fairly unique tactic to become a responsible corporate citizen: it partnered with the World Food Programme in 2002 to provide logistics support for distributing food parcels in developing countries. The aim was to inspire and motivate employees by giving people the chance to offer their knowledge and expertise to a 'good cause'. This applied to everyone within the company, from post delivery people to those in management and executive positions.

TNT also introduced an internal volunteer programme where employees can work for three months with the WFP in a developing country. Employees are also encouraged to fundraise money for the programme – including taking part in the annual 'Walk the World' event (pictured here), which is open to employees and their families.

The partnership attracted huge publicity and has significantly boosted TNT's reputation, both among employees and externally. In 2004, it was voted as one of the top ten European employers in Fortune magazine.

interview

Michael Hockney, Chief Executive, D&AD

How relevant is branding to design?

I think that branding sits at the absolute core of everything.

Branding is about creating an entity in the consumer's mind so that they have a representation. But behind this representation what they actually have is a whole series of images, beliefs and actions as a result of effective branding.

So when someone asks 'what is a brand for?' I say it's the means by which you stay in a market longer, and more profitably because you've created a brand property.

What do you believe is the relationship between the brand and the product or service?

The brand helps carry a product through a difficult time. It could be a contamination or a situation where a competitor comes in, but the brand is an incredibly powerful business tool. Brands can bounce back because of their credibility and integrity.

The better brands are where the image in the customer's mind is well-rounded so the pack or the logo is the image or identity you seek out. But it's more than that – it is a whole series of mental images about quality, about appropriateness to task, about (if appropriate) longevity, and about price. The combination of those values comes out of the brand and says to the consumer 'this costs x, but it's worth it'.

So the consumer takes on board the rational, emotional and visual aspects, which together create something that they want to ascribe to.

"Branding is about creating an entity in the consumer's mind so that they have a representation"

Creative of the brand: An expression often used to refer to the 'creative' output of the brand including the design and words.

"People do great creative work where they have supreme confidence and pressure of deadlines, but ideas can be killed off and watered down"

Do you think the rules of branding have changed recently, given there is so much more competition and a more complex audience?

There is a brand language that hasn't changed in 30 years. And when it works, it works as well as it always has.

There is a lot of talk about scepticism around brands, and designers and brand managers need to work hard to meet the consumer's needs. But people latch on to brand values in exactly the same way they did 30 years ago. Strong branding is still there, the issue is that it is harder to do well for lots of reasons. There's much more competition and consumers are more savvy, but the mechanism works in the same way.

The way that the designer or the advertiser has to think about the communication is utterly different from 30 years ago. It is just harder to make the communication heard because of communication clutter and segmentation. The designer and advertiser are now forced into narrow casting – segmenting an audience starting with the generic savvy consumer, then segmenting the media.

Price, packaging and product are one communication vehicle, but now there's a multifaceted approach to communicating the brand, which includes digital technology, direct mail, direct marketing and retail. There are now more channels of communication and this multitude of channels and fragmentation of the audience makes it harder to make the breakthrough with the customer.

Within the context of a fragmented audience, how should the designer best approach a branding project?

They need to start with an identifiable personality – an individual – and build their communication around that, then design what is right. The designer then makes a choice about the media to use. Ad agencies are very aware of this and develop multi-approach solutions.

When you put the package together to reach that audience, the branding rules are still the same: you have to win people's minds, people's hearts, people's money, and then win their footfall to buy your product over something else. So the underlying principle has not changed. Life has just become more complex, more varied, and so people are more difficult to classify.

People do great creative work where they have supreme confidence and pressure of deadlines, but ideas can be killed off and watered down.

Do you think branding is understood by most businesses now?

Marketing is generally misunderstood within business. There are fewer marketing directors on the main board and fewer chief executives with a marketing background. There is also a short-term approach in business based on quarterly rather than annual reporting, but branding needs longevity to work.

Agencies: Companies that offer brand expertise to service clients. These are often branding agencies, digital agencies, design agencies or public relations agencies.

Channel: The medium or media format in which the brand is used for marketing.

CHAPTER 05

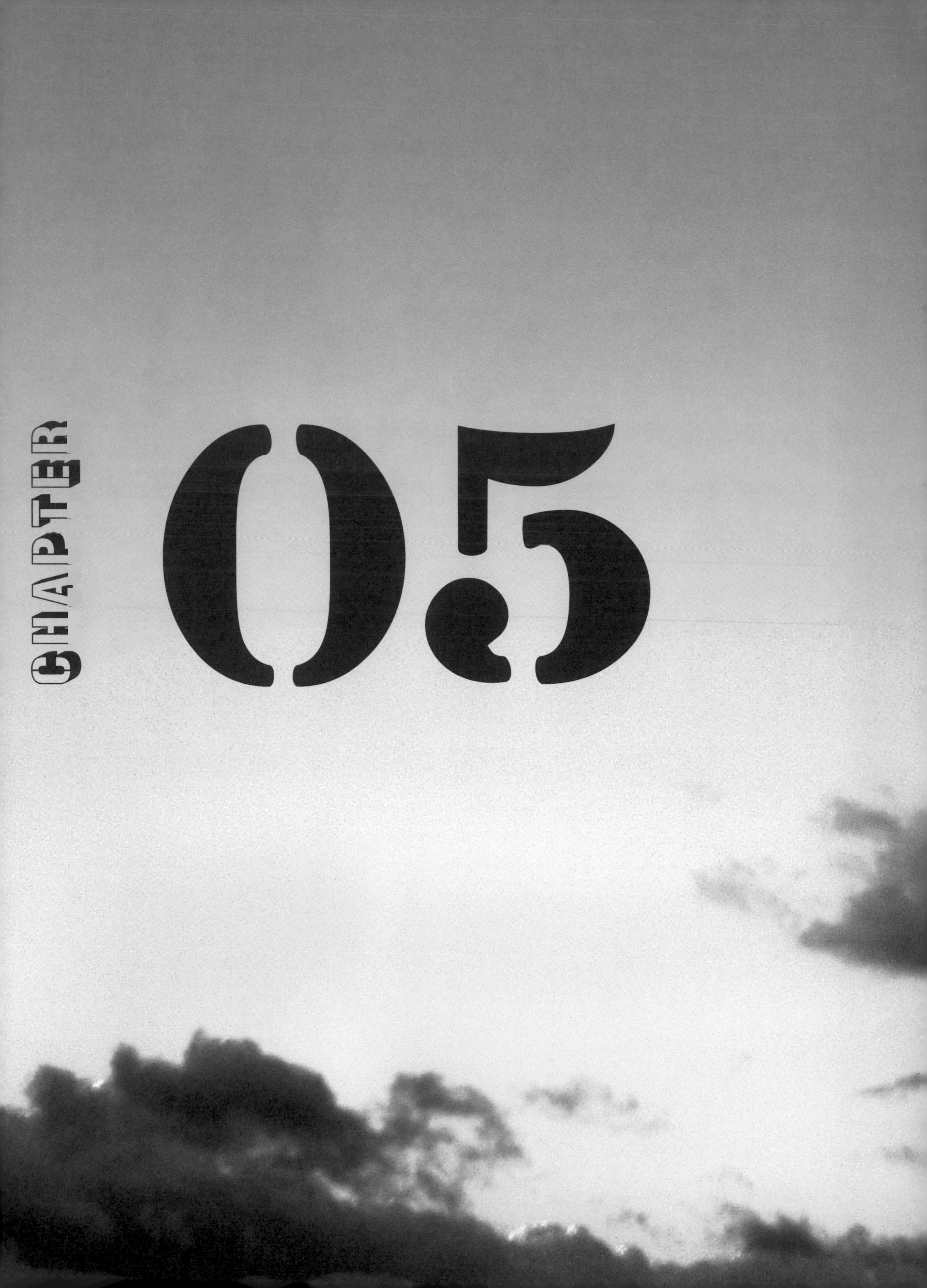

CURRENT TRENDS IN BRANDING

INTRODUCTION

A good designer will not mimic a trend, but use it to create something new. The best designers start trends.

The theory at the start of this chapter on brand trends discusses how a product's life is determined. 'Risk and Reward' analyses the different ways that companies can introduce new products to customers, with varying degrees of risk. The success of a product will also be influenced by wider trends – such as global events, street trends and key people such as celebrities or top designers.

This chapter identifies some of the major trends in today's branding environment and looks at their impact on brands such as: the evident trend in branding to address the individual, rather than speak to the masses; a move towards less branding, more fun and better service; and a positive trend in making brands more responsible. Branding the unusual is on the rise, including branding countries as well as people, and there's an increase in 'own brands' – where prominent brands are now offering extra products and services under their own name.

Simon Anholt, government advisor and author on branding, discusses what branding a country really means. Shari Swan, a trends expert who has a network of 'moles' around the world in fashion, music and on the street, gives an insight into how trends work and where things are going.

Chapter 5 Contents:

THEORY CHAPTER 05 /

++

Risk and Reward

To help decide if the rewards outweigh the risks of launching a new product, companies use an 'Ansoff Matrix':

	MARKET PENETRATION	PRODUCT DEVELOPMENT
EXISTING CUSTOMERS	Market penetration (Low risk)	Product development (High risk)
NEW CUSTOMERS	Market development (Medium risk)	Diversification (Highest risk)

Many businesses are happy to sell known products to people they already do business with, and there are examples of companies who have essentially done this for hundreds of years (some banks and brewers, for example). But sometimes the 'low risk' strategy hampers growth and innovation. You can only grow so much within a known market and if tastes suddenly change, or a threat emerges from a new company, a customer base can disappear overnight. Equally, if something goes wrong with your one product (a health scare or technological problem) it can actually take a long time to recover confidence.

Three alternative strategies are available. Firstly, you can develop new products for existing customers. But this risks cannibalising your existing sales, or alienating or confusing people. Secondly, you can sell your current product to new customers, locally or globally. But this means overcoming preconceptions about your product or service, spending money marketing yourself to the new group and, possibly, alienating your existing customers.

The clothing brand Burberry – for over 100 years associated with the English gentry and royalty – found that young people on the street were wearing their products. Burberry caps and handbags were becoming trendy. The problem for Burberry was how could they take advantage of this without alienating the customers they already had? As several nightclubs in the UK began to ban anyone wearing Burberry because of the association it had with hooliganism, the dilemma became even greater – especially as a rising trade in fake Burberry goods was damaging sales and reputation. The choice for Burberry was either to develop the market or to diversify, both risky strategies – but doing nothing was also risky and would indicate a lack of any control over the situation.

The third, and riskiest strategy available is to develop new products for new markets. This requires a lot of investment in research and development that takes time and money – or a company could just purchase another company that is working in that area, or acquire a brand that is already known and respected. This is particularly prevalent in the technology

"You can only grow so much within a known market"

arena. Apple bought a software company that had already developed a well-respected music player that later became iTunes – recruiting their engineers saved them having to start from scratch and removed a potential competitor. Microsoft bought Mac game developer Bungie, who were working on a game called Halo; they spotted that it would make a good launch title for their new Xbox game console. Adobe bought Aldus in 1994 for their Pagemaker software, but declined to purchase Freehand, a competitor to their Illustrator software, which was licensed to Aldus by a company called AltSys. AltSys and Freehand were in turn bought by Macromedia who then, in 1997, bought a would-be competitor called FutureWave whose FutureSplash animation tool eventually became Flash. Recently, Adobe have bought Macromedia and so now owns Freehand anyhow.

Of course some companies start up with a great idea just in the hope, that it will catch the eye of a bigger player who will then offer a great deal of money to buy it – either to develop it themselves, or to kill it off, depending on whether it is seen as an opportunity to address a weakness, or a threat to their current success.

BRANDING IN THE CONTEXT OF TRENDS

Trends can help guide the direction of the brand and trend-prediction is a growth industry. Brands like to know what is popular to help them plan their direction. Knowledge of trends can be used to generate ideas or campaigns, or be fed into a longer-term brand strategy. A brand might want to create a campaign for the elusive 18–24-year-old male and so hire a trends expert to tell them what these people wear, watch and like. The 'trend-spotters' are not only tapped into the world around them, but to everyone else's world.

Identifying brand trends helps as a starting point for big brand ideas. While clever brands set trends, many brands react and respond to trends. If a brand can recognise, predict and drive a trend, then it will have a stronger connection with its audience. However, branding is long-term, while trends are often, by their very nature, short-lived. Brands can jump on a trend and alter it in the process: they may amplify a trend by making it mainstream, or smother it.

For those who can successfully predict the future, brand trends are a lucrative and booming industry. Companies pay people to observe street influences such as lifestyle and retail directions. This includes looking at fashion, art and restaurants; finding out what the 'cool' or wealthy people are doing; and observing different cultural behaviour and interplays. A key trend is often referred to as an 'insight' and can be the factor that drives the creative direction of a brand campaign.

Trends do not work in isolation. They are driven by people heavily influenced by their environments. Global events, politics and the state of the economy all affect our mind-set and behaviour, although often in unpredictable ways – some trends simply take off while others don't. Malcolm Gladwell, author of *The Tipping Point*, observes that trends stick for three key reasons: the 'law of the few' (i.e. some individuals are able to create trends

through their influence or connections); the 'stickiness' factor; and the 'power of context', that is, your environment.[1]

In the context of Gladwell's 'law of the few', celebrities often work as 'connectors' to the brand. In many countries they endorse a product or service simply by being seen to use it. Product placement by brands has been a public relations tactic for over two decades and it still works. Celebrity mums like Kate Moss and Gwyneth Paltrow immediately boosted pram sales by being photographed with their babies in a particular Dutch brand of pram – despite a hefty price tag. The endorsement did not seem to be staged (the manufacturers were taken by surprise), but when a brand is associated with an influential person its value is raised.

Brand trends often respond to social issues. Health is now a big issue in most developed nations due to rising levels of obesity and related diseases like diabetes. There is a greater awareness of food sourcing and malpractice in the supermarket supply chains, making many people more aware of what they eat. One of the most surprising and evident responses to the health trend has been that of the king of the fast-food chains, McDonald's, introducing salads. Other brands, like Unilever, are using their own corporate brand as an identifier on packaging, to show that the food has been sourced by its own farmers who have adopted sustainable farming techniques. These issues are now being discussed openly: when the movie *Super Size Me* was released in 2004, which documented the filmmaker's declining health while eating McDonalds constantly for a month, the fast-food chain gently responded by issuing advertisements that explained its stance. The approach was surprising for a company renowned for its litigious actions.

However, recognising trends is one thing; successfully adapting to the business and

direction of the brand takes skill. Many brands adopt trends based on advice or industry expertise and get it wrong. Alternatively, they may ignore a key trend at their peril (the music industry took years to acknowledge the growth of online music, for example). The successful adoption of a trend is often dependent on timing: to have impact, big brands want trends to spread into the masses and this can take years. If the brand is too heavy-handed it can over-commercialise a trend and so lose its perception of being 'cool'.

Other brands may simply be ahead of their time with trends: there are many brands that have failed by basing growth around too small a market of 'early adopters' – the people who invest in new technology because they enjoy being the first to own it. The Apple Newton MessagePad was the first PDA (hand-held computer) on the market that recognised handwriting. It was introduced in 1994. The concept was right – hand-helds were, eventually, to take off, but the technology, like the hand-writing recognition, was not able to deliver to market expectations when it launched. Consequently, the product failed to cut it with the masses. While the Newton was a leader in terms of being the first to market with hand-held technology, other companies, like Palm, emerged with smaller, more relevant technology. Analysts believe Apple would have had a hit on their hands if they had stuck it out, but that long term, they were correct to get out of the market as Palm's declining fortunes have shown.

A designer who is aware and informed of broad trends and market trends will be at an advantage. Trends can influence design as much as design influences trends. This chapter highlights some general trends in branding that have been identified from interviews and research at the tail end of 2004.

1: ANTI-WAR DEMONSTRATIONS

Since the War in Iraq in 2003, studies on brands have shown a waning popularity and lack of trust outside of the USA among some prominent American brands.

Trends also affect the way brands respond to their audiences. As life becomes more stressful and difficult to manage, brands respond by promoting characteristics such as safety, efficient time management, less complexity and aspects that make people feel more comfortable like heritage, tradition and brand authenticity.

Images courtesy of CND and Sue Longbottom (Anti-war demonstration in London, 15 February, 2003)

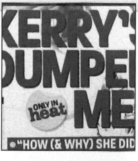

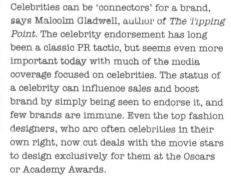

2: THE POWER OF CELEBRITY

Celebrities can be 'connectors' for a brand, says Malcolm Gladwell, author of *The Tipping Point*. The celebrity endorsement has long been a classic PR tactic, but seems even more important today with much of the media coverage focused on celebrities. The status of a celebrity can influence sales and boost brand by simply being seen to endorse it, and few brands are immune. Even the top fashion designers, who are often celebrities in their own right, now cut deals with the movie stars to design exclusively for them at the Oscars or Academy Awards.

Many celebrities are also brands in their own right: David and Victoria Beckham are probably the most famous celebrity brand who have carefully cultivated their own image. David Beckham now has his own logo, thanks to Adidas.

THEORY   PAGE / 100
See 'The Product Life Cycle (PLC)'

1. Malcolm Gladwell, *The Tipping Point*, Abacus, UK, 2002

THE INDIVIDUAL

Brands used to target whole sections of the population, but now they are targeting you as an individual – a creative person who thinks for themselves.

There are various elements that have led to the rise of the individual. More buying power has broken down previous barriers where good products and services were limited to the elite. It is also possible that people have turned to smaller, more innovative brands as an alternative to the often homogenous approach of global brands. Greater individual wealth, awareness of trends, accessibility and choice have also made people more confident in expressing themselves as individuals.

Brands are responding to the individual with buying power by appearing to shift from a 'one-size-fits-all' approach – where people have been classified as a group demographic – to appealing to individual tastes and attitudes. In reality the individual is still part of a mass, and it is the clever packaging of services that makes for individual appeal. Mass brands, like the furniture warehouse IKEA, encourage an individual 'mix-and-match' approach to their mass-produced products. Other brands try to get closer to the individual by adopting a more direct, intimate approach.

Starbucks says to 'make it your Starbucks' in ordering 'off the menu' by customising our own coffee .

The rise of the individual, particularly the creative individual, and their spending power means many brands are improving services, recognising that a single service approach does not work for everyone. It also offers an opportunity for smaller, more innovative brands to capture an individual's attention by offering a specific product or service of quality.

"They are targeting you as an individual – a creative person who thinks for themselves"

What's Your Flavour?

Add A Syrup To Your Favourite Starbucks Coffee.

= A Double Tall Caramel Skimmed Cappuccino.

MAKE IT Your STARBUCKS

1

1: STARBUCKS A-BOARD ADVERTISING

This Starbucks poster advertising encourages people to try a tailor-made approach by designing their own latte or adding their preferred flavour. The campaign reflects a trend among mass brands towards the customisation of product ranges, acknowledging that people desire something a bit more special rather than being limited to brand homogeny.

The 'creative' individual has also become a target for brands, most obvious in the branding of technology companies: Apple Computer is for those who 'Think Different'; HP says it's 'You and HP'; while Sony tells us to 'Go Create'. This approach is also responding to where the money is – these individuals have spending power and make up a high percentage of the working population.

"Simplicity is wisdom. Wisdom is simplicity"

Simon Anholt, Government Advisor and Author

SIMPLICITY

Simplicity sticks. A simple idea behind a creative output is much easier to grasp and retain than a collection of complex ideas. We are surrounded by so much noise and brand 'clutter' (advertising messages, billboards, a huge variety of information vying for our attention), that we have shorter attention spans and less time. Only clear, simple messages are likely to stick.

Simplicity helps to make sense. In business today, there is a desire to return to simple approaches that don't need reams of documentation to convey. For example, design company IDEO drives the development of a product idea to prototype stage as quickly as it is able, so that the client has something physical and tangible as soon as possible. Language in business is becoming simplified to avoid the use of business jargon. This is a significant change from a decade ago when complex words and brain-baffling legalese and management-speak was perceived by many as proof that you were getting value for money.

However, simplicity can be difficult to achieve. It is not a style, but rather a simple communication through a product or service, arrived at by the filtering of complex ideas and developments. It requires time and an ability to view the problem from the audience's perspective. Presenting a simple idea requires confidence. In the branding world this

means working in streamlined structures with open communication. Simplicity is hard to achieve, particularly when branding projects or campaigns often involve numerous parties with different aims and tight deadlines.

The trend towards simplicity is likely to stay for the foreseeable future, because people want it. One brand consultant said that the biggest plea among people when she researched brand trends was to "get rid of the bullshit". In design terms, simplicity has an elegance that is modern and contemporary. It is also different and so, for now, makes the brand stand out.

1

1: CLAUDIA SKODA BOUTIQUE, BERLIN
MARC NEWSON

Australian designer, Marc Newson, is currently one of the most prominent product designers in the world. Newson does not limit himself to one particular design output, such as furniture. He is probably best known for his earlier furniture designs (including famous pieces for the Italian manufacturer, Cappellini), objects (from Alessi coffee sets, to Nike trainers, to a female sex-toy), interiors (including a private jet), to designing a prototype aeroplane and, most recently, a chain of hotels.

The Claudia Skoda boutique, a designer boutique in Berlin, is an older design of Newson's, but reflects his style of modern simplicity.

Viruses cost organisations $55bn a year. Protect yours with networked IT services from BT.

25,000 multi-site organisations have chosen BT's unrivalled network expertise. We block over 40,000 viruses and prevent more than 14m unauthorised access attempts every month. So, BT helps ensure that your business-critical information gets to the right person, in the right place, at the right time, without interference. Securing your organisation to keep on doing what it does best. Discover more about succeeding in the digital networked economy at bt.com/networkedIT

*As reported on Silicon.com in Jan 2004, from a report from Trend Micro.

BT
More power to you

2: BT ADVERTISING
ST LUKES

A BT advertising campaign promoting its broadband technology for businesses had a huge street presence, on billboards and posters throughout the UK in 2004.

Visually, the campaign is noticeable, with a single strapline. Yet, what attempts to be a simple campaign has many messages running behind the images, which are difficult to grasp from the single images and strapline. What is the 'digital networked economy'? What do the images represent? (Some express data security and other digital issues encountered by business, although this is hard to interpret.) The campaign is striking and noticeable as well as surprisingly creative for a business campaign, but its message lacks true impact because of its complexity.

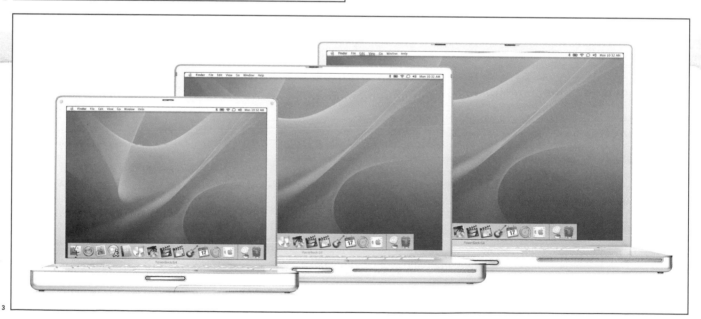

3: APPLE COMPUTER POWERBOOKS

Simplicity of design and image is a key characteristic associated with all of Apple Computer's products – from its iPod, to the PowerBooks (pictured), to its desktop range. A computer as simple as a PowerBook is not just about beautiful design, but involves complex engineering and sophisticated technology to achieve such a clean look and ease of use.

Jonathan Ive, Apple Computer's head of design, tried to define simplicity in a talk at London's Design Museum in 2004: "When people talk about simplicity as a style it drives me nuts. Apparent simplicity is one of the most difficult things to do. It's not obvious how hard it is."

Images courtesy of Apple Computer Inc.

"Less branding builds creativity amongst an audience"

LESS BRANDING

Some brands are so recognised by their design, products or tone of voice, they do not need to promote themselves through a logo. If the name is not known and the campaign or product is good, people will investigate the brand for themselves. As a consequence, branding is now becoming more subtle and clever.

This subtlety is a way of standing out by doing things differently. If the execution is clever, it will make people talk. The tactic is like a viral campaign, travelling by word-of-mouth and recommendation rather than being forced on people. Less branding is also possibly a response to brand-overload. The anti-brand movement and Naomi Klein's book, *No Logo,* successfully encourage a weariness and distrust in brands.

Stephen Cheliotis of Superbrands, an organisation that annually encourages votes for the 'coolest' brands in the world, believes that less branding will become more common. "The physical aspects of the brand design, such as the brand mark, will matter less. Clever communications can be done where the character of the brand is expressed without mentioning the name," says Cheliotis. People are more interested in the brand attitude and impression than the identity.

Unbranded brands have already done well. Japanese home brand Muji and clothing brand Uniqlo have successfully supported a no brand culture, while at the same time becoming successful brands in their own right. In summer 2004, BMW hosted a party for London's creative industry with a 'no logo' approach, to launch its new car. There was no BMW promotional material present (except for the car) and, significantly, no BMW staff at the party. Instead the company commissioned artists to create art installations about the new car. The idea behind the approach was to be seen as 'cool' and innovative among London's creative scene.

This creative approach is being used by consumer brands in their communication materials. Some brands distribute materials based on an idea or story, rather than the brand itself. Initially there seems to be no connection to a brand – no name, no logo – just a quirky idea behind the communication. For example, the lager brand Grolsch ran an alien abduction campaign where the direct marketing and website told stories about alien abductions, without mentioning the brand. The vodka brand, Smirnoff, has launched a new brand of vodka called 'Norsk'. Journalists were sent a fairytale book called 'Norsk' about the discovery of a spirit. At no point in the tale is the spirit connected to Smirnoff vodka .

These kind of creative concepts and campaigns are a way for brands to be associated with clever ideas conveyed by word-of-mouth or viral campaigns, rather than clumsy overstating of the brand's benefits. Less branding builds credibility among its audience.

1: A FLAGSHIP APPLE STORE

Apple introduced its own branded retail stores in the USA and the UK in 2004. There is little to mark that the store is Apple – there's no signage – except for a simple flag. Apple's stores show how simplicity in style can be carried through to the retail elements – less branding is powerful if the store will be recognised just by its distinctive style and look, simply because people know about it already.

2–4: 'THE ROAD TO LISBON' ADIDAS ADVERTISING CAMPAIGN
180 AMSTERDAM (PART OF 180/TBWA ALLIANCE)

The Adidas 'Road to Lisbon' campaign was based around a story leading up to the UEFA EURO 2004 and set to the soundtrack of the epic 1969 film *The Italian Job*. Ad agency 180 Amsterdam designed scooters for 13 of the world's best players to travel from their respective home countries to Lisbon for the championships. Each scooter was customised in the national team colours and reflected the player's character – a mod-like number for Beckham, a leopard-skin seat-cover for Dutch player Makaay. Meanwhile the cameras follow as the players meet up for kick-arounds in forests, lay-bys and on anything remotely resembling a pitch. They eventually end up in the main square of Lisbon.

The story behind the campaign takes more prominence than the logo. The campaign was rolled-out globally in the run-up to the championships.

"Brands will use clever communications, rather than their identity, to express their character because people are more interested in the brand's attitude and impression"

5: NORSK TALES FAIRY TALE
6: THE DIAGEO BRANDING

The fairy tale *The Norsk Tales: The Town That Night Forgot* was created for the launch of Smirnoff's Norsk vodka and copies were mailed to journalists and press outlets. Although the story concerns the discovery of a new, magical spirit to be drunk, nowhere in the book was the Smirnoff brand referred to by name. The only traditional branding on the publication was that of parent company Diageo, discretely tucked out of the way on the back cover.

MORE FUN

Brands that provide enjoyment will stand out in the future. It is a differentiator and a way to get noticed. So, according to brand gurus like Wally Olins, consumer brands will be adding fun to their offer. This means that brands will aim to take the dullness out of life's administration: banks will have coffee bars and supermarket shopping will become fun. Brands will offer practical solutions to make life easier, like having shops in a Post Office that sell things you want to post (a logical solution that has been offered in places like New Zealand and Australia for years, but is still not common across Europe).

Fun is a way of enhancing the brand experience and giving a good impression. After all, it worked for Disney when its founder created Disneyland. Fun things also make good use of the expensive retail space that many brands own, but under-use. If a bank has unused space then why not house a cafe? They may successfully attract a few new customers and make existing customers feel good about the company. Associating fun with the brand

also attempts to create an emotional connection between the consumer and the brand: in that good service and convenience leaves a good impression.

This new approach means that traditional product brands with basic retail outlets will now create spaces where people can meet, eat and learn.

Apple Computer is one major brand that has adopted 'fun' into its services: its new-style retail stores have internet cafes, a kids' zone, training sessions, a theatre for workshops and demonstrations and added extras like a 'genius' bar, where the Mac expert answers customer questions.

Meanwhile many women's clothing brands have learned that entertaining boyfriends while women try on clothes is a practical solution. Clothing retailers FCUK and H&M have PlayStations and seating areas for the men. The lingerie brand Coco De Mer has gone a step further by introducing peep-holes in the changing room doors for partners to view the lingerie 'in situ'.

At the other end of the fun scale, an entrepreneur in Montreal, Canada, has created a funeral parlour with designer furniture, a funky bar, a library (with books to help the grieving and offer spiritual guidance) and, of course, options for 'accessories' (a crucifix or the Koran, you choose) to mark the denomination of the service. Driving the trend for fun in branding is only limited by ideas.

> "Brands will aim to take the dullness out of life's administration: banks will have coffee bars and supermarket shopping will become fun"

"Fun is a way of enhancing the brand experience and giving a good impression"

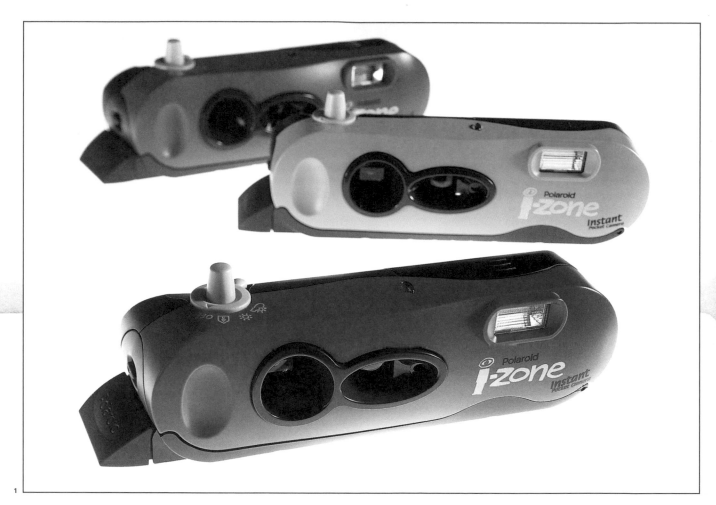

1

1: THE I-ZONE BY POLAROID
IDEO FOR POLAROID

Simplicity in design and function makes the kids' Polaroid I-zone such a striking and noticeable addition to the Polaroid product line that it has captured a new market, becoming the best-selling camera in the USA at the time of print.

The Polaroid I-zone was designed by IDEO. The industrial designers only started designing after interviewing children from the 'tween' to teen years to understand their likes and dislikes. They discovered that kids use cameras for 'photo play' – an expression of creativity and a way to connect with friends. These findings were applied to the design to create an appropriate form and function – the colour, soft-grip edges, and compact size are deliberately easy to hold and use, and the camera will fit in a pocket.

"Many new brands have succeeded by simply taking an existing product offer and repackaging it with extra and efficient services"

BETTER SERVICE

For many brands today, service is the key differentiator. This is because it is often difficult to distinguish one product over another if they are sold at similar prices. If Dell, Toshiba and Compaq offer computers to a business at the same price, with similar functionality, it is the service offered that will swing the decision to buy. Service includes how those products will be supported, maintained and repaired; how quick turn-around on those repairs are; and what deal the customer will get on their next purchase.

Brand-owners know this – there is constant talk of 'focusing on the customer' – but few still deliver good services even though a lack of service can damage a brand. This lack of attention to service has its roots in history. Branding emerged from a product-based culture where brands were (and, in many cases, still are) managed by marketeers who often know little about delivering customer service. Product branding is based on a manufacturing culture, where the product is made and sold to fit a purpose or need of the consumer, and the focus is on delivering the product. What happens afterwards has historically been of little interest to those who made it.

The trend towards better services is in response to human behaviour. Many people are made uncomfortable by the increasing amount of technology they find in their lives. Customer Service has commonly been moved to call centres fronted by queuing systems and internet-based communications. People generally prefer to deal with another person, particularly if something goes wrong and they want a human contact with whom to discuss their needs. Service is also being demanded by customers whose buying power gives them access to serviced products and thus the knowledge of how service should be. If a celebrity can have personal shopping in expensive stores, then why shouldn't other shops offer the same to its customers? A basic level of service was previously something for those that paid high prices, but has now shifted to the mainstream. And if you have money, you get more.

Good brands offer a service package to suit the individual – if you need personal service and advice then a relationship manager should be available; if you know what you want, and want access to information quickly and easily, then an online service is preferable. Good brands also speak directly to the consumer – if you have any problems or comments on our product, simply call the helpline. This is a significant shift: customers have often been treated as a mass audience once they have bought a product. Many brands hoped that technology would solve the service issue and replace the need to employ more people. As retail banks have discovered, replacing branches with computers to cut costs has not worked very well. Brands are now developing individual services for different types of customers.

Attention to service works and many new brands have succeeded by simply taking an existing product offer and repackaging it with extra and efficient services. Richard Branson's Virgin brand emerged at a time when Europe was synonymous with bad service. He took existing products and reintroduced them with easy-to-use services and friendly staff. Virgin's approach was to give the customer something familiar but do it better.

Other brands, like mobile phones, are attempting to offer an 'integrated' customer experience – where knowledge of the customer's needs is visible to any employee who serves the customer. This means that bills, finances and usage patterns can be viewed at one point. The ability to provide an integrated experience requires sophisticated technology systems – an expensive undertaking.

A service approach is also a natural progression for brands where the products have reached their buying peak (or 'saturation point'). For example, most people in the UK now own a mobile phone, so how can the phone providers continue to make money and differentiate themselves? Introducing customised services, such as a personal advisor who can tell you all the benefits of your phone, gives brands an opportunity to sell more services and an upgraded product.

Product: The engineered designed product that is often the basis of the brand.

1

1: OCADO ONLINE DELIVERY SERVICE

Ocado is an online grocery store, based in the UK. It is the brainchild of three former Goldman Sach's bankers who formed a partnership with the top-end UK supermarket Waitrose in January 2002.

Ocado was not the first in the market for online groceries, but it differentiated itself by promising – and delivering – a commitment to service and quality: no rotten vegetables and delivery within a one-hour time slot.

Everything, from the tailormade Mercedes-Benz fleet to the training of the van-drivers, to the quality of the food, is focused on customer service – or, as Ocado's website states to "create an exciting new grocery experience in which our actions speak louder than our words". While the brand sits at the top end of the market (it is a little bit pricier than others), it is simply marketed at people who are busy. Customer feedback, so far, indicates that it is delivering on its brand promise.

2: ORANGE CONCEPT STORE

The stores of the mobile communications company Orange are indicative of how brands are attempting to provide a personal service to customers, by offering a spectrum of service from self-management of your phone and accounts (through online access) to a dedicated personal phone manager: "We're covering all bases with the consumer, from the inexperienced to the techie", says Adam Scott, Brand Experience Manager at Orange.

Orange opened its first retail shops in 1994, and later developed 'concept stores' that are aimed at offering more comprehensive services, demonstration areas, and products.

"The successful uptake of technology relies on people buying it, and technology takes time to be accepted by the masses"

EASY TECHNOLOGY

Technology can aid a great brand experience by making services run smoother, adding extra benefits to the customers, and improving communication. It can provide a better product; as technological devices become smaller and more flexible, their application becomes more exciting, such as their integration into home furniture or clothing. As access to technology becomes easier and cheaper the world over, technology will become the facilitator for brands, rather than a substitute for services.

The learning curve in the application of technology has been a steep one. In the lead up to the dot-com boom, technology was hyped as the solution to every company's and individual's needs. Many businesses, banks for example, used technology as a short-cut for customer service and a way to cut costs and personal service.

After the dot-com bubble burst, many brands rejected technology, believing that the end of the hype meant the end of its application. The music industry, for example, took years to see technology as a potential threat to its business because of web access to music and the easy pirating of music through technology. Although technology has forced us forward and sped up the pace of the world, in reality, the most common technologies available now have been in the making for over ten years – mobile phones, digital assistants and video conferencing.

Technology in the home, such as sound-systems embedded in furniture, is only now being developed by companies like Philips, even though it has been talked about for years. The successful uptake of technology relies on people buying it, and technology takes time to be accepted by the masses.

The uptake of technology can happen by accident – SMS was never intended to be marketed as a product but it took off. Innovative brands are also seeking smart ways to integrate technology beyond physical product use. This includes using technology, such as SMS and internet-based technology, in marketing promotions. Technology should now be truly integrated as part of the brand experience.

1: WIRELESS TECHNOLOGY

'Online oxygen' is about having wireless access to the internet wherever you may be. There are 'hotspot' wireless zones in café chains. As our lives become more mobile and more communication is reliant on email, rather than voice, the ability to get online anywhere will not just be a bonus, but a necessity.

Reinier Evers of Trendwatching.com says that: "Eight years after the first websites started popping up, and email made its way from science labs to office desks and living rooms, 800 million consumers worldwide are beginning to see online access as an absolute necessity, comparable to oxygen. And there are no signs that the pace of integrating online access into daily life is slowing down. Being in control and communicating whenever or however is just too tempting."

Images courtesy of trendwatching.com

SMS: To send a text message using a mobile phone.

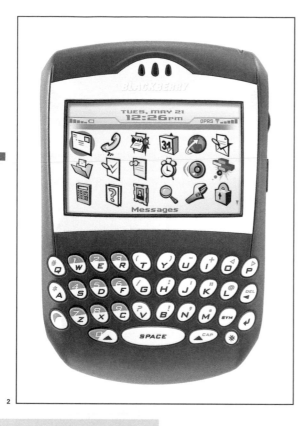

2

2: THE BLACKBERRY PDA

On-the-move technology has taken
off. There's no excuse not to be connected
to web or email constantly and the
Blackberry is the solution for the 'mobile
professional'. The technology was developed
and manufactured by Research in Motion and
is licensed to the mobile networks. Of all the
digital mobile devices available, this one
seems to be the most popular, offering a
keyboard and 'always-on' access. Owners
invest emotionally in their blackberries and
claim that they are addictive.

Image courtesy of RIM

"Technology is now truly integrated as part of the experience and is a facilitator, not a substitute"

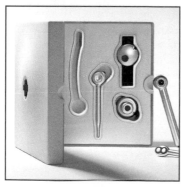

3

4

5

6

3: PHILIPS TECHNOLOGY IN THE HOME: MEDICAL BOX (3), RECHARGEABLE SHELF (4) AND INVISION TV (6) FOR THE BATHROOM AND TILE SPEAKER (5) FOR THE KITCHEN
PAESAGGI FLUIDI BY PHILIPS AND CAPPELLINI

The idea and possibilities of being
fully networked in your home through
sophisticated technology has been talked
about for years within the technology
industry. The technology just had to be small
enough and affordable enough to justify
embedding it in everyday furniture.
Philips and world-renowned furniture
designers, Cappellini, have teamed up
to produce some concept pieces where
technology is embedded elegantly in
furniture so as not to be obtrusive.
The hi-tech consumer market in Japan
has moved on even further: the latest
'must-have' technology for the elite home
is a domestic robot.

THEORY   PAGE / 126
See 'Risk and Reward'

RESPONSIBLE BRANDS

> ## "Responsible branding asks more of companies than the donation of money or resources"

A brand that behaves responsibly is able to boost its reputation, motivate staff, and build a positive profile for itself. While it is unusual for brands to focus solely on responsibility as a brand message (with the exception of brands selling 'ethical' products, Non-Governmental Organisations (NGOs) or charities), 'responsibility' is becoming part of the repertoire for major brands, as consumers and other stakeholders proactively demand more responsibility from them and it is likely that, where choice is ubiquitous, a brand's responsible agenda could be a differentiator in the buying process.

Responsible branding in its current form has countless interpretations. Many view responsible branding as Corporate Social Responsibility. This is where a brand contributes to the local community or undertakes sponsorship efforts (such as providing technology or services to the local school or community) to improve its reputation and image in the eyes of the consumer and other stakeholders. This can involve working with international organisations, like the United Nations, and NGOs.

But responsible branding asks more of companies than the donation of money or resources to good causes. It concerns the behaviour of the brand as a whole, from head office to the operations level (such as those in the field). Brands need to behave responsibly in their product sourcing, their supply chain, their behaviour to staff and customers, and in their implementation of community investments. Responsibility also covers 'good governance' procedures: how the finances and internal workings are run to ensure that they comply with laws and regulations.

Is a brand truly responsible if it gives money to a community while it ignores human rights or environmental issues? Oil companies are one of the most vocal industries in talking about responsible behaviour as their core business creates environmental damage, involves relocating people, and often causes conflict zones (impacting on human rights issues). In response, the companies argue that people want oil. The companies limit the damage, and maintain their reputation by actively engaging in dialogue and programmes to improve areas such as corruption, human rights and environment issues. However, many people still believe there is a disparity between what is said and what is done. As one BBC producer said after investigating the building of a pipeline to serve the world's oil needs: "It may be good publicity for the oil industry to say that it's becoming more open, but our experience suggests that these fine-sounding words are not being put into practice as much as the industry would like us to believe. Things may be changing but it seems to us that it will take a long time before this leopard really changes its spots."[2]

The majority of brands have a long way to go before they can be deemed to be behaving responsibly, and a brand's greatest fear is a consumer revolt. Yet the returns on responsible behaviour are huge, in terms of boosting the reputation of the brand and improving brand image. It can instil pride in those working for the brand, it can help attract new employees, it can be a deciding factor in the purchasing process and boost spending power in the communities in which it invests. Responsible behaviour is a board level issue that must be built into the core of business behaviour and values.

NGOs: An acronym for Non-Governmental Organisation. This is an organisation that is not part of the government (either local, state or federal), for example, Greenpeace and Amnesty International.

1

1: SHELL ADVERTISING CAMPAIGN, 1999

The oil industry is a sector that is leading in the area of 'responsible branding' because of the nature of its business. Shell has been one of the drivers of its industry, increasing awareness of its more positive actions to reduce environmental impact and contributing to local communities. At the time of release these advertisements were the first attempts by an oil company to engage stakeholders in the difficult questions surrounding responsible energy production and consumption; Shell was, perhaps, ahead of its time. Companies, particularly in the oil industry, are expected to have good social and environmental policies and a commitment to minimising environmental impact. It is likely that branding and advertising around responsible business initiatives, such as environmental impact, will become more common. The current debate is if and how such activity should be publicised and communicated. Stakeholders may expect corporate responsibility – both social and environmental – as part of doing good business. The question is whether the communication of the activities that companies pursue to fulfil this expectation contribute to differentiation within the market.

2. www.bbc.co.uk/bbcfour/documentaries/
storyville/oil-diary2.shtml.

> "Branding a country is deciding the fate of a nation. Yet the design industry is starting to do nicely out of a misunderstanding about what brands need to do. They think of branding as a logo, identity and promotion."
>
> Simon Anholt, Government Advisor and Author

BRANDING COUNTRIES

Brands and branding exist in areas where there is competition. Yet, there are some areas that seemed immune to the branding wand. One of those was the idea of branding a country.

At one level, countries have undertaken brand exercises for a long time, competing for our tourist dollars. What is shifting is that many countries now see the need to create an identity for themselves in a global society. How do the new entrants to the European Community differentiate themselves in the eyes of those who are already part of the European Community? How do they make themselves attractive to foreign investors or to reconstruction efforts? Or when making an Olympic bid?

Branding a country is not about running a tourism campaign or creating a country's logo. Beneath the identity, branding a country requires an in-depth understanding of how countries operate: economically, financially and culturally. This means knowledge of the affairs that affect governments, such as international relations, foreign investment, domestic budgets and the level of skilled population.

For this reason Simon Anholt, a specialist in 'branding' countries, argues that it is a dangerous thing to put the future of a nation in the hands of a branding agency. The rebrand of a country can be viewed by a branding agency within the narrow context of creating a logo and brand identity, while newly branding a country really, according to Anholt, is 'deciding the fate of a nation'.

Branding here is about building the perceived value and worth of a country. A newly branded country can also help

change perceptions in a post-conflict phase. Croatia was a major tourist destination in the early 1990s, prior to the war in the Balkans. It is currently attempting to reinvent itself to be attractive to foreign investment as well as tourists. Vietnam has successfully changed its image from being that of a post-war country in poverty, to a successful tourist destination and base for foreign companies.

In some circumstances, it is possible to brand a country as separate regions – one part may be a holiday destination, another attractive to foreign investment due to an educated workforce, another a conflict zone needing donor money. This can be relevant for countries that have been recipients of aid and press attention and the perception may have stuck. Ethiopia, for example, is now being covered in the press as a new tourist destination, while many still perceive it as a country that was once overwhelmed by famine.

Like a branded corporation, a branded country requires self-analysis. The subject (in this case, the country) needs to look inwards to ascertain what it stands for, what its values are and how it wishes to be projected to the outside world. Brand consultant, Kristina Dryza, says that countries, or those responsible for them, must do some soul-searching: "A country needs to reconnect with its culture. To look at its traditions and language – the bedrock of what makes that country what it is. Then they need to reinterpret that in a modern setting."

1: NYC OLYMPIC BID LOGO
WOLFF OLINS

New York City not only competed for the 2012 Olympics but its mayor, Michael Bloomberg, commissioned a UK branding agency to give the city a 'rebrand'. The rebranding initiative was believed to involve creating a more coherent image of the city. A new image for New York may be a positive step after the lasting images of the city on September 11th, 2001.

2: LIECHTENSTEIN COUNTRY REBRAND WOLFF OLINS

It may seem odd that a country wants to be represented by a logo or brand mark when it already has a flag and a monarchy. In 2004 Liechtenstein became the first country to 'rebrand' itself with a new country logo. To date, regions and metropolitan areas have adopted brands to help change an existing image, promote a new image or to simply get noticed.

Liechtenstein is a tiny principality slotted between Austria and Switzerland and mostly overlooked on the European tourist map. It has rebranded to boost tourism and investment. The new symbol, called the 'democratic crown', is intended to be used on a line of upmarket products, on government and official documents, as well as by the private sector. The brand, according to the agency that created it, Wolff Olins, represents the "beliefs and values of Liechtenstein as a whole".

3: 2012 OLYMPIC BIDS

The perception of a country or region is incredibly important when it comes to competing to host international events. The Olympics tops them all and countries spend millions on the bid campaigns. Each country bidding for the 2012 Olympics developed their own logo, but the branding goes a long way beyond developing a brand mark: to win the bidding wars the International Olympic Committee and the city's own citizens must be convinced that the city can cope with the pressure on its infrastructure, security, crowds, of building an Olympic village and stadium and all associated complications. London's successful bid carried a strong identity that played with the idea of scale, featuring athletes using London landmarks as sporting equipment, against a background of blue sky.

OWN BRANDS

Own brands are those which introduce new product lines under their own label, outside of their core business offer.

Supermarkets that introduce their own name brand ranges are the most obvious example. The aim here is to extend the brand, building on their existing and established brand name. The 'own brand' also offers a one-stop shop for the customer – if they trust the brand they can buy all their goods under the same label.

In the 1990s, the idea that a supermarket would sell their own financial services under a brand was a new and risky notion. It's a bit like super models taking up acting – something that works well if the core brand proves talented in both areas; or it may threaten a reputation if the new own brand falls below existing standards. Yet own brand introduction of products outside of their core area of business have been successful.

There are different tactics that brands can use in extending their reach to introduce new product ranges in their name. They can buy in the expertise and rebrand it under their name, such as BP's buying of the 'Wild Bean Cafe' chain. Or they can introduce a product range that is an obvious extension of their core offer – such as a hairdresser selling its own branded hair-care products.

Or a safer technique, requiring less investment, is to move into a form of co-branding, where a brand teams up with other brands to offer a joint product that combines the two names (Green & Black's organic chocolate is sold at the cafe chain Pret-a-Manger in branded packaging with both names). This technique builds on the strength of both brands.

1: WILDBEAN CAFE IN BP FORECOURT SHOP

Brands can bring in new services under their own banner by buying in the expertise. BP bought a catering company and rebranded it as its own Wild Bean Cafes that now form part of their service stations.

2: GREEN & BLACK'S AND PRET-A-MANGER COLLABORATION

The collaboration between two well-known brands to produce a unique product is becoming a popular way of introducing new 'own-branded' goods. In this case, food outlet Pret-a-Manger offers organic chocolate made by Green & Black's. The product has a new packaging with joint logos and is sold solely at Pret-a-Manger outlets. The advantage is that the partnership can carry the weight and positive perceptions of both brands.

"The 'own brand' also offers a one-stop shop for the customer – if they trust the brand, they can buy all their goods under the same label"

PERSONAL BRANDING

Branding 'me' has become a huge growth industry, particularly in the USA. Branding the individual is something that is most evident in celebrity culture – for those such as David Beckham, Martha Stewart, celebrity chefs like Jamie Oliver, and popstars like Madonna and Kylie. Many of them painstakingly reinvent their image on a regular basis to show the world that they, or their product, have changed. Rebranding themselves may relate to their talent – Madonna invents a new image with every new album – or come after a high-profile personal battle to show that all is OK – Nicole Kidman seemed to become more famous and glamourous after her much reported break-up with Tom Cruise. David Beckham appears to 'rebrand' himself with each new hairstyle. Now the branding gurus are telling us that you too, should tactically brand yourself.

Branding the individual is not new, but its increasingly mainstream popularity is indicative of the times we live in: most people will not work in the same job, or even in the same industry, throughout their life. Most people will not be with one partner all their lives. Any change, particularly on the career front, requires a new outlook and, with that, say the brand gurus, a reinvention.

Essentially branding yourself is a self-development technique made easy by perceiving yourself as a brand. By being your own brand, you are able to view yourself objectively, and that is the power of personal branding. 'Rebranding' a person can be used to improve an image, to help progress a career, to get back into the workforce, to even, perhaps, find a new partner. It encourages the individual to question their values and behaviour, but

like all branding, the 'brand' must be authentic to its subject, otherwise the branded creation is unlikely to work.

Personal branding can be interpreted in other ways: the tattoo is the ultimate personal brand – particularly if the tattoo is a brand. Naomi Klein in her book, *No Logo*, reveals that many Nike employees have the Nike 'swoosh' tattooed into their skin.

Personal branding is part of the greater trend that recognises and focuses on the individual, and encourages the person to take control. Whether it will take off among a more cynical European audience, with less of a taste for self-help methods than their American counterparts, remains to be seen.

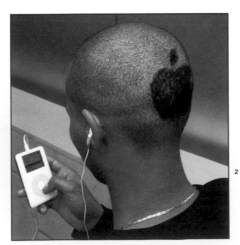

**1: DAVID BECKHAM LOGO
DESIGNED BY ADIDAS**

The footballer, David Beckham, is possibly one of the most well-known faces in the world and he is so much his own brand that Adidas have created a logo for him.

Personal branding is carefully managed and manipulated – involving every move from the career choices made, to how every action and event is publicised, to the style of the subject's haircut. It is also a growth area, no longer limited to celebrities.

2: WEARING THE APPLE LOGO

Choosing to wear a company logo as a hairstyle or a tattoo shows a sincere mark of loyalty, and is an ultimate advertisement for the brand. This trend has led to people auctioning their bodies as advertising surfaces on the internet.

Image courtesy of Linda Nylind

"Personal branding is part of the greater trend that recognises and focuses on the individual, and encourages the person to take control"

interview 1

Simon Anholt, Government Advisor and Author

Brand expert Simon Anholt is experienced in branding countries from his work with Placebrand in the UK. This type of branding involves much more than creating a brand identity and promoting the brand. To develop a brand strategy for a country requires months of in-depth analysis about the state of a nation – its economic situation and plans, its state of development, its foreign policy and international relations. Designers who are appointed to simply create a logo for a country, city or region should proceed with caution.

Why would a country want to brand itself?

All countries already have a brand, because they all have a reputation. But not all of those brands are fair, and most of them are indistinct, outdated, incomplete, and don't provide the country with real competitive advantage. So countries usually approach us because they want to take some control over their brand.

Some poorer countries want to brand themselves because the rest of the world perceives them as a country that can only survive on hand-outs. This is a perception carefully crafted by the aid agencies for the excellent reason that it brings in donor funds, but the image becomes deeply ingrained and can effectively prevent the country from developing tourism, exports, cultural relations, or attracting investment. Taking control over its brand can therefore be a poor country's first step towards economic independence.

> "All countries already have a brand, because they all have a reputation. But not all of those brands are fair, and most of them are indistinct, outdated and incomplete"

"A country doesn't need an identity because countries have flags. A logo can be good for an internal initiative, but externally it will just confuse people"

What do you think about the branding agency approach to branding countries? This seems to be a huge growth area for agencies.

Branding a country is effectively deciding the fate of a nation, yet branding agencies tend to approach countries as if they were dealing with a simple consumer product. Of course this approach is not only ineffective; it's irresponsible and dangerous. Countries, like corporations, are mainly composed of people, but in some of these countries the people do not have a voice; in corporations they do, or people can choose to leave.

Branding a country is not to do with communications, it is something the country has to do for itself. It is not about being creative or designing brands, it is about having a plan and coordinating the actions and behaviours of the government and the people, in harmony with those plans.

What about countries that find themselves on the international stage, such as the new entrants to the European Community, or a country that 'competes' for aid from donor countries. Do you think 'branding' the country helps and how important is it?

It is a valuable and interesting construct. Brand is one of the few apropos that helps a country's perception.

For example, if the composite brand is the EC, then you add an accession country, the main players are thinking "does this slightly dodgy brand enhance or detract from the main brand?". The main driver is largely emotional and branding is a good route into that — it is the path through the minefield of emotions.

interview 2

Shari Swan, Trend Predictor, Streative Branding

How do trend projections play a role in branding?

Progressive brands are moving away from traditional advertising methodologies and opting for consumer insights to connect authentically to the market. Still, traditional brand-owners are not yet ready to accept that qualitative trends and consumer emotion are driving the market.

The interpretation of trend can be tricky as trend is often influenced by personal opinion and personal experience. There is also so much trend information available that brand managers have a difficult time prioritising the most relevant trends that are affecting their business. In addition, we may identify up to 40 global and local trends, but most corporations are only able to address two main trends per season.

How are people interacting with brands and incorporating them into their lives?

Today's youth interacts with brands that connect with it on an emotional level. They want to feel that a brand belongs and connects to their lives. They are interested in co-creating with brands and want to feel that they can influence product design, marketing, events and communications.

The 18–24 youth market is wired, educated, cynical and irrational. They're into brand authenticity. They know everything about the brands that surround them and have grave concerns about social and ethical responsibility. They believe that companies should give back something to the world in which they operate.

More brands are collaborating to create new products and designs. What significant trends do you see in partnering among brands?

At the moment, we've identified four partnership models:

• Promotional Sponsorship such as Lance Armstrong and the yellow armband or Motorola and the NFL Ingredient Partnerships, where one seeks a partner in another industry. Another example is the concept of Intel Inside, which partners with computer companies like Microsoft.
• Value-Based Partnerships occur when a service and product come together to create new experiences, such as Vodafone and Sony creating mobile music content.
• Innovation-Based Co-branding where two brands get together to create something that has never been done before, for example Burtons and Apple in creating their iPod jacket.
• Design is yet another discipline that is fast developing branded partnerships – Karl Lagerfeld has designed clothes for H&M and to celebrate the 150th anniversary of Steinway & Sons, Lagerfeld also created a commemorative piano for Steinway.

How do you advise companies to look out for trends?

So many companies focus on their immediate competition for marketplace trends. I preach the gospel to brands about 'looking sideways' at products and brands in markets beyond their own. Radical innovations come about when elements from very different worlds are brought together. That could mean a company like Coca-Cola should be tracking what is happening in pharmaceutical branding or telecommunications rather than only studying beverage trends.

So, where are trends in branding heading? People seem to be seeking simplicity in brands, both in the product and in their communication – is this a trend?

We are heading back to basics; to the uncomplicated, to human connection and emotional experience. Today's consumer is exposed to, on average, 20,000 to 30,000 advertisements and new products a year and the youth today is tuning-out all this information. People are weary of all the messages screaming at them from every aspect of their lives. We will be going back to the basics in a more sophisticated way. Brands now need to be authentic and real; it's about honesty and sincerity.

Do you think there is a role for ethics and responsibility in branding?

If corporations don't take their ethical ethos and corporate principles seriously in the development of their brand – from design to development to logistics, operations and marketing – then they are going to struggle. Social and ethical responsibility is now a given for doing business in today's environment.

"I preach the gospel to brands about 'looking sideways' at products and brands in markets beyond their own. Radical innovations come about when elements from very different worlds are brought together"

CHAPTER 06

DELIVERING THE BRAND EXPERIENCE

INTRODUCTION

Brands today are experienced through numerous different media and in different contexts. The graphic designer is the scriptwriter of the consumer's experience with the brand.

This chapter defines the brand experience and highlights some of the key points where people interact with the brand: in retail and public environments; through product design and packaging; through partnerships and advertising; through technology and in different ways around the world. Drawing on examples, it looks at how the designer can choreograph and influence that experience.

The theory section looks at the marketing mix of a brand: product, price, place and promotion – a necessary grounding for any product or service.

There are two interviews in this chapter: Stefano Marzano, head of design at electronics company Philips, talks about designing on a global scale and the design process within Philips, in the first interview. Jonathan Ive, head of Apple Computer's design team and creator of products like the iMac and iPod, then talks about design in an open 'question and answer' session at London's Design Museum – his first public appearance in seven years.

Chapter 6 Contents:

◗◗

THEORY CHAPTER 06 /
++

The Marketing Mix – The Four 'P's

The four 'P's are key to any product or service. They are:

• Product (or service)
• Price
• Place
• Promotion

Each of these represents a use of resources that, if mixed correctly, offers enormous rewards. But if the mix is not quite right, disaster beckons.

PRODUCT	Benefits for the customer Quality of the product Design of the product Features Branding Packaging After-sales service	PLACE	Type of store it is sold in Ease of access to store Website Direct sales (catalogue, telesales etc.) Point-of-sale display Customer service/staff knowledge Retailer relationships (see The Pareto Principle p98)
PRICE	Discounts Add-ons or free gifts Perceived value Rebates Loyalty schemes Loss-leaders	PROMOTION	Advertising Direct Marketing (mailshots etc.) Telephone sales Brochures Trade exhibitions Sponsorship, PR Sales force Gifts Branding

Here are four examples of brands in terms of price, product, place and promotion:

WAL-MART	Price, customer service, convenience, opening times, range of goods	QUANTAS	Customer service, convenience, range of destinations, online booking, comfort
WASHING DETERGENTS	Features, promotions, advertising, money-back guarantees, recommendation by washing machine manufacturers, discounts	SMITHSONIAN	Tradition, respect, value for money, quality, archives, public service

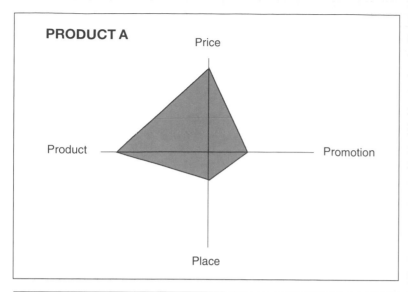

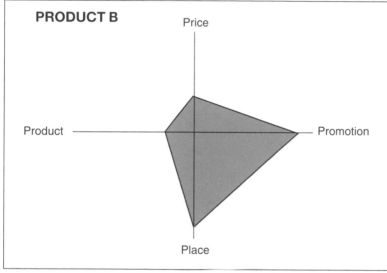

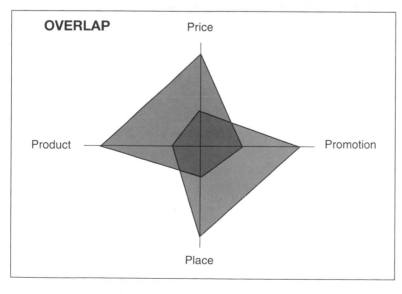

Checking for overlap

Some companies will plot their marketing mix on a simple graph to see if it overlaps either with a competitor or, more seriously, with one of their own products.

Product A is an exclusive product with high design and functionality values, and extremely well manufactured. As such, it is priced at a premium. Because of its status, the product does not need to be particularly well promoted and can only be found in a few exclusive outlets.

Product B is a low-cost, low-quality version of the same sort of product. It is heavily promoted and can be found virtually everywhere.
Do these two products compete?

There is some overlap, but not a great deal. Both products are, however, competing for the same customers who occupy the overlapping areas.

If the products belong to different companies, this might not be a problem, but if they belong to the same company then one product may be damaging sales of the other, or consumers may be confused by what each has to offer individually.

Loss-leader: A product that makes a loss but money is made elsewhere. For example stores sell best-selling books at a loss, but gamble that customers will buy other things too once they are in the store.

THEORY CHAPTER 06 /

++

Brand Differentiation

A key tool in the fight against too much overlap between a company's own brands, and between competing companies' brands is differentiation. Making sure consumers can see clear differences between brands is an easy way to develop a clear 'offer' or 'unique selling point' (USP) that it otherwise might not have.

In the early 1990s Apple had a bewildering array of computer models available, and brought new ones out regularly. This confusion led to a drop in sales. Eventually the company focused on four areas: professional and consumer desktop and laptop machines, as illustrated in the table below.

As sales grew and customers began to understand the differentiation between products, the range expanded and now includes business/scientific models called XServes, and educational models called eMacs. There are several models available in each category depending on intended use – and generally the differentiation works in that customers know which product is aimed at them.

APPLE MAC COMPUTERS	DESKTOP	LAPTOP
PROFESSIONAL	G-series (G3, G4, G5)	Powerbook
CONSUMER	iMac	iBook

"Making sure consumers can see clear differences between brands is an easy way to develop a clear 'offer' or 'unique selling point' (USP)"

Kraft, the USA-based multinational food company has several coffee brands around the world including six in the UK. Although all are owned by the same company, they are promoted and managed separately and, though there is some overlap, cater for different consumer groups, as can be seen on a price/quality comparison (see below).

KRAFT	QUALITY			
PRICE	Economy	Standard	Good	Superior
High				Kenco Rappor Carte Noire (Superior taste, premium price)
Above average			Kenco (Instant coffee with the taste and aroma of real coffee) Cafe Hag (Decaffeinated coffee)	
Average		Maxwell House (Instant coffee)		
Low	Mellow Birds (Mild instant coffee)			

"The brand experience is the real and tangible showcase of the brand and is expressed through dozens of individual opportunities"

CREATING A BRAND EXPERIENCE

Brand experience is how the audience reacts to a brand at any contact point, and it is the basis of consumer dialogue with the brand. The experience of a brand is a series of interactions that, over time, can encourage brand loyalty or marginalise a product or service. The consumer is buying something larger than the product or service: they are buying into the philosophy and the spirit behind the brand. This is why IKEA speaks about the 'IKEA way', why the founder of Starbucks, Howard Schultz, says that Starbucks offers a 'lifestyle' rather than just coffee, and why brands like Nike promote ambition and commitment through selling sports clothing into a highly competitive market.

People judge a brand by their experience with it, and so every contact with the brand must reflect its essence and core values, and deliver on expectation. While many brands go to great lengths to create a homogenous experience across countries and cultures (Starbucks, Holiday Inn and McDonald's, for example), the product does not need to be physically identical at every point of consumption. It is the brand's values and essence that must remain the constant experience, while the product itself can be translated in many different ways with regional variation or seasonal flair.

The brand experience is created from a brand vision. The experience itself is everything your audience senses about your brand. Every resulting perception and insight will support or denigrate the brand. An experience may have a product or service behind it, but this is not essential – a brand experience can become a reality even though it may be based on a concept (the War on Terror, for example) and it will always result in an emotional response. Brands can also use promotion to set a brand experience and product expectation even before the product or service is launched. As spending power increases and choice blossoms, audiences now have an expectation that just about every purchasing opportunity should deliver some degree of delight. We want a high level of service and an ever-higher quality of product and this poses a challenge for the creators of the brand experience.

Disney was one of the earliest and most successful purveyors of the complete brand experience – Disneyland is a shrine to a legion of animators and storytellers and the personality and beliefs of Walt Disney. An experience with Nike is intended to inspire and motivate us into an action response – to 'Just do it'. If you buy a Body Shop product you are buying into a philosophy of caring for your world and your environment and when you buy Apple computer products you are implored to 'Think different' and be creative.

1

Mobile phone operator, Orange, based its market introduction around a spirit of optimism summed up in an iridescent colour identity ('The future's bright, the future's Orange'), while Vodafone

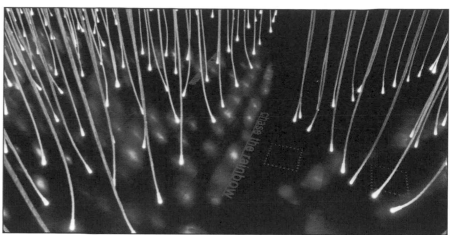

1, 2: THE ORANGE IMAGINARIUM
IMAGINATION

The Orange Imaginarium is an exhibition space for children found at a science centre called Explore@Bristol in the UK. Orange is one of the main corporate sponsors of the centre. The idea of the space was to create an environment that would be fun for children while educating them in wireless technology. There were limits in place due to Orange's corporate policies about promoting to children, such as no SMS to be used. Yet, the space had to be transformed to appeal to the 4–16 year-old age group, which is a broad spectrum of ages in terms of tastes and attitudes. It has to be interactive and genuinely innovative.

The Imaginarium was created by brand experience agency, Imagination Ltd. It is a good example of how spaces can be used to provide an experience that both reflects the brand and moves it forward. The exhibition space seeks to engage children in a learning environment by demonstrating, through interaction, how wireless technology works. At the start of the journey, animated stories illustrate to children the connection between the technology on show and everyday needs. Then children are able to interact with a directional speaker to say their name and the computer responds in different pitches. The third stage, called 'Chase the Rainbow', has been created as an example of how technology can personalise an individual's space, as kids move through fibreoptic cables that change colour. The final stage of the experience uses voice-activation technology to recognise children's individual voices, to tell them jokes at their request.

plays on the idea of intimacy (its strapline is 'How are you?'). Orange, in keeping with its avant-garde company name, set up an expectation that relates to hope, but the subtext that the future of mobile communication lies with Orange has proved difficult to deliver. In contrast, Vodafone's engineering roots display more of a pragmatic focus in its company name and use of the phrase 'How are you?' as its brand link relates right back to pragmatic use of the phone – 'How are you?' is the second most commonly used phrase next to 'Hello'. Brands can convey an expectation or a promise, and experiences that follow through on this promise strongly promote the brand values. Those that fail to deliver on expectations can breed buyer regret and dissonance.

Yet, while the brand experience is a mainstream concept in branding, many still get it wrong. Iain Ellwood, Strategy Director at branding agency Interbrand says: "Many brands focus on the promise not the experience – 80 per cent focus will be on the promise, 20 per cent on the experience, with the customer at the centre. But the balance needs redressing. 60 per cent of the brand should be about the experience, and 40 per cent on the promise."

Experience matters to every brand and just how the audience interacts with the brand must be consciously developed across every interaction. The designer is the creator and translator of the brand experience – they are often involved in conceptualising the brand and turning the brand promise into a tangible reality, acting as the link between the audience and the brand. This is the starting point for a positive brand experience. "Like a movie script, the designer is in control of managing the emotional journey. Whether it's about designing a bottle of liquid detergent or a website," says Ellwood. It is the designer who 'scripts' how the user interacts with the bottle, such as the actions of opening it and using the contents.

The designer creates the narrative of the brand experience and this is best understood by working from the customer's viewpoint. The designer must seek to engage the audience and create an experience that is relevant and appropriate. Ralph Ardill, former Strategy Director at Imagination, a company that has specialised in creating the brand experience for over 25 years, explains: "It is possible to communicate without engaging; but it's impossible to engage without communicating well. A communication perspective is one size fits all. An engagement perspective is thinking about the audience, what they are interested in, when they need it, how they need it. You have to understand what it takes to make me want to buy one – that is engagement."

To engage, the designer must understand how the audience will be interacting with the brand and its environment, the consumer's frame of mind, as well as what the brand is 'saying'. Then the customer journey must be scripted to apply to different forms of media, managing the consumer experience of the brand at every point – the retail experience, the product itself, the service, the phone contact, the brochures, the posters, the price and the follow-up customer care. Scripting the brand experience offers huge opportunities for creative scope and innovation. The use of alternative techniques for promoting the brand message should be considered: a website is a more flexible medium than retail because of its immediacy and availability; events and partnerships offer new ways to promote a different aspect or personality of the brand, while ambient media and advertising can take the brand experience to the audience, often in unexpected ways.

Brands are now seeking to capture an experience that moves beyond triggering the five senses. Brand experts talk about capturing a 'sixth sense' or brand 'spirit', which establishes a deeper connection with the audience. The brand experience is extending into more unique and original ways of 'living the brand'. In Japan, Chanel has opened a restaurant in its store in association with restaurateur Alain Ducasse, where the food will, according to Chanel's PR people, "pay homage to the Chanel spirit" and is designed to reflect Chanel's fashion collection.

The experience, in any form, should be simple in execution and uncomplicated in its message. An experience must be easily identifiable with the brand-owner, without necessarily a logo in sight.

Some brands create a focal point for the brand experience, such as a major retail store. If the experience created is powerful enough, people will associate it with the brand. Topshop's Oxford Street store in London is their showcase for the brand to the world and is constructed like a middle-eastern market of independent retailers under an umbrella brand, yet, the brand's local shops do not match this experience. The 'flagship' store was revamped in 1998 and is their most popular store, attracting over 200,000 customers each week. The 'experience' is created by in-house DJs, a cafe, themed collections, changing interiors, and a constant turnover of stock and ranges.

"Designing interiors for Topshop is like working with a big theatre. The first thing I seek to do is to create a lifestyle, a fashion feeling. I want to create a 'wow' factor when people walk in the store," says Ben Wittman an interior designer for Topshop. "We work closely with the fashion design team, who explain the product range for the season and who we want to appeal to. I take influences from other stores, trends and cities – the design has to be cool."

1

"Brand experts talk about capturing a 'sixth sense', or brand 'spirit'"

"The experience, in any form, should remain simple in execution and uncomplicated in its message"

2

3

1–3: MAKING NASDAQ ACCESSIBLE
IMAGINATION (USA) INC.

A brand experience does not necessarily need to be linked to a tangible product or service. Brand experience agency, Imagination (USA) Inc., was asked to create an experience to mark the opening of the financial markets for NASDAQ, an electronic screen-based service that shows the financial security markets in real time. NASDAQ was competing for media coverage with Wall Street, which opens its markets with a bell, and is screened on channels like CNN. NASDAQ wanted more coverage and public awareness of its brand.

Imagination (USA) Inc. created an experience that attracted attention to the opening ceremony. Every morning a high-profile person was invited to digitally sign their name to signal the opening of the market. This signing triggered a multimedia experience of music, light and graphics, that culminated in the market formally opening. At the same time, the signing was projected across all of NASDAQ's available media, including a huge screen outside its headquarters in the centre of New York. The new opening ceremony doubled broadcast coverage for NASDAQ.

RETAIL AND PUBLIC SPACES

A controlled brand space – whether it is a retail space, exhibition space, office space, hotel or restaurant – is one of the most powerful forms of the brand experience and provides a unique venue for brand expression. It offers a multi-sensory showcase for the brand: sight (the space itself), sound (music), the smells, touch (the product, the materials and fabrics used) and taste (the restaurant or cafe associated with the brand, if there is one). A space, even temporarily dedicated to a brand, is able to project the brand character in a unique way, either as an intensely focused display or by using promotional partners to indicate support and industry strength.

These brand spaces are ideal for launching a brand, changing perceptions and attracting potential new customers. A space is more than a three-dimensional view of the product or service – it can offer a brand experience that is immersive, reflecting the philosophy of the brand.

The retail space is also becoming more important to brands as the style of consumer shopping changes: people are looking for ways to participate with the product rather than to simply view the product in a display case. People want to interact and try out products, to see new concepts, and to learn about how they can get the most from their existing product. Apple in the UK tried an experiment like this in the late 1980s by franchising a retail concept called the Apple Centre. To the consumer these environments were consistently represented with the same furnishing and training, and appeared to be Apple-owned, but the user experience was variable and the brand impact on Apple degraded over time. The new Apple stores are a non-franchised solution and

offer one of the best examples of how brands are moving forward in the retail space. Each store has an internet cafe, a kids' zone, training sessions, a theatre for workshops and demonstrations and help points under one roof. Sony followed Apple into the franchising of Sony Centres, which now proclaim their independence from Sony Corporation. Time will tell whether Sony follows Apple with a Sony Store retail concept.

The 'day out' shopping experience, epitomised early on by IKEA, is now becoming centred on entertainment rather than retail. Retail space also offers opportunities for service brands, like banks, to maximise precious square footage by offering other services and partnerships within their own outlets. A UK bank, Abbey (now owned by Spanish bank, Santander) partnered with a cafe chain (Costa), creating a meeting space and social area from a space that was purely functional in the past. It is difficult to determine if the cafe is part of the bank or the bank part of the cafe.

Despite the dominance of large, often global brands in the main shopping streets, many of these are trying to create a sense of intimacy and personal service with their customers in-store: "We're going back to the corner store approach, when you knew your local shopkeeper or bank manager," says Orange Brand Experience manager, Adam Scott, who has helped develop the Orange retail shops. "The store is the environment for the customer to find out what they can do – it is the touch and feel of the brand. It needs to reflect the brand values and use materials that reflect the brand language."

1: THE RETAIL EXPERIENCE OF IKEA HOME STORES

Swedish furniture company, IKEA, is one of the most successful retail brands of our time. Its huge stores bring well-designed furniture to the masses at a low price. The key is the do-it-yourself approach: select what you want, pick it up from the warehouse and self-assemble.

The 'IKEA way' has stemmed from the philosophy of its founder, Ingvar Kamprad, who initially started the company as a mail-order business. A particular style and culture runs through the company with egalitarian principles dominating. Within the company there are flat management structures and minimal hierarchy. The brand experience offers a deliberate 'day out' with everything available at the store – including facilities for children and a family restaurant.

There are few people who have not experienced – or endured – the IKEA retail experience and customers, from all cultures and countries, continue to clamour for more: sales totalled 12.8 billion Euro in 2004 ($US15.5 billion) and there are now stores in 44 countries. An opening of a new store in the UK in early 2005 caused injuries after people fought over opening-day bargains, and three people were killed at a store opening in Saudi Arabia in late 2004. While Europe still tops the list for sales revenue, new markets, like China, represent huge growth for IKEA.

Franchises: Shops that are linked to a brand, but are individually owned.

"The retail space is becoming more important to brands as the style of consumer shopping changes"

1: PRADA DRESSING ROOM, NEW YORK CITY STORE
IDEO

The ultimate brand experience is still best epitomised by luxury brands or services that offer a seamless experience of quality and sanctuary, from the clothes to the shop interiors to the interactive dressing rooms.

Italian haute couturier, Prada, opened a groundbreaking store in 2001 in New York City, designed by the Dutch architect Rem Koolhaas. Design company, IDEO, worked on the dressing rooms and in-store devices which allow the staff to focus completely on the customer. The dressing rooms – a glass booth – include design features like a 'magic mirror' that is a camera and display that adds a four-second delay so the customer can spin around and view all sides of the garment. Sensors in the closets detect the electronic tags on store items, which trigger a touch screen with all information about the item, from availability to permutations of colour, fabric, and size.

Spaces can also offer opportunities for brands to participate within a community. Some brands have created permanent exhibition spaces and parks aimed at entertaining, educating and providing the ultimate brand experience. The Orange Imaginarium is part of a science centre for young people in the UK, and uses its own technology to create play areas that can demonstrate technology to children. The Guinness Storehouse is a centre in Dublin for tourists, employees and people wanting a connection with the brand – and a taster of the product. It is six floors of a formerly disused brewery and includes exhibition spaces, bars, a conference and training centre, a gallery and an events venue. The building is more aptly described by its designers as a 'cultural hub' rather than a visitors' centre and embodies the Guinness brand experience.

The graphic designer may be involved at a number of levels in creating an interpretation of the brand in a spatial environment, and work as part of a much larger team that could include architects, set designers and engineers. At the concept stage, the scripting of the customer journey and experience within a space is an interesting part of the designer's role. The journey must balance what the brand is trying to achieve with how the customer will connect with the brand and participate at different points – the design team are the 'scriptwriters' who can guide them through a journey. This means that the designer is able to influence human interaction within that space and control the entire experience: from the point of entry at the door, to how people interact with the product, services or other people within that space.

"You must know the landscape as well as the consumer and design from there," says Adam Scott from Orange. You need to understand the market and what is being achieved at the location – for example, if there are lots of children, you need to provide services for them. The key thing is finding a reference point that you can build from, and once you have that you can then work from an existing design palette. Our shops have standard 'hygiene' factors that are the basics that you build into the store to reach your audience, such as a cash-point or a link to customer service. You then build from that level. Retail spaces can take two to three years to roll-out, so the design agency has to be aware that materials and layout are not overly fashionable – they must not date."

Yet spaces can be costly and dominated by larger brands. It can be difficult for smaller, newer brands to achieve a retail presence and so many opt for partnerships, where merchandise can be displayed in another brand's shop (called 'concessions' in retail terms). In these scenarios, there must be careful consideration given to the type of partnership to ensure that the brand association is of benefit to both brands. The physical display of the merchandise, within its space confinements, is also important. Other new retailers prefer to use a website as the 'shop front' and avoid retail space altogether. The design, presentation and ease of shopping through the website need to be carefully considered.

"The journey must balance what the brand is trying to achieve with how the customer will connect with the brand and participate at different points – the design team are the 'scriptwriters' who can guide them through a journey"

2: SAMSUNG WINTER OLYMPIC PAVILION, SALT LAKE 2002, WINTER OLYMPIC GAMES
IMAGINATION (USA) INC.

Samsung Electronics sought to create a venue at the Salt Lake 2002 Winter Olympic Games that brought its tagline to life, 'DigitAll, Everyone's Invited'. With this as the main brief, design and communications company, Imagination (USA) Inc., created an environment at a Winter Olympics pavilion that could be used as a meeting place for athletes and the public, and show off Samsung's wireless technology capabilities.

Each piece of design and product relates back to the main theme – digital for all. Visitors could play games, communicate with the athletes by digital means and share views that are then broadcast on to the façade of the pavilion. There were over 12,000 visitors per day to the Samsung venue.

"The scripting of the customer journey and experience within a space is an interesting part of the designer's role"

Journey: Often used to refer to the audience journey or 'user journey', particularly in relation to websites. This is the way the audience will physically connect with the brand.

Roll-out: The time it takes to launch the product often from pre-launch through to post-launch phase.

"The product is the face behind the brand – the focus of the user's brand dialogue and the physical interface that they react to. Brand and product cannot compensate each other; a dog in a dress is still a dog!"

Steve Everhard, Multos (a division of Mastercard)

PRODUCT DESIGN

Before branding, there were products and trademarks. A good product is often at the core of a brand – its quality, design and function are a critical part of the brand experience. The impact of a well-designed product should not be underestimated – people have always bought into uniquely designed products and many are prepared to pay a premium for a specific design approach. Many brands are built around services rather than a physical product as part of the core offer, and service design, in itself, is a form of product design. Competition in banking, insurance and internet service provision are all examples of service industries that place considerable emphasis on brand development as a visible differentiator.

The approach used by a good product designer can also be applied to graphic design in brand expression. The end product involves a product vision, validated by a careful analysis of user needs, testing and experimentation, form and function tradeoffs, and interpretation of the brand language into design. The product designer has a good understanding of the impact of their design on the user. As design company, IDEO points out, any product must integrate the core make-up of the brand. "The DNA of the brand must come through the product," says Ingelise Nielsen from IDEO, a design and innovation company. IDEO includes the design of services as a 'real and tangible' example of product design.

Although each company is different, product design will often work separately from the branding division. The relationship and level of involvement between the two will depend on the company. Marketing and R&D will come together at specific review stages of a product design process.

The need for a product will often emerge from the marketing department (including branding) which, after senior management approval, passes to R&D for technical feasibility and reports. Initial prototypes of the product or service may form part of this stage. There will be review stages in the development process where checks are made that the product development from R&D reflects the aims of the business and brand, often involving the marketing or product management team. In parallel, industrial design expertise will be called upon to translate market needs into physical form and user interface.

Although it is possible that a graphic designer may be involved at the conceptual or ideas level of product development, normally this function is a specialised task much closer to engineering or industrial design than graphic design. A graphic designer may also have a specific role in the product design, such as validating interface design, an area where brand values can be reinforced to the consumer. The brand team within an organisation may monitor the product design based on their knowledge of the brand experience and what the customer expects from the brand.

However, the main ideas for product design should come from the product design team – knowing what the customer wants, what makes good design, and balancing form and function to address the audience needs.

The key to good product design, according to Jonathan Ive, Vice President of Design at Apple Computer, is to care about what you are creating: "It is about focus and caring. We know every bit of the product inside-out because we need to understand what is possible. Bad products testify to people not caring. Our goal is to develop the very best products we can. Some things you rely on intuitively to say 'yes, this is right'."[1] Ive is known to work closely with the CEO of Apple Computer, Steve Jobs, in the early ideas' phase of the design process – perhaps a key element of the company's new-found success. In contrast, design company IDEO, has every team member involved throughout the product design creation process – including anthropologists, industrial designers and graphic designers. On the other hand, the 'brand experience' team at Orange will feed in ideas to the product design team based on what people want at the retail end.

The design solution itself does not always have to be easy and intuitive to the consumer: "Something that is appropriate does not always have to be totally intuitive – if the benefit people get from using the technology is maximised, you can bend the rules a bit," says Nielsen from IDEO.

From the branding standpoint, the graphic designer must translate the essence of the product or service into the brand communications. They must capture the essence of the product from both the aesthetic and functionality viewpoint. John Williamson, a board director at branding agency Wolff Olins, believes that one of the most successful products this last decade, the iPod, is more than simply an iPod: "Apple has created an icon – an object of desire. It has reinvented the music world with the iPod. It could be that the iPod is the Bauhaus of product design, the pure aesthetic, but it is really a piece of tribalism. They have successfully built a community around the iPod as people can tell by the design of the earphones whether you have one – whether you are in or out. It is a cult and cults are now inclusive."

A good product is an essential piece of a brand's identity. A brilliant product, from the Sony Walkman to the iPod will, for many people, be the brand and therefore the purest expression of the brand's values.

1, 2. Jonathan Ive, Vice President of Design, Apple Computer, talk at Design Museum, London, 2004
3. Marc Newson, Product Designer, talk at Design Museum, London, 2005

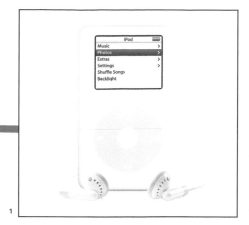

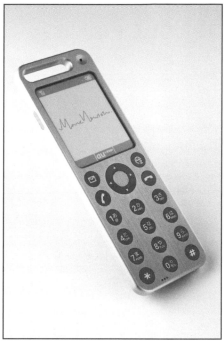

1: APPLE IPOD
2: iPOD® U2 Special Edition

Apple Computer is one of the world leaders in product design. Head of Design, Jonathan Ive, and the Apple design team, have created a revolution in the computing industry, creating design classics to replace the ubiquitous 'beige box' computer.

The first Apple iPod is an MP3 player, which was first launched in 2001. Since then Apple has sold more than 10 million iPods and seen its profits rise four-fold by early 2005. The success of the iPod has persuaded many users to shift to the Apple platform, boosting sales of other products.

When Jonathan Ive was asked about the creative process in designing the iPod, he said: "It had to be simple. It holds and retrieves data and is designed to be part of a much bigger system – part of your PC. The iPod was about making a really nice object that would play music."[2]

3: PORCELAIN CUP
4: 'STAVROS' BOTTLE OPENER
5: 'MOJO' FEMALE SEX TOY
6: 'ROCK' DOORSTOP
7: 'TALBY' PHONE
MARC NEWSON

Australian Marc Newson is one of the leading product designers in the world. His design style carries a bright pop aesthetic. Newson started out by making his creations himself, such as his furniture pieces. The perfection in design in terms of form and shape is possibly due to his desire to experiment with different materials: "I am technically obsessed with materials and technology. There are no new technologies out there – it's not so much the material itself, but the way it is being used. It's important to learn how to really understand materials, to make things and learn how things work."

Humour, Newson claims, is also an important element in his work so that it "doesn't take itself too seriously." Perhaps that's why he agreed to design a female sex toy (pictured here, called the 'Mojo'). The project required Newson to work in close association with the women in his office for customer feedback: "I was quite stunned to be asked to design that. I decided that I didn't want to design anything that looked like a dildo – that was too cliched."[3]

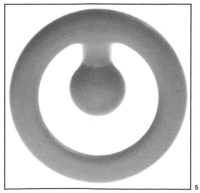

INTERVIEW PAGE / 187

See Jonathan Ive

"What use is a great wrapping if the consumer cannot open it?"

PRODUCT PACKAGING

Product packaging is another key part of the brand expression and includes the physical form of the product as well as its wrapping and configuration. The box in which the product is presented, the bag in which it is carried, and the branded vehicle that transports the product are all part of the packaging. Packaging is part of the journey that is concerned with the safe and enticing delivery of the product to the consumer: it adds to the brand experience by providing yet another opportunity to project the emotion and character of the brand, setting expectations for discovery, consumption and customer delight. The packaging is like a book cover – it can draw you in even if you're unfamiliar with its contents.

Packaging has become ever more important when so many brands compete in the same purchasing environment. This is particularly true when brands try to establish themselves as part of a concession (a shop within a shop, such as selling a brand in a department store), a technique employed by some brands to launch themselves into a new market. Packaging can also enhance the experience of buying the product; perfume brands have always made the art of opening the box a major part of the experience, and the packaging, brand development and promotion are complete long before the fragrance is designed.

Many brands now use different forms of packaging to promote a key brand message or simply to promote themselves. The sandwich shop and cafe, Pret a Manger, uses its individual packaging on each sandwich to tell people about the freshness of its products. Clothing manufacturer, Ted Baker, has always included amusing instructions on its labels about caring for the garment. UK-based fruit drinks company, Innocent Drinks, started writing cheeky anecdotes on its product labels as an alternative to advertising: "You have 30 seconds of someone's attention while they're drinking your drink. Why not use it?" says Dan Germain from Innocent and creator of its drinks labels. The labels successfully express the tone and style of the company, as well as the quality of the product.

For the graphic designer the configuration and packaging of the product offers another opportunity to reinforce the brand values. The messages, the tone, the style, the materials used, all affect the emotional associations with the brand. Product packaging, in its immediate physical form (such as the bottle), sets a style for the brand, and this can either attract or alienate depending on the way it projects itself to the audience. For example, a shampoo that is packaged in a transparent bottle may be perceived as more 'honest' than one in a solid colour that hides the view of the product itself. Most importantly, what is said by the packaging (in tone, style and language) must match the product's branding objectives. A well-designed presentation for a poor-quality product – something that 'looked so much better on the box' – will be regarded as fraudulent by most buyers.

Despite opportunities for creative scope, many brands still underplay the role of packaging in its wider forms such as bags, vehicles or documentation as part of the brand narrative. Creative and innovative packaging can involve complex regulatory negotiation in many markets. Food and trading standard rules and hygiene statutes may need to be considered and legal documentation (such as guarantees) presented in a strict, formal way with no room for creative treatment.

Clever design can still be used to guide the customer even when there are restrictions in place – there is an opportunity to create an appropriate and relevant experience, to entice the customer through the journey of discovering the product inside, and to reinforce the buying decision as a good one. Tell the customer what is most essential they should read, tell them the bits they shouldn't throw away (the guarantee, for example), and help them fill in forms. The Apple iPod packaging opens in a series of slow reveals to build product excitement, the styling is clean and minimal like the product, and small indicators of product pride extend to a simple 'Enjoy' message on the package that contains the manuals.

Another key consideration of product wrapping is the environmental impact. Many brands and brand-owners claim to be doing more to reduce environmental waste, yet most still use chemical-based products for packaging (like plastics and polystyrene). The selection of materials is often recommended by the designer, so why not recommend packaging that has less adverse environmental impact? This is especially true now that consumers are aware of these issues and may make buying decisions based on an overt display of social and environmental responsibility.

Any packaging must also be appropriate and functional: what use is a great wrapping if the consumer cannot open it? When the liquid packaging market was revolutionised by Swedish paper-products manufacturer Tetra-Pak, the containers were often criticised by consumers as being difficult to open without spilling the contents. It's an example of a design that worked perfectly for the manufacturing process, but not for the purchaser until the basic product was redesigned. Packaging should enhance the product experience, not limit it.

"Despite opportunities for creative scope, many brands still underplay the role of packaging in its wider forms"

1: INNOCENT DRINKS' PACKAGING

Packaging that stands out is a great way to reinforce a brand. The packaging of Innocent Drinks, a fruit drink company in the UK, is designed to make people laugh, but also cleverly promotes the brand. There is always a point to the label – it starts with an anecdote and ends by reinforcing the freshness and quality of the product. But packaging is more than a bottle – the company styled 'cow vans' and vans covered in grass in order to stand out and promote their drinks.

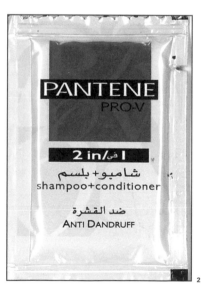

"Packaging has become ever more important when so many brands compete in the same purchasing environment"

Concessions: A store within a store.

Journey: Often used to refer to the audience journey or 'user journey', particularly in relation to a website. This is the way the audience will physically connect with the brand.

2: SACHET PACKAGING FROM MOROCCO

Brand packaging is in response to the market. In the poorer markets found in Asia, India and the Middle East, the packaging of basic household brands differs from that in supermarkets of Western nations. Here the price, convenience and accessibility are reflected in the packaging – such as the Surf washing powder sachet that sells for one rupee in India, or the single-use sachet of Pantene shampoo in Morocco. Certain brands seem to dominate excessively in particular developing markets, depending on which battles were won to corner the market in the late 20th century.

"The value in engaging me is that they get something different. There is a benefit for the culture within the company by doing it differently to the way they would usually approach it"

Product designer, Marc Newson, on working with Nike to design a new shoe.

CO-BRANDING PARTNERSHIPS

As brands seek new and more innovative ways to extend their presence, partnering with other brands and co-branding deals are becoming a common tactic. While partnerships themselves are nothing new, the extension of this area with new ideas is exciting. A partnership may be used to extend the reach of the brand or product into new markets, to offer a better service, or to build on a reputation by associating the brand with an event or a partner. It can also be a low-risk investment for a brand that wants to gradually gain a presence in a new market or sector.

Partnering offers opportunities to apply the brand in different ways through associations, sponsorship, joint product developments and licensing. A partnership between brands can come in various forms including monetary exchange, technology or knowledge transfer, a sponsorship deal, a non-financial exchange of services or a licensing agreement (where one product may license the right to use the trademark or intellectual property of another, such as Hewlett Packard producing iPods). "A partnership must fit within the scope of the brand," says Charlie Graves, former head of licensing at National Geographic. "To serve the mission of National Geographic we need to reach as many people as possible, therefore we need to be in other products and other mindsets. Partnerships give a broader reach of our product base and a broader reach of National Geographic."

To an audience, the partnership must make sense. Either through the solution created or the natural fit of the partners. Effective partnerships are based around the core skill, service or product that a company has to offer and the combination of the two (or more) brands must offer something extra. Brands like those of cafes can extend beyond a street presence to establish outlets in retail and office spaces; and well-known fashion designers can design for the mass market by teaming up with a popular high-street brand, without losing credibility.

There are now some new and unlikely partnerships being formed offering unusual new product innovations: cosmetic company Shiseido and Coca-Cola have joined forces to launch a new cosmetic and beverage products – these include a 'diet water' and a 'toning mist', which claim to have slimming qualities based on a grapefruit extract. Partnerships in retail and office spaces are also becoming more ubiquitous as brands open outlets in local shop premises. The employees can take comfort in recognising a familiar brand, while the brand has an easily accessible customer.

Another new area for partnerships is the charity and not-for-profit sector: high-profile charities are teaming up with third parties, like clothing and furniture manufacturers, to introduce branded products under the charity name, with a percentage of the profit donated to the charity. It's an innovative way of funding a sector that can no longer rely solely on donations to survive; it makes the consumer feel good by choosing to buy from the charity; and the third-party brand is able to extend their brand range and reach through the association.

Partnerships between the public and private sector are also common as corporations team up with international organisations, like UN bodies and not-for-profit organisations on issues that contribute to their social responsibility agendas. Some public sector and international bodies are encouraging involvement from brands (and the companies behind them) to help support programmes relating to development and social issues – choosing the right brand association is a critical step for a not-for-profit organisation, where maintaining an objective reputation is often crucial. Sector partnerships among businesses are also becoming more common as a way of collaborating to develop sector initiatives or new products.

A partnership can say a lot about a brand through its associations. The designer must understand the nature of the partnership and the role of each partner – this will impact on the outcome of the combined brand identity such as the placement of logos. Innovations in the area of partnerships also offer creative opportunities for the designer – the collaboration should be maximised from both sides so the designer must consider if there are any other ways of combining the two brands that are currently not being explored, such as creating more innovative marketing collateral that promotes the partnership.

"Partnership marketing is becoming key to branding. Two cool brands together make an impression"

Stephen Cheliotis, Superbrands

1: VODAFONE AND FERRARI

Celebrities can create successful partnerships with brands. Vodafone in Spain used both national and international celebrities – Rubens Barrichello and Michael Schumacher – to support a public relations event with the aim of enticing wider press coverage.

Images courtesy of Vodafone Spain

"Advertising remains the guardian of the brand and is often the central messenger of the audience-brand relationship"

ADVERTISING

Advertising has always been the most high-profile way of making us aware of a brand, from the early days of daubed shop-signs to internet banner advertising and advertorials in print, on TV and on the radio. Branding became a publicly pervasive discipline with the advent of commercial television and TV advertising was the brand darling for many corporations. Advertisements with an excellent idea, good creative execution and tactical timing often worked. If all else failed, sheer repetition was always a tool that could be used to drive home the brand message.

The advertisement for the launch of Apple's first computer is entered in the annals as one of the best in advertising history – an ad created by film director, Ridley Scott, in the style of George Orwell's novel, 1984, in which IBM was portrayed as Big Brother, computer users as grey drones, and Apple by a woman athlete throwing a sledge-hammer into the projected image of the face of Orwell's 'Newspeak'. It was radical in its challenge that 1984 wouldn't be like the Orwellian 1984 thanks to Apple, and also in the use of a woman to break the male-inspired ideology of control from the centre. The ad was only shown once during the half-time interval in the Superbowl – yet its power and impact endure even today. Benetton made its name through Oliviero Toscani's controversial poster ads in the 1990s, which challenged people's opinions on issues like AIDS, capital punishment and racism. The tactic was deliberately provocative and the company was often forced to remove ads – a good tactic for brand publicity. At the time, the advertisements succeeded in making the company known, even though the main Benetton product range of woolly jumpers was fairly conservative.

The difficulty for brands today is that TV-based advertising no longer has the monopoly on people's attention that it once enjoyed – ten years ago TV was the only broadband medium that guaranteed an audience and immediate brand profile. The challenge for advertisers now is the proliferation of channels and the cost of coverage. Viewers have alternatives to the standard broadcast TV: we can block out ads with our interactive TV and stay informed or updated through other media. Neither is it possible to select similar capacities and investments in media that can be applied the world over. Different countries and cultures tend to favour different media: press advertising is more important in the UK than it is in France; radio advertising is more prolific in the USA than the UK. The strength of local radio stations

has provided a cheaper and often more pervasive broadband medium for advertisers. This has offered a creative opportunity for audio brand marks, like Intel's 'inside' jingle, and it makes advertising affordable for smaller brands.

In response to a multi-channel, diverse world, more novel approaches to advertising have been developed. Ad agencies now apply their talent to other media beyond billboards and TV, to include events, online advertising, sponsorship, ambient media and guerrilla or 'buzz marketing' – high-profile event marketing that creates excitement. Smaller brands are also using alternative techniques instead of spending big budgets through the ad agencies, including the use of labels or bags to promote products and ideas, and viral marketing campaigns based on word of mouth.

Yet advertising still remains the guardian of the brand and is often the central messenger of the audience-brand relationship. Good advertising is a necessary part of reinforcing the brand experience and this offers broad creative scope for the graphic designer. Car advertising has always been backed by large budgets and exotic locations to evoke an idealised 'experience' of driving that vehicle. Luxury brands spend a lot of money on photography and models to reinforce that feeling of selectiveness and elitism, while beer ads tend to be more irreverent and fun. Advertising done well – with a good and relevant creative idea behind it – has the ability to make a dramatic success of a brand or rebrand. It can help change perceptions around a product or reinforce the character and style of that product and brand. Most importantly for the brand, good advertising gets talked about.

Like any branding medium, there are dozens of challenges confronting today's advertisers: how to connect with the consumer, overly complex messages, a lack of brand narration or a disconnection between the product and the ad (a great product and poor ad, or vice versa). Advertising can also overplay or distort immediate brand concerns, such as the desire for brands to have a closer connection and understanding with their audience. There is a current proliferation of ads that use direct or emotional language in an attempt to establish this connection – LloydsTSB is 'your bank'; retail shop Marks & Spencers is 'your M&S'; Velvet Toilet Tissue tells us to 'Love your bum'; while McDonald's says 'I'm luvin' it'. The idea that a brand or its product has been

"Designers need to create design communications, not pieces of art. The design must be based on a design proposition and ensure that it has a practical application – a beautiful design may be too expensive to implement. The most important thing is to be realistic with the client: mad ideas are often diluted, and that defeats the original idea"
Britt Iverson, Mother

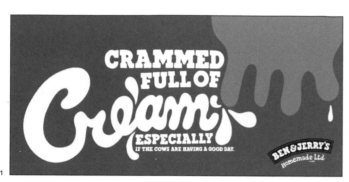

1

designed for 'you' can be difficult to prove if it doesn't confer a sense of ownership or interaction: "This is indicative of the communications industry grabbing a trend and then sticking it on," says Ralph Ardill, Experiential Consultant, formerly of Imagination Ltd. "The brands want you to fall in love with them and that's where it comes unstuck. Most people do not love inanimate objects. I think there's going be a point where this perception and reality will come to a head."

Advertising must be considered as part of other promotional elements – rather than the mainstay of the brand – and it needs to work in harmony with other media. Many brands now talk about executing 'integrated' campaigns: a campaign is executed across different media with one main message or campaign idea, hopefully exploiting each specific medium for greatest impact. This enables the brand to extend the reach of its campaigns to target as many people as possible through different channels. The role of the ad agency becomes extended and can lead to some blurred boundaries across the spectrum of creative agencies: events and sponsorship opportunities that used to be in the hands of the PR may be given to an ad agency as an ambient medium opportunity; online ads might be created by both digital agencies and the digital arms of ad and PR agencies.

In multiple agency scenarios, it is often the ad agency that projects itself as creative director and takes the lead, creating the main message and brief for all the other agencies and ensuring that the tone of voice and the concepts are consistent and integrated. It is the creative director who then leads the direction of an ad and overall integrated campaign.

1: BEN & JERRY'S ICE CREAM

Ben & Jerry's successfully uses one simple strapline to get the main brand message across in a humorous, creative way. The ads are noticeable, they always play on the product benefits (such as 'more nuts'), and have a recognisable style in their wording and cartoon-like graphics.

Agencies: Companies that offer brand expertise to service clients. These are often branding agencies, digital agencies, design agencies or public relations agencies.

THEORY   PAGE / 158
See 'The Marketing Mix – The Four 'P's'

"One of the greatest challenges for brands in the new media environment is to integrate the technology with other areas of the brand"

BRANDS AND NEW TECHNOLOGIES

Online branding is often viewed as an add-on, with less budget and less time committed to it than other areas of branding, and yet can be an effective and cheap way to project a brand. Although websites and modern mobile phones give brands an opportunity to reach new people, the challenge is to make it work with the context. Brand positioning needs to be thought out in technology environments to be relevant to the audience and the interface. Websites can offer an easy way to reinforce an ad or product campaign; they can give a campaign a longer life by improving brand efficiency through online services; and the creative execution can be certainly more daring and playful than in other environments, simply because the technology supports interactivity and gives the designer more to play with.

The popularity of online advertising seems to have stalled in recent years. According to eMarketer, a research company specialising in online advertising analysis, USA online marketing spend fell from a peak of $8.23 billion to $6.32 billion between 2000 and 2002, with few signs of recovery in 2003. Stalwarts like eBay and Amazon defy the trend but for most companies promotion is just one element in a cross-media branding campaign. The impact of successfully branded websites can also rely on misleading figures that are based on counting 'hits' or 'click-throughs' on pages – the frequency of more meaningful second-click action (of where the user intends to go within the site) technically difficult to track.

Websites and technology-based environments are still relatively new forms of media in branding and have a long way to go before the majority of brands use the medium effectively. In the run up to the dot-com days, there was a lot of pressure for brands to have an online presence and use technology as a marketing tool. In this rush, many organisations misunderstood how technology could be harnessed to deliver innovative promotion for their business, instead often using the web as a dumping ground for materials or as a bland marketing tool that offered customers little more than a phone number. The fall-out of the dot-com bubble burst and trends such as CRM (Customer Relationship Management where technology is used to manage customers) led to a lot of confusion of how, exactly, technology could facilitate brands and business. But the web presents an opportunity for business and service industries to improve customer service and develop fully-fledged web services that are easy and convenient. The potential of the internet is enormous, but often takes more vision and energy than companies are willing to expend.

Consumer-facing brands have used the web most effectively as a creative medium that projects a single message and supports their social campaigns. Brands like Diesel run clever, attention-grabbing campaigns seemingly unrelated to the brand; Lavazza and others have their own radio stations and DJs; the BBC promotes the web as a portal to the world and a quick source of information, as well as a low-cost way to increase audiences in parts of the world where the conventionally broadcast channels are not available. Levi Strauss uses the web to reinforce the lifestyle statements rather than promote itself as a jeans-wear manufacturer; there is no hint on the site of a heavy work-wear product but, instead, downloadable music, games, insight into future products and a high degree of interaction. The web can create a brand experience in its own right and the skilled designer is able exploit the unique characteristics of this medium to help expand the effectiveness of any brand communication.

Whether for business or consumer purposes, the application of new media to a brand must be relevant and appropriate. Most importantly, the content should engage the audience. It is an environment where an impatient audience has control, receiving information quickly and with shorter attention spans. Any promotion using these digital media still needs to reflect the main message and positioning of the brand with a navigational journey that has a clear purpose – to reach information or, simply, to entertain. The technology must enable and not confuse – unless the disorientation is deliberate. Text is a vital part of the experience of the media, but reading long passages is tiring and often a lazy solution given the rich ways in which the brand can communicate within the medium.

One of the greatest challenges for brands in the new media environment is to integrate the technology with other areas of the brand, so that there is a seamless experience for the customer. For example, a retail store should know what is sold online and what is available and in stock, or one department in a bank should know the full status of your account and implement reassuring security that isn't overly onerous to the visitor. This means that brands need to invest in technology and training, and most are still struggling to do so. Historically, the internet or 'new media' part of a brand was viewed as separate from the core brand and marketing mix, in the domain of a separate department or contracted agency. The trend now is for increasing integration with other areas of the brand.

With the introduction of newer technologies, such as SMS (mobile phone 'text messaging') and 3G (mobile videophones), there is huge potential for more creative brand promotion. Although there are current restrictions on screen size, and the depth and quality of images, technology is evolving rapidly and the performance is improving to add extra creative dimensions. Brands are moving forward by combining different media through clever campaigns, such as the use of TV to encourage people to send SMS and linking this to websites and viral

1

1: BT INTRANET
RUFUS LEONARD

Intranets work in a similar way to the internet, but are closed digital systems usually used within organisations to cut down on administrative processes. These images are from the intranet of the telecoms company, BT. Designed by agency, Rufus Leonard, the intranet was updated in 2004 to make it more 'user-friendly' and a better resource for employees of BT. The information is grouped in a portal-like style with links to other websites within BT.

marketing. The internationally popular TV show *Big Brother* generates a huge amount of income from mobile 'text' voting.

Texting and 3G technology offer huge opportunities for branding campaigns and promotions. But this new style of mobile and online promotion also carries ethical issues – should companies and brands be encouraging children or teenagers to text someone they don't know or is it now accepted behaviour? Are people aware of their own data protection when they register on websites or take part in a competition? Most mobile phone operators have policies that restrict the brand from encouraging children to text. Yet other mobile phone operators have community sites for teenagers that are branded under a different name, these sell services as well as offer support and advice to teenagers. The brands will argue that they provide services for young people that are in demand and they promote these services within ethical boundaries. The brand trends people say that teenagers do not mind being branded to, as long as they have a choice and the quality of the content is good. But by masking the brand association there is a concern that the operator exploits the trust and loyalty won, by using the site as a means to sell services.

Design Challenges

Communicating the benefits of digital media is important to enable people to use and understand it. It is important that a unified brand image is consistently

disseminated across a brand's various websites. This means that the brand identity, palette and, to a degree, the tone of voice of the sites should reflect the same brand character.

Another challenge for brands is how to adapt a brand identity to a new media environment, without diluting the brand. Digital formats offer a degree of flexibility and clever ways of interpreting the brand, but need to be done in the context of the brand's graphic limitations.

Basic design rules apply in making a good brand experience and Jakob Nielsen[4] is probably the best source of reference. There are particular navigation principles and 'web-sate' colours that should be used and tested across a range of computers. Certain levels of service need to be attained such as quick email response, and a stable technology backbone that ensures fast loading and little waiting. Don't let animations and technical wizardry get in the way of the user and the message – a frustrating user experience is always damaging to the brand.

Intranets

Using the web as a communication mechanism within companies spawned what is known as the 'intranet'. These are websites for employees or a group of employees. The idea is to encourage communication and inform people of general company information, project updates, events and practical information like phone directories and people profiles.

Creating intranets is a lucrative undertaking and a relatively easy task for design agencies (intranets tend to follow basic design principles and navigation). A well-designed intranet will be a part of a company's brand. It can help generate ideas within a company, share information and connect people within the company. Most importantly, it can be used to connect 'management' with the workers – often something that fails when a company has acquired a new business, grown quickly or been through changes.

The potential for good intranets is extensive: they can be used for online 'chats' between the top people and employees on specific subjects; they can be used among a select group of people to help run projects; they can connect global teams or be used for in-service training at their desk. Some multinationals use intranets to 'brief' management on what they should be saying to the press and how to deliver that message. For the designer, the same principles apply as designing a website – start with the audience and work out what they need, then design the site accordingly.

4. Jakob Nielsen, *Designing Web Usability*, New Riders, UK, 2000

3G: Third-generation mobile technology with full multimedia applications such as video and cameras.

Consumer-facing brands: Brands that sell products to a consumer market rather than the business market.

Hits: The number of imprints on a website created by a mouse, to determine the pages people are visiting and how many visitors there are.

"Another challenge for brands is how to adapt a brand identity to a new media environment, without diluting the brand"

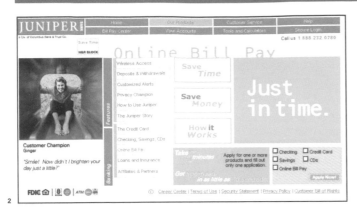

2

2: WWW.JUNIPER.COM
IDEO

The journey taken by users of a website is as important as the content. An intuitive, well-planned website will have an impact on the perception of the brand. Most websites are mapped out by a team of strategists, information architects, content experts and designers. Design company IDEO is known for a more unique approach based around observing human behaviour.

The technique is specific to IDEO, and applied to any kind of design project, whether product or website design. The Juniper Financial website, for a US financial start-up, was created by a team consisting of specialists in human factors, business factors, design strategy, and interaction and environment design.

To build a customer-facing website, IDEO conducted observations of the bank's customers in different environments, including at home, in the bank and at cash machines. Those studied were asked to define what money meant through drawings. This was an abstract exercise to understand attitudes that were difficult to convey in words. These people were then categorised to help determine the ideal customer for Juniper and determine how Juniper could differentiate itself in its market.

1

1: WWW.GOOGLE.COM

Google is the world's largest search engine and one of the most well-known online brand names in the world (up there with Amazon.com). People now refer to 'googling' when they mean searching online. The concept of Google is simple – type in what you are looking for and it will present a range of matches. Its efficiency, ease-of-use and accuracy in searching has made it the market leader, despite not being the first commercial search engine. Google makes its money from advertising.

The name comes from the mathematical term 'Googol', which is a 1 followed by 100 zeros. The wordplay is meant to reflect the company's ability to organise the immense amount of information available on the web.

TIPS FOR DESIGNING WEBSITES:

01 Understand your audience and their environment

02 Be bold

03 Use direct language

04 Have clear navigation: the major issue with many websites

05 Give the website character

06 Change it often – use technology that supports easy content change and gives visitors a reason to return

07 Make it function well: ensure it displays on as many platforms and devices as possible

08 Be aware of any special needs of your audience, such as text-only for anyone with impaired sight, and not relying on audio for anyone with impaired hearing

09 Push the boundaries of the medium, but not to the point that they don't work

"Don't let animations and technical wizardry get in the way of the user and the message – a frustrating user experience is always damaging to the brand"

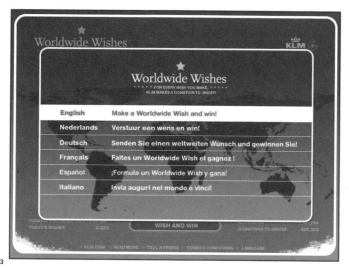
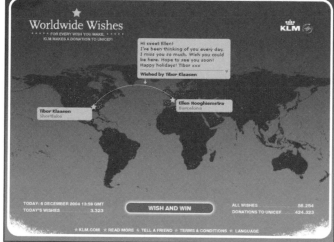

3

3: WORLDWIDE WISHES ONLINE VIRAL MARKETING CAMPAIGN, KLM ROYAL DUTCH AIRLINES
LOST BOYS

In December 2004, the Dutch-based airline KLM launched a viral marketing campaign for KLM.com visitors to send their seasonal wishes to loved ones around the world. The most original travel wish from every country was to come true, granted by KLM. When the wish was submitted, the sender and receiver could see how it bridged the world among all the other sent wishes. This created a lively image of stars on a map with all the various seasonal greetings in many languages.

The campaign ran for nearly two months and nearly 100,000 people participated – resulting in five wishes per second. In the seasonal spirit, KLM donated ten airmiles to UNICEF for every wish made.

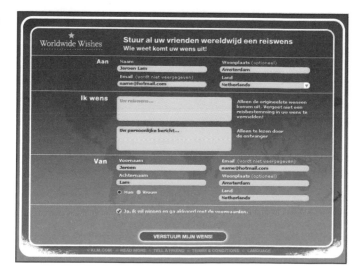

"At BP there is less flexibility now and greater levels of consistency and homogeny so the customer knows what they are getting. There are basic elements of consistency like the proposition and positioning. While the product offer may be tailored according to the market and the execution may be slightly different, the underpinning message is the same"

Duncan Blake, BP

GLOBAL BRANDS

"If a brand achieves success at home, the next step is usually to think about which other markets to enter"

With the globalisation of business has come the globalisation of brands. If a brand achieves success at home, the next step is usually to think about which other markets to enter. The large global brands are constantly eyeing up new countries or may seek to expand their local presence into any emerging new markets. For the big players, the countries to watch are the ones with large populations, fairly limited brand presence (at the moment) and a growing middle class with money to spend. These countries are Brazil, Russia, India and China (referred to as the 'BRIC' nations, a term coined by bankers, Goldman Sachs) and large brands are working to understand more about what makes these populations tick. The other interesting countries from a brand perspective are the new players on the global stage, such as the 13 countries that joined the European Community in 2004.

Managing a global brand – or designing for one – is not easy. One of the biggest issues is cultural misunderstanding: trying to apply what works in one country to another, and assuming that everyone does things the same way. A lack of effective communication links or knowledge of other markets also presents problems. Many companies have limited knowledge of what goes on at the local level in other countries and it is not until a global campaign or website is instigated that the local nuances and customs are unravelled – in terms of consistency in images and execution, there can be little consistency in images and creative execution.

Faced with these choices, many brand-owners have elected to centralise and control the brand from one point. The term global/local is often banded about, meaning that although the brand is centrally controlled the local markets have some flexibility to implement as they like. In practice, brand-owners like control and materials are dispersed from head office with little or no room to manoeuvre, apart from allowing for language translation. The truth is that brands struggle with the notion of being global and this may be because of inflexible corporate structures. Once a process is in place, the corporation may well decide to 'restructure', 'decentralise' or cut down the brand portfolio, creating an entirely new way of managing the brand once again.

Whatever approach is taken, brands have to be adapted in some measure to fit a local market, and the best way to do this is to speak to those living there. Different cultures interact with products and services in a different way, and this must be taken into account. Design and innovation company, IDEO, uses observation techniques to understand how people in different markets use a specific product and adapt the product accordingly. Mobile phone service provider, Orange, will roll-out a centralised brand strategy that is adapted by the local market, and then use the best ideas from each market. Philips Design has trend and research teams that focus on understanding people in different countries; they look for commonalities within each market and design and customise accordingly.

Different channels of media and naming must also be taken into account. National Geographic initially tried working with one tag-line across its international markets and variety of media. What worked for the magazine did not work for other media such as the TV channel. Karen Rice Gardiner, Director of Creative Services at the National Geographic Society believes it to be: "because the type of media application for our content makes a very big difference in the way our content is applied."

Design Practicalities

Consistency in the appearance of the brand is perhaps the most important part of global brand management. One issue is how far to apply consistency without restricting creativity. As a basic minimum there should be consistent application of the brand identity – how it should look, its placement and colour palette. This can still be difficult in practice for brands. For example, an organisation like the ICRC (the International Committee of the Red Cross), encounters practical difficulties in managing a consistent brand roll-out at local level, where people in 'the field' may not have access to the internet, to printing resources or simply have a different interpretation of style and colour. "We can't dictate all the time what people are doing in the field. We give them the tools to be able to produce materials and encourage them. They then produce materials for different needs in the field," says Michelle Rockwell from the ICRC's international headquarters, based in Geneva, Switzerland.

A degree of flexibility should be given to the brand holders of each market because they understand their local markets best. There needs to be an element of trust and autonomy. The best way is to create a framework and let people apply it.

Stefano Marzano, Chief Executive of Philips Design outlines its global approach. "The creation of our products depends on where the strategic centre is within Philips, for example technology products are based in Singapore and Hong Kong. Then within the global markets, we look for commonalities – what are the common technologies? What are the customisations? Lifestyle products are customised more. For example, we take into account local food traditions and local habits for our domestic appliances. Our professional products, such as our medical products, have more commonality. There may be different things to take into account, like obesity in some countries, but the human body is the same."

"Globally, we can take the best from each market"
Adam Scott, Orange

1: BP AROUND THE WORLD

It is important to have an element of consistency across a brand's execution around the world. The question is how much consistency? Brands like Starbucks, have almost identical interiors in their coffee stores whether in New Zealand or Seattle. Yet, many brand managers state that it is important to offer some local flavour in the application of the brand.

Images © BP P.L.C. 2000–2005

2: BRAND CAMPAIGN WINDOWS AND STATIONERY FOR NIKE EUROPEAN CUP FOOTBALL CAMPAIGN

Nike rolled out their campaign in their stores across Europe, issuing detailed guidelines on implementation to maintain consistency. Small details like campaign stationery contributed to a coherent and powerful campaign.

Roll-out: The time it takes to launch the product often from pre-launch through to post-launch phase.

The proposition: The way a brand projects itself or what it says about itself.

The positioning: Where a brand 'sits' in relation to its competitors.

ACID PIGS FLY OVER ME AT
DIESEL.COM

1

"A degree of flexibility should be given to the brand holders of each market because they understand their local markets best"

"One of the biggest issues is cultural misunderstanding: trying to apply what works in one country to another, and assuming that everyone does things the same way"

1: LOBO FROM BRAZIL 'ACID PIGS FLY OVER ME'
2: DOUGLAS AVERY FROM USA 'THE GEISHA WILL SHOW ME'
3: TOM BARMAN FROM BELGIUM 'MY WALL IS SCREAMING'
4: DA JOINT FROM HONG KONG 'I MUST DESTROY THE EVIL BEAR'
DIESEL ADVERTISING CAMPAIGN: PRINT AND VIDEO

Behind each of these posed Diesel images is an eclectic series of videos created by visual artists around the world for the 'Diesel Dreams' campaign – the theme of Diesel's Autumn/Winter 2004 campaign.

30 different artists – or 'Diesel dream-makers' – were commissioned from 17 countries to produce a video. The result is a mix of original videos and animations with some unusual titles. All are related to the interpretation of dreams.

Many brands around the world now use artists to communicate or launch new products. The idea is that they produce a unique piece of work for the brand, which generally offers a more subtle or creative interpretation.

interview 1

Stefano Marzano, Chief Executive, Philips Design

What is the role of product design in branding?

Design is an integral part of the brand proposition. It is the visual articulator of what the brand tends to be and the expression of the brand.

Brands often do the same thing and compete in the same field. What makes the difference between one company and the other is how they do it. So the design is what translates this into the tangible – the interaction, the function, how it works. It represents the way objects are shaped and the way services are delivered. Design is how the brand proves itself.

People buy into design. It is the definition of the brand because it forms the experience, both physically and mentally.

Where should designers start when designing for a brand?

Most design starts with an abstract concept that has to be translated into a behavioural model. This shaping is the profession of a designer, who takes it from an idea to execution. For example, you'll have a model in mind of how a service is delivered and it is design which shapes that service.

The designer must also realise that design is an act of communication. So the shape, character and how it is done must match with the audience's expectations.

Philips designs for the mass market. And how do you ensure that the design is appropriate for a global audience and mass market? We have a broad spectrum of people working as part of the design team including psychologists and 'human factors' people. Our research teams focus on understanding people in

different countries, across different generations. We conduct this research at different levels:

• We look at mega-trends. These are the major trends in society, with a seven-to-ten-year window.
• We also do a cultural scan to analyse the 'street' trends of today, such as visual, language, art and cinematic trends.
• We then look at the personal trends. This is analysing the character of the different groups of users. We do generational research looking at people of different ages, and also observe specific people.

This qualitative research feeds into the quantitative research, which then feeds into design.

How do you manage the design process globally?

A company must first consolidate its practices to be cost-efficient and offer consistency before it can be capable of managing innovation. We have a fully integrated business creation process from upstream to downstream, and locations around the world. The creation of products depends on where the strategic centre is within Philips, for example technology products will be made in Singapore or Hong Kong.

Then, within the global markets, we look for the commonalities such as the common technologies and customisations among the products. Lifestyle products, like domestic appliances, are customised based on local habits like local food traditions. Our professional products, such as our medical products, have more commonality and consistency.

To create successful and desirable solutions, you have to first design with complexity. But your focus needs to realise a solution that is accessible. This means producing simple solutions from complexity.

What do you think about graphic design in branding today?

Quite often graphic design in advertising and communications does not communicate authentically. It creates an impression of something that is not real.

Graphic designers need to maintain authenticity to challenge and to not compromise. It is about being honest. There is too much in this world which sketches a reality which is not real, but there is always a clear interaction which is possible. Graphic designers need to be authentic and genuine in their expression.

How do you personally approach design?

My basic principle is that design is about people and nature. People can live in harmony with the world. When design serves its purpose, it works; when it does not, it is wrong. It is about sustainable development and the 'liveability' of the planet.

Human factors: Referred to as specialists who look at human behaviour as part of the design process. These people are often trained in anthropology or psychology.

interview 2

Johnathan Ive, Vice President of Design, Apple Computer

The following is based on a talk at the London Design Museum, to an audience in an open question and answer session on 28 October 2004. It was the first public forum that Ive had spoken at in seven years.

What is the creative process at Apple?

There is no rigid creative process at Apple. Nothing is documented and there's no design brief.

What we do is understand what the opportunities are, but if the problem is not identified it's tough to design. Sometimes we spend time figuring out how to develop a ready-made product to make it better.

What was the creative process in designing the iPod?

It had to be simple. It holds and retrieves data and is designed to be part of a much bigger system — part of your PC. The iPod was about making a really nice object that would play music.

Do you work closely with the team that designs the Mac Operating System (OS)?

We are the only company that owns an OS and the hardware so we are able to exploit stuff that other people can't. But we're not opportunistic — we make things that we personally like.

We try to find the simple solution and it can teeter on the edge of being almost naïve. I think the first Apple products, like the Mac Classic, are almost naïve in their design — and that's a good thing.

How did design within Apple change when Steve Jobs returned as CEO in 1997?

The old Apple company lost its own identity. The defined agenda was around everyone else, and we tried to copy that. There was a disconnection between what we were doing [in the design team] and what we were shipping.

When Apple does stuff well it is out of the context of what everyone else does. We always think out of context and work in a fluid way. If you design from the outside you get screwed up — you can't design with integrity that way.

Are there products you design that are never seen in the market?

What you don't do can be way more important than what you do. We try and do less and make it count.

How much does design drive the technology?

We focus on what will make a good product rather than using technology for the sake of it.

We have to push and drive to solve problems — to believe that we can do all this stuff. So we work really hard to pursue problems because we want to make nice products. We end up solving some hard problems that [the consumer] does not know about and we don't have to shout about the cleverness of the solution.

Often the product ranges look similar, such as the iBooks. Do you design for product ranges and coherency?

We don't pursue coherency as a goal at all. We design individual products, not a range.

We have a small stable team with a set of principles that are important to us. It's much more important that you have a nice product and the freedom to design the next one.

Do you have any tips for design students?

You need to care and focus. If you are prepared to keep on doing stuff, you develop a set of behaviours from caring.

We know every bit of the product inside-out because we need to understand what is possible. Bad products testify to people not caring — our goal is to develop the very best products we can, rather than aim to make money.

The setting of constraints is as important as the solution. For example, with the iMac we were trying to create a stand made from one piece and we had such a hard time working it out. But there are some things you know instinctively are right.

Do you make products that care for the environment?

We're aware of [the environmental impact] at a number of different levels. The most important thing is that we design nice products that you won't throw away.

> "You need to care and focus. If you are prepared to keep on doing stuff, you develop a set of behaviours from caring"

07

WAYS OF WORKING

INTRODUCTION

Good design happens when teams work well together, including having an excellent relationship with the client. The start of this chapter looks at the way teams are structured within both design agencies and companies, and the different players who may make up that team. There's also an insight into the brand methodology process. This takes the previous theory in the book and details how to structure its application.

Yet executing creative work for a brand is often only the first stage of a wider process. This chapter looks at how the brand design is sustained through practical maintenance like creating brand guidelines to ensure that the brand is consistently applied globally.

It details the fundamental elements of guidelines including visual elements and tone of voice. Examples of brand guidelines from Nike, London's National Portrait Gallery and DHL are provided.

Mike Tiedy from Nike Europe talks about the design process within Nike. And the designer behind the rebrand of logistics company DHL, gives an insight into the brand maintenance process at DHL.

Chapter 7 Contents:

++

The Brand Methodology

"It is essential that you keep abreast of the latest developments in marketing, business and branding by reading trade journals"

Brand values: The characteristics of a brand.

Theory is all very well, but how does it work in practice? Throughout this book we've introduced you to some key concepts in marketing and branding, so how do these affect the designer working on a brand? The process below will appear in various guises depending on the design company and the client (or the in-house design department as is often the case), but the advice below should apply broadly in most cases. The most essential advice is to arm yourself with as much information as possible before beginning work.

STEP 01

Establish the relationship with the whole team and the client.

STEP 02

Define the business issue. Use tools such as the Ansoff matrix (page 126) and PEST (page 72) and SWOT analyses (page 40) to help you understand why a brand is being launched or changed. Chances are, these analyses will already have been done, but if not, you could talk to your client and ask questions to help you work out the reasons why you are being asked to work on the brand. Proceeding without this key information risks producing an inappropriate proposal.

STEP 03

Question the brief: Does it effectively explain the proposition of the brand? What is its relationship to its audience? What does the audience think of it and what does the brand think of the audience? Are the brand values clear?

STEP 04

Start the creative conceptualising by defining key messages: what is the brand, product or service saying to its audience?

STEP 05

Work with the copywriters to define the visual and verbal identity of the brand. It is crucial that words and images work together.

STEP 06

Check that the output matches the brief – does it fit with the brand proposition and business objective? Does it enhance the relationship between the consumer and the brand? Does it express the true values of the brand?

It is very rare that successful brands arise out of instinct alone. What some people call instinct is actually experience – the more experienced you get at working on brands the easier it will be to assimilate the required information. To help with this it is essential that you keep abreast of the latest developments in marketing, business and branding by reading trade journals and using online resources.

> "With a product brand you can spend 75 per cent of your time, money and energy trying to influence customers and 25 per cent on everything else, while with a service brand you have to spend at least 50 per cent of your time and money influencing your own people. In order to get an effective service brand, people have to be taught to live the brand they work with"

Wally Olins, Wolff Olins[1]

WORKING STRUCTURES

There is no magic formula for working on branding projects. The best work happens in small cohesive teams where everyone has a full understanding of the job and its goals. Every agency or structure within a company is different and structures tend to reflect how those running the company prioritise the 'brand'. It is ideas that drive every brand campaign and ideas that make brands stand out. The best structures – either within the company (in-house) or within an agency – are those that facilitate the free flow of ideas from all teams involved in the brand process. Graphic design is the visual output of those ideas and a fundamental element of the brand execution.

Branding, in general, is the responsibility of the marketing team within companies. Although some businesses do not have dedicated brand teams, the perception can be that the area of branding is a nebulous element compared to other departments like financial, legal, sales and communications departments. The brand burden may be shared between the marketing and communications teams. At the other end of the scale, some large global brand-driven companies structure teams specifically around the brand and design, breaking away from the traditional corporate in-house structure.

While there is little structural consistency among either companies or the creative agencies that work on the brand, the most effective structures are those that encourage team-working, shared ideas and communication. This leads to a more powerful creative execution of the brand. A good working process is even more crucial when brand campaigns are

executed across a range of media. This 'integrated campaign' approach is used when the brand seeks to project a core message or insight to as broad an audience as possible. Integrated campaigns can involve a variety of creative agencies, including advertising, direct marketing, digital, public relations and campaign agencies. Excellent direction is essential in these scenarios as each agency's role and responsibilities need to be clearly defined. Often there will be an agency that leads the integrated campaign (usually the ad agency).

In every project, the relationship between the agency and the client – who holds responsibility for the output of the campaign – is of vital importance. Specialist creative agencies have a duty to 'educate' the client on the approach to design, if necessary. The agency should push the boundaries of creative ideas, within the context of the brand and goals of the project. There are so many agencies today offering similar services that the client chooses on the quality of the creative output and, often, the people and personalities who will be working on the project.

1. Wally Olins, *On Brand*, Thames & Hudson Ltd., UK, 2004

Agencies: Companies that offer brand expertise to service clients. These are often branding agencies, digital agencies, design agencies or public relations agencies

"In every project, the relationship between the agency and the client – who holds responsibility for the output of the campaign – is of vital importance. Specialist creative agencies have a duty to 'educate' the client on the approach to design, if necessary"

THE CLIENT RELATIONSHIP

A good relationship with the client can help the creative execution. The process between client and the agency is one of collective discovery: innovation happens when business strategy and positioning are teamed with creative insight.

The client's role is to understand the business and direction of the brand and brief the agency. A thorough analysis and understanding of the audience is crucial, and this is often undertaken by market researchers before other creative agencies become involved in the brand project. Once an agency is briefed on a project, there is a process of interactive refinement – the creative agency needs to push and question the client and the brief. They are in an ideal position to challenge – the agency is an objective outsider and expert. They need to ensure that the ideas are relevant to the audience – too often projects are executed that suit the needs of the client rather than the audience.

Many agencies will assign the client relationship to their own project managers or account handlers – the people responsible for ensuring that the project is delivered on time and within budget. But there also needs to be a good, open communication between the client and the designer. The way the client speaks, their approach, the words they use when describing the brand, are all insights into the brand for the designers, and can help the creative process. An open dialogue between the client and the designer, from the outset of the project, will enable the designer to influence the direction of the brand execution. It also helps if things go wrong!

Many agencies now promote transparent structures between the agency and the client. The client will have full insight into how the agency works (often called their 'methodology') and transparency may extend to the financial workings of an agency. In many cases a creative agency will be an extension of the in-house brand team, which creates an intimate relationship based on trust and understanding between the client and agency. A lot of knowledge and brand value will rest with the agency so a transparent structure will help facilitate the key working relationship with the client. Many agencies build their business on just one key client.

TIPS FOR GOOD CLIENT RELATIONS BY TOM GEISMAR:

01 **Approach the project with an open mind**
02 **Listen carefully**
03 **Be flexible**
04 **Don't accept the problem as being as stated**
05 **Take time to understand the issues**
06 **Do something new and different**
07 **Involve people**

[Chermayeff & Geismar has been responsible for the branding of global companies including National Geographic, NBC and Mobil]

"The process between client and agency is one of collective discovery: innovation happens when business strategy and positioning are teamed with creative insight"

AGENCIES

Excellent teamwork and shared ideas lead to excellent creative output. Today, when multimedia expression of brands is becoming increasingly common, the development phase can involve many disciplines, coordinated by a brand 'producer'. The team may also consist of all types of employees, from full-time to freelancers. Those running the project must decide on the talent they need to execute the best brand delivery.

These disciplines can cover a range of talent and skills – from those who understand human behaviour (the anthropologists, psychologists and 'human factors' people), to those who can translate this into tangible brand communications (the strategists, designers and writers). Every role plays a crucial part in the project delivery and an agency needs to ensure that none of the disciplines work in isolation: for example, the business strategy – sourced by the business strategists – must feed into the creative process (the designers and writers), and be supported by project managers or planners who are responsible for the coordination and delivery of the project. Holding everything together is a narrative or story that describes how the output relates to the customer and the brand direction. Some creative agencies and companies now prefer people who can bring a range of skills to the job, working across the traditional structures within the agency.

Throughout the process, the relationship between the designer and copywriter is a crucial one. Ideas start with words and the creative output is dependent on the words and visuals working together. Advertising offers a good example of a harmonious relationship between words and graphics, as agencies are structured around art director/copywriter teams and this is often imitated within design and branding agencies.

The more progressive branding agencies have loose structures where designers have a broad range of skills and work across teams of creatives. UK Advertising agency, Mother, moved away from a traditional ad agency structure where the client relationship is guarded by an account handler. Instead, the creatives have a direct relationship with the client and have four key parties on every project: the client, the creative, the strategists, and the 'mothers' who coordinate the project. All parties are exposed to the problem and work together.

> "There are few marketing directors on the main board because there are fewer chief executives with a marketing background – marketing is often misunderstood"
>
> **Michael Hockney, D&AD**

"Strategy cannot be developed in isolation from the creative, and the creative without a strategy will not work in the long term; this poses a different way of working for many clients"

Britt Iverson, Mother

Human factors: Referred to as specialists who look at human behaviour as part of the design process. These people are often trained in anthropology or psychology.

Brand producer: The person who holds a brand project together; the central co-ordinator.

Narrative: A story that supports the brand.

Strategy: An overused and often misinterpreted word. Usually means the overriding thinking and science behind the brand (for example, where it should be positioned in its market to attract its desired audience).

INTERVIEW   PAGE / 210

See Mike Tiedy

IN-HOUSE STRUCTURES

Increasingly, many companies prefer to have their own in-house design team rather than work with external agencies. There is no doubt that designing for a company versus an agency are two very different environments.

Some claim that it is more effective to keep the branding process and creative development within the company (in-house) as those working on the inside are the most knowledgeable about the brand, and therefore have the best ideas. At the same time, some companies seek their ideas in agencies, believing a more objective approach is beneficial.

In theory, in-house teams should be able to work more effectively across the different company divisions, simply because they are often in the same building. In practice, this is dependent on individuals and a willingness and ability to encourage the free flow of ideas.

In-house structures should enable better sharing of knowledge and ideas, and an ability to reprocess campaign executions and approaches. It can be easier to enforce change if you are working from the inside – but you need patience and diplomacy skills to play the necessary politics.

In-house teams also reduce the risk of losing knowledge to an external agency, particularly if that agency is fired. On the other hand, many agencies and companies work in partnership for years.

Is it better to work in-house or within an agency? It simply depends on which landscape you prefer.

For the most part, in-house teams are smaller than a corresponding team on the agency side, and this is often the reason why agencies are used – for the simple reason that it is not worth employing the full teams of staff needed to execute various brand campaigns. In-house teams sometimes retain an advertising agency as the 'keeper' of the brand ('retaining' means that they are paid a monthly fee), while design and branding agencies might be used on a project-by-project basis, for special occasions such as creating a new identity. However, many in-house teams often choose to work with particular agencies that they know and love.

The brand (and brand projects) should, ideally, have a representative at the board level of a company. Branding is a discipline that is as important to a company's survival as the finance or legal division. Sometimes this person will be the head of marketing. However, many company structures still undermine the role of branding and relegate the roles to below executive level.

The in-house brand team will be responsible for 'owning' the brand and managing its direction. If they work with an agency, it is their role to keep other people within the company informed of project progression so that there are no surprises at launch. This also makes the approval for campaigns quicker and simpler by ensuring it has sign-off from all major parties concerned. Some companies may have only one or two people committed to the brand – even in a company of thousands of employees – and will use agencies who work as an extension of the company.

One of the issues with larger organisations is that there may be separate teams responsible for differing brands or sub-brands within the company, each with its own goals and marketing targets. This can make integrated working and a consistent execution difficult. Although consistency may not be a priority, separate aims, objectives and budgets will invariably mean that people are repeating work within teams, within one company. Ideally, there needs to be clear direction from the top about the brand communication and messages.

Some brands, like Topshop and Innocent Drinks, drive the campaigns from within the companies, but use specialists to advise them on execution. The Topshop model makes campaign execution easier: they have interior stylists, graphic designers, and fashion designers all working together on one brand campaign and they can do that with their own talent. For photography and advertising they employ a 'stylist' to devise the creative style. In this scenario, the graphic designer has more influence and control on the brand output.

The interior layout and design of Topshop's flagship London store is changed seasonally and influenced by the clothes, fabrics and colours used by the fashion designers. The styles are fed into the graphic design of campaigns; for example, the launch of a new range of clothes or a service needs bags, posters, invitations or other marketing materials created. Often a particular design aspect of a clothing range is translated into the marketing.

Flagship store: The main store which best represents the brand.

"Is it better to work in-house or within an agency? It simply depends on which landscape you prefer"

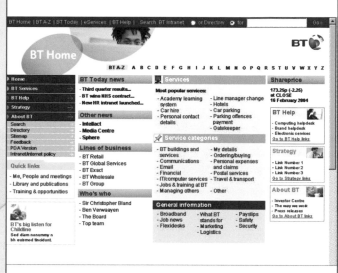

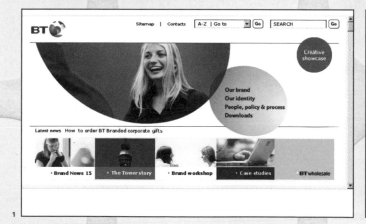

1: BT WEB-BASED BRAND MAINTENANCE
RUFUS LEONARD

BT has had a brand extranet for many years. Its purpose is to offer guidance and tools for anyone working on a branding or marketing campaign. The site ensures that there is consistency in the application of the brand.

The brand site was updated by digital branding agency, Rufus Leonard in 2004, to include the latest BT brand mark. It offers a comprehensive set of rules about the brand, including the brand mission; vision and values; legal information; image styles and typefaces; examples of the brand in action and downloads; an image library and resources; and policy and procedures about the brand, such as co-branding and sponsorship guidelines. While all the information is online, support is provided by a helpline.

THEORY   PAGE / 192
See 'The Brand Methodology'

"Design as an industry is poorly paid compared to other professions"

THE BRAND TEAM

The structure and composition of teams will differ from agency to agency. These job descriptions give a rough idea of the type of people involved in the immediate creative teams and their earning potential.[1]

Project Managers: These people are the lynchpin of projects and teams. A good project manager is invaluable. They will have the main client contact and are responsible for ensuring that the project is delivered on time, within budget and answers the brief.

Strategy Team: Often called 'consultants' or 'planners'. This is the team that defines the direction of a branding campaign based on the business needs of the client and the customer's requirements. They will develop the brand proposition, positioning and values. Many agencies recruit strategists with business degrees (MBAs) although this is not a necessity. What is probably more important is an understanding of people and what motivates purchasing decisions. The strategist's key input is at the beginning of a project, but they are involved through the life-span of the project.

Creative Directors: A creative director is often considered the pinnacle position for designers. These are the senior level people who drive the creative direction, concepts and final creative output of what it is that is being created, be it a campaign, product, packaging, corporate identity or website. They need to work closely with the client, inspiring the creative execution and ensuring the designers and writers understand the issues. Underneath the creative director may be copywriter and art director teams.

Designers: There are often different levels of designers within agencies. 'Mid-weight' designers will have two to three years' experience, whilst senior designers range from five to 20 years' experience. Many creative directors say that they now look

for designers with generalist / integrated skills – i.e. those people who have a good understanding of typography, design, business and user needs. However, design teams can consist of a number of specialists – animators, typographers, web designers, graphic designers, and more – it depends on what the team needs. Whilst agencies expect designers to have proficient Mac skills in all the usual programs, creativity would be the main reason for employing somebody.

Production Team: These are the people working on production and layout of the design. They are the 'factory' of the team, responsible for creating the physical form and tend to be experts on a Mac. They are organised, need to be able to work under pressure and handle stress well.

Information Architects (IAs): IAs are employed in digital brand and communication agencies. They work closely with designers to create web pages and define the 'user journey' – how people will interact with information. They are required to have a strong appreciation of design and customer experience requirements, as well as a strong appreciation for the business drivers of the website or mobile application. Information Architects are able to direct the development of easy-to-use websites, that are simple to navigate and satisfy the brief.

The Writers: Copywriters may be paired with a designer to work on projects – the two specialisms need to work together. Like designers, writers can come from a number of backgrounds – advertising copywriters, journalists or online writers. Different writing specialisms require different talents – writing an ad requires different skills to writing a brochure, or developing brand names. Some agencies also have 'content' teams, which work closely with information architects to map the content of websites. One of the key roles of a writer is to help

develop the narrative behind the brand – that is, the story of the journey the customer in contact with the brand takes. This area of writing and scripting is becoming more common in business.

Salary Levels: Salary structures within agencies and in-house are not clear-cut. In general, though, a junior strategist will earn more money than a junior designer or writer. However, the role of the senior level creative is an important one – a creative director and head of copy will be on decent salaries as their contribution is significant to the direction and style of the agency. Salaries will vary among people dependent on how their contribution to the agency is viewed. If you're good, then fight for more.

Often agencies will work on 'billing' structures where each person and team must spend the majority of their time on projects that are billed to clients. As a general rule of thumb, agencies often work on the model that the employee must bill three times their salary. However, this will depend on how well the agency is managed – many projects are over-worked and the agency can lose money, so 'billables' can be erroneous. Meanwhile, in-house salaries can be lower, but this is usually compensated by a 'package' that can include sustainable job perks. In theory, there is more security working within the company, as agencies can always be fired by the client. However, with talent and experience, you can eventually, call the shots.

"In theory, there is more security working within a company as agencies can always be fired by the client"

1: BRAND AND RETAIL CAMPAIGN GUIDELINES FOR NIKE EUROPEAN CUP FOOTBALL CAMPAIGN

These images demonstrate the design process for a retail campaign that was run across Europe by Nike Europe, who are based in the Netherlands. The guidelines include fundamental design details for the colour palette, wording, typography, fonts and placement of imagery.

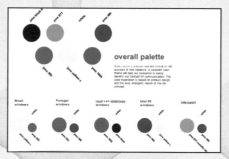

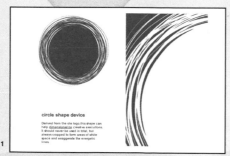

Journey: Often used to refer to the audience journey or 'user journey', particularly in relation to a website. This is the way the audience will physically connect with the brand.

Brand values: The characteristics of a brand.

2. Additional information provided by Gabriele Skelton, Recruitment Consultants in London, Peter Giles – ex- brand strategist at Interbrand and Razorfish, the London personality branding agency.

WHY MAINTAIN THE BRAND?

Once a brand is created and has found its place in the market, the branding budget is directed towards maintaining and developing that brand. There needs to be consistency in the brand execution and this is a key part of brand maintenance. Defining some basic brand identity principles at the outset of a brand's life is the best way to help this.

"There needs to be consistency in the brand execution and this is a key part of brand maintenance"

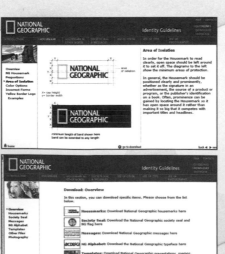

1: BRAND MAINTENANCE WEBSITE FOR NATIONAL GEOGRAPHIC

The National Geographic Society was founded in 1888. Its magazine – National Geographic – has long been the main media for the brand. Now it has television channels, online media and numerous licensees who are permitted to use the National Geographic brand.

Pictured here are screen-shots of the brand's online guidelines after a rebrand in 2004. These guidelines are used across the various media and among suppliers to keep the brand identity consistent. A digital version of brand guidelines enables people to download tools, such as the logo, and to use it as a central source for 'best practice' examples. Although all the brand tools are available online, the brand application also needs to be checked and enforced. National Geographic – like most global companies – has a team committed to 'policing' the presentation of the brand.

"Most global companies have a team committed to policing the presentation of the brand"

Why Maintain The Brand

Brand guidelines (or Brand Manuals) ensure that the identity principles are kept intact. They outline the visual and verbal language of the brand and give instructions on how to apply the brand in different contexts and media. Brand guidelines will define the standards for those using the brand, both within and outside the organisation, and let people know the parameters of what is acceptable. The alternative to brand guidelines is to enforce the brand using a team from within the marketing function – this is also done in addition to guidelines within some companies. This function can sometimes compromise the objective of quality brand proliferation – it can increase the time taken to approve a new project, introduce subjective assessment, and is reactive rather than proactive.

Brand guidelines are created by the agency or in-house team that has developed the identity. It can be a lucrative task for a branding agency, but it is also time consuming. Every detail needs to be checked and approved and the process can take months. Comprehensive guidelines will include specific details on the identity, including colours, layouts, measurements, logo application and tone of voice. These are all discussed in further detail within this chapter.

Guidelines will be used by anyone who produces material that includes the brand identity. This includes brand teams, creative agencies (advertising, design, online, PR and marketing agencies), suppliers, partners, licensees, product managers (those responsible for marketing products) and sales people. Guidelines need to avoid design jargon and be as straightforward as possible. The publication of the brand guidelines encourages effective use of the brand and reduces management overheads by allowing marketing teams to move quickly, yet deliver consistently.

A brand without guidelines can become diluted over time. Most brands now operate across a number of different media, and if no rules are established at the outset regarding brand consistency, the brand can look completely disparate, compromising the brand and its values.

While there are obvious benefits in providing guidelines, implementation need not be regimented. The purpose of guidelines is to guide, rather than dictate, defining the way the brand communicates in a visual and verbal style, and providing an understanding of brand values and behaviour. Guidelines should not stifle creativity or ideas. Brand owners must accept that what works in one country may not work in another, and people need to be able to apply the brand within the context of their own marketplace and media. This is why many companies speak of a 'global / local' approach, where the local market is able to implement the brand within the perimeters of the guidelines. However, brands can vary enormously in terms of the degree of implementation flexibility. The objective of guidelines must always be to allow sympathetic brand promotion within the limitations of specific media and technology, and to encourage local cultural empathy. At the same time, it must maintain the strategy of global brand delivery.

Global/local: An expression used in marketing meaning that a global brand will be implemented with a local approach and flavour in individual countries.

"While there are obvious benefits in providing guidelines, implementation need not be regimented"

"A brand without guidelines can become diluted over time"

BRAND GUIDELINES

Visual Guidelines

Visual guidelines are important for any designer who works on a brand. A designer who is involved in creating a brand is likely to also create the visual guidelines for that brand. Visual guidelines include the specific graphic design elements that enable people to recreate the brand identity in the correct format, structure and colours. These graphic elements are not limited to the logo or positioning of the name, but extend to all design elements. The visual guidelines need to show how the brand is executed across all media – from brochures to websites.

It is important for the designer to understand the technical limitations of each medium where the brand might be used. For instance, the impact of TV interference on finer elements of the logo may affect TV advertising strategies and the minimum or maximum size of the brand mark. There is also considerable difference in colour reproduction across film, TV, web-based graphics and print that may affect both the visual brand mark and its interplay with any background. Certain typefaces are also less flexible in web-based or TV media compared with most printed forms. The designer needs to demonstrate how the identity is projected in different formats and channels, and also to cover scenarios such as co-branding and working with partner brands.

TIPS FOR DESIGNERS: WHAT TO INCLUDE ON VISUAL GUIDELINES

01 **Design elements of the logo, including how it can be adapted in size to suit different media and applications**

02 **Colour, including details on tones. This should cover the elements of the logo as well as a colour palette that can be used across all brand communication materials and media**

03 **Typeface, including typographical elements of the logo, headings and body text. The typeface may also differ for specific media if the main 'corporate' typeface does not work well on the web, or TV for instance**

04 **The 'look and feel' of the visual elements. These demonstrate how the visual elements work together on a page or frame and how they interact with the background and other foreground elements**

05 **Photography, including the style of execution and where to source it. Some brands maintain online image libraries for sourcing images. If this is not possible, show examples of appropriate photography**

06 **Tone of voice. This is the language of the brand, both written and spoken. It is as fundamental to brand guidelines as the visual identity and is often the most difficult element to express in the guidelines**

Co-branding: When two or more brands appear together in marketing communications.

Auditing exercise: An 'audit' in the branding context often means an early assessment into what branding collateral exists.

"The tone of voice is developed at the same time as the visual identity and, like design, is created from an in-depth understanding of the brand"

Tone of Voice

The purpose of defining the 'tone of voice' is to create a consistent syntax for the brand. It is the verbal expression of the brand and must work in harmony with the visual elements. Many designers view the brand language as distinct from the design, adding words as an afterthought to the graphical layout. This is not the correct approach. The tone of voice is developed at the same time as the visual identity and, like design, is created from an in-depth understanding of the brand. Excellent brand communications only happen when the two (design and language) work together.

The tone of voice is likely to be created by a writer or brand communications expert. A comprehensive tone of voice document will detail how the brand should 'speak' across different communications – for example, in spoken areas like customer communication and phone manner, as well as written communication like websites, brochures and brand messages on vehicles.

Brand messages are also a key element of the tone of voice. Brand messages should capture the spirit and aims of the brand – they are not things that people would say, but should help employees and external parties who work with the brand to understand its values and direction. Key words can also be included in the tone of voice document. These are words that characterise the brand and can be used in any written copy or spoken language of the brand.

A brand's tone of voice needs to be as flexible as the elements. An overriding tone of voice will establish the character of the brand but different products – and the people representing the brand – will have a distinctive style. For example, a car manufacturer may have a distinctive tone of voice for each car model, although there will be some consistent characteristics that help the customer recognise the brand.

1

1: NATIONAL PORTRAIT GALLERY BRAND GUIDELINES RUFUS LEONARD

The National Portrait Gallery is a world-renowned gallery based in London. These guidelines were created as part of a review of the gallery's brand and visual identity. Prior to creating these guidelines, the design agency, Rufus Leonard, was involved in a detailed assessment of the gallery's competitive position and a visual audit was conducted to see what materials existed. Rufus Leonard then shaped the brand positioning, personality and values.

Guideline Implementation and Online Brand Centres

Once guidelines are created they need to be communicated and promoted. Many brands have in-house teams that are responsible for 'policing' the brand to ensure that it is not misused or abused in any way. Ideally there should also be a mechanism within companies to update and recommend changes from those who are implementing the brand. In most cases the guidelines should expect to cover the vast majority of implementations, but a process is needed to handle the exceptions to the rule based on experience and brand consistency.

The simplest way of managing the basics of the brand identity is through online brand centres. These are specific websites built to house the guidelines and tend to be accessed with passwords. Websites offer a more effective way of managing the brand as images, materials and logos can be easily accessed and downloaded. They can show best practice examples and give people the opportunity to feedback. A central website is also ideal to keep people informed of changes to the brand. Some brands support their 'online brand centres' with dedicated phone lines to answer any tricky brand questions.

Brands usually offer guidelines in paper format as well. This is particularly relevant if the brand is being used in more remote places, where internet access is slow or unavailable.

> " The simplest way of managing the basics of the brand identity is through online brand centres. These are specific websites built to house the guidelines and tend to be accessed with passwords"

Best practice: A piece of work that is recognised by the industry as representing the best way to apply the brand.

1: DHL BRAND MAINTENANCE WEBSITE
NITSCH DESIGN GMBH

DHL is an international courier company that was bought by Deutsche Post World Net. The buy-out led to a rebrand and the need to create guidelines. The guidelines are a crucial step in the branding process when former brands merge or change.

The website for these guidelines is simple and comprehensive in its navigation and application of the brand. What is impressive is the extent to which each section of the brand guidelines site is supported by people: DHL set up a range of phone lines that have dedicated support for every aspect of the brand application – from DHL signage to logo placement to sportswear.

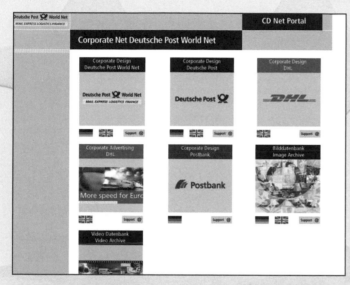

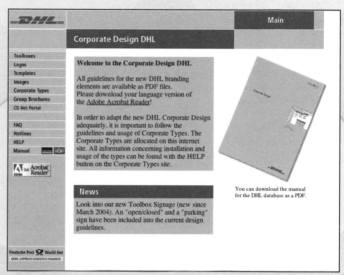

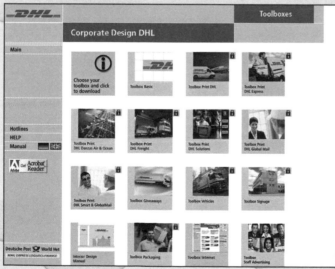

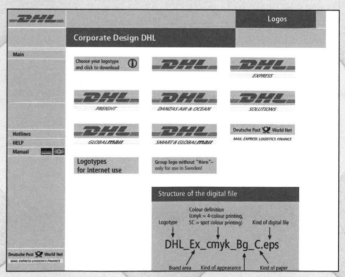

interview 1

Mike Tiedy, Creative Director, Brand Design EMEA (Europe, Middle East and Africa), Nike, Europe

Mike Tiedy has a team of 22 designers, including film and video designers. His team designs for the retail base of Nike Europe creating the formats, fixtures and designs of the retail interiors, as well as events and materials for campaigns. The product design comes out of Nike US.

What is the structure within Nike and how does your design team work within that structure?

Nike is initiative-based – we base our campaigns around events. A lot of our work is based on a product launch or an event. We have tiers of initiatives – a tier one initiative will involve advertising: a television commercial, or an outdoor campaign, or a mix of both.

When we design the retail fixtures we start by looking for the places of integration so that there is some consistency, but the integration throughout the initiative can also be very slight. I don't think integration always happens on purpose – sometimes timing can be a factor. When you're working on something like a fixture for 3,000 shops across Europe, there's a timeline that pushes far back – so the integration may just be through a colour, a texture, or a surface reflection, like deciding we want to use a shiny white plastic.

How is the brand controlled in the design process?

Take something like football where every two years we have a big event. At the start we work with our global partners and the product engineers to define some directional pieces – something that says "here's where we want to go" – maybe we're trying to be technical, or fluffy and soft, or clean. There are some characteristics. So we create a style guide that helps to inform the product. Or the style guide

might be informed from the product and development – it's always a circular thing that goes on between the product and us.

At a certain point, people working on the campaign will come into contact with that style guide – but it is not a bible. Once we have this style guide, we can start working against it in different ways. The main point of contact especially, I think, for Wieden & Kennedy [Nike's long-standing ad agency] will be an 'insight' – the consumer insight, or concept, which the campaign is based on.

Is a style guide always based around a theme? Can that theme be as simple as just five words?

The themes for the style guide are elaborate. It will cover colours, textures, materials, flows, shapes, everything. It's the starting point. You're taking apparel, equipment or footwear, and you're trying to give people some guidance and some direction that ties this altogether.

At the same time there may be a very determined insight which will support the campaign and marketing. For example, the Olympics was about speed and being fast. For football our insight was called 'brilliant football'. It's the offensive game – about leading and being a bit showy. By calling it 'brilliant football' you start setting your mind in a direction of materials, forms and colours and other design elements for that concept.

But there's always a process of reinvention as well. You can look at something we did well before and consider how to re-jig it. We need to change direction all the time.

Do you opt for slight shifts or radical change in design style, or is it campaign dependent?

It depends on the consumer. If you look at something like running, there tends to be slow changes. People who are into running are absolutely into every technical feature, and when they get something that's right they don't want to change. It's a different breed of people.

But in football, you're dealing with a younger, more vibrant game that's changing much faster. The teams and the characters that surface change a lot, and that's part of our attitude too. We don't look for change for change's sake, though – it's really about defining the characters of the next season.

Is the audience tougher to define today?

We're pretty determined about who we're aiming at, but there's a sharp point to it, with a wide body. When you hit that sharp point – the person we're aiming for – then it's going to have a reverberation effect. It's almost like when you break the speed of sound, you have these repercussions that occur.

The sharp point could be a 14 year-old boy we're aiming at who plays football in the street every day – that's really the definition that marketing brings to it. In design, we try to dive in deep about what that person is doing, what influences him and what he is seeing, and that leads us to some of the visual insights.

Fixturing: The interior fixtures of a retail store, such as shelving.

"For us, simplicity is huge right now, especially in the brand design group"

Can you give me an example of how you apply an 'insight' to a campaign?

For football '02 we were working with bright orange plastic on the product design side. It was smooth and clean, and the product was very highly designed with simple, graphic shapes. Yet the insight for the TV commercial was built around the idea of a secret tournament.

When you visualise something secret you think in a language that is undercover, clandestine and secretive, with graffiti pieces and a particular look. Yet the product is technical and clean. It was interesting to see how the things melded – the TV commercial was an old ship where the secret tournament happened and we were doing events that replicated that. Yet we had this really strong pure colour coming through – the orange – which was coming from the product design. There was almost a confrontation between the design of the product and the insight. Inside the events we had a lot of elements that were hi-tech-looking and a lot of opposing elements like rusty old cages and barrels. And the product looks beautiful with it – the product comes alive. You have to learn to take both languages and be able to compromise and change them to fit the best communication means.

So sometimes the insight and the product work side-by-side and sometimes they are diametrically opposed. It's always an interesting thing that happens when things are in conflict to see how they end up gelling, whether we're working on a women's campaign or a running campaign or football.

So is it these insights that keep Nike at the creative edge?

Definitely. I think this company makes sure that there's a story that we can tell – that's a very important part of our philosophy. The story could be conceptual, or technical and beneficial. There's not a whole lot of "invent something to sell this today", but instead there is a real effort to make sure there's a story to be told. People always ask "what's the concept?" It's just part of the culture of working here.

It sounds like you have a lot of creative freedom. Are you able to set the direction on these campaigns?

Depending on the initiative, we play different roles. Sometimes we are designing, sometimes we are directing . Because a design language can influence everything from product to point of purchase, we are sometimes given visual directions – photography and other content – to make sure all aspects of an initiative marry together.

How do you maintain the creative momentum, particularly working within a large global company?

There are a lot of things to inspire designers here. Firstly, they see a lot of incredible design all the time from their peers. Whether in footwear, or apparel or equipment, there is a huge design community. Here [in Nike Europe] it's smaller but we still see the influences of what happens from that design community in the USA.

Putting yourself at risk is culturally accepted here. People aren't too scared to throw out crazy ideas – in fact, it's encouraged to try to push the limits and be different.

I think there's an evolution of design that happens throughout Nike. You see phases of things happen all the time, and it may start with one person or one group and take root, and you can see these things spin across the company. It is absolutely organic. Sometimes this can be a trend like trying to simplify things in keeping it cleaner or more streamlined. But you see waves of things that are happening in design come through our whole design group.

Are there any particular trends that you see in branding at the moment that influence you?

We have our own in-house trend and research department. We also get our influences from tours, shows, books and magazines. We're just trying to cut down. I think it's a response to almost too much information out there. People don't know where to start.

So even in our visual looks, we're trying to streamline and clean things up. Not that this is exactly new for us. We're trying to make sure that we're telling the right story at the right time.

What about outside influences? Do you look at trends and feed them into the design?

We use influencers like WGSN.com [the 'worth global style network', a web-based trends tool] as a resource, as well as tours, shows and magazines. The influence in Europe on design is so much stronger than in the USA. The Netherlands [where Nike Europe is based] has a huge design culture.

Each city in Europe has so much going on historically whereas in the USA this just happens in major cities. The USA is one big market; people tend to adopt large, general trends that spread across it. I think the USA has some very strong points but as a culture everyone adopts the same things. Whereas in Europe, you speak a different language within a few miles' distance from each other; communications across Europe are more diverse, and culture and history have an effect on branding trends.

We try to share the things that we do among the design teams and show best practice – designers have a tendency to want to do the opposite if it's already been done. The idea is to set up a common DNA and interpret it for your market; to share best practice and put it back into a central source.

interview 2

Frank Heemsoth, DHL Account, Nitsch Design GmbH

What is the history behind the DHL rebrand and how did you, as the design agency, approach the rebrand?

The rebrand was undertaken when the logistics group Deutsche Post World Net bought the majority of DHL (51 per cent). As the design agency, we had to integrate the DHL logotype into the existing Corporate Design of the group – this design is strongly based on the yellow Deutsche Post.

In its former brand architecture the group owned three brands, Deutsche Post, Danzas and Postbank. They shared the same frame of a common design, all using a yellow background. The old DHL brand was within a white box, because before the ownership of the majority of the shares, the logotype was not allowed to appear on yellow. This always made DHL look like a foreign brand within the brand portfolio, as there was a lack of integration in the visual relationship between it and the groups' brands.

When Deutsche Post World Net bought the remainder of DHL, the decision to implement DHL into the groups' Corporate Design structure was obvious.

What process did you go through, as the design agency, with the rebrand?

We had to be really careful with the redesign. The basic principle was to maintain the well-known character of this globally known brand. We started with a lot of proposals aimed at giving the DHL logotype a slightly new look.

Of course all our proposals used red on yellow. We also had to make sure that the proportions of the brand fitted the existing proportions of the so called 'brand-field', similar to the Deutsche Post and Postbank brands. This was essential because the design represents the structure of a common global player – the group logo Deutsche Post World Net includes five different 'brand areas', offering different postal services – mail express, mail, finance and express logistics products. So, DHL had to fit within this corporate design.

A challenge for brands is to keep the brand intact and consistent after a rebranding process. What was the process for DHL?

DHL has outlets and offices all over the world, so we had to find a way to communicate the new design to all employees and agencies.

We decided to build 'toolboxes' that could be used by everybody involved in the rebranding process. We also built a website called the DHL Corporate Net where employees and agencies can find all the branding tools they need for projects. There are sections covering areas like toolboxes, logotypes, fonts, images and templates.

There are also regional brand managers in place who are responsible for ensuring the brand is being maintained in different continents.

"The new logo type became a strong symbol for the internal integration of the employees of three former express and logistics brands"

Guidelines, particularly online guidelines, are common within companies today. Did you use any other techniques to communicate the brand?

As part of the rebrand process we also set up several 'hotlines' – dedicated phone lines for branding matters – open ten hours a day. So if somebody has a question concerning one of these topics, they can either contact their local rebranding manager or call the design agency. These hotlines are:

The DHL Corporate Design Hotline: This advises on all corporate design matters and provides initial basic guidelines; explaining rebranding rules, application guidelines and logotypes. The Hotline assists employees or agencies all over the world.

The Corporate Wear Hotline: For questions concerning the new Corporate, Sports or Event Wear.

Corporate Colours and Materials Hotline: For all questions concerning colour. This hotline team is concerned with answering all types of questions concerning print media, coatings, foils or other materials.

Technical Hotline: For employees, suppliers or agencies all over the world who have technical problems with the online guidelines or image library. This covers downloading fonts, ordering images, searching for high resolution images, and general technical problems, like ISDN-transfers or other downloads.

Vehicle Hotline: This assists in the worldwide rebranding of DHL vehicles.

Signage Hotline: For questions on exterior and interior signage for local buildings and offices. The team checks signage rebranding proposals and gives feedback concerning visual looks, measurements or technical constructions.

Advertising Hotline: This is concerned with advertising guidelines for print at the start of advertising campaigns.

How was the brand launched?

There were several events around the world for each country to show employees and customers the new brand. This was also supported by two major advertising campaigns – one in Germany and a worldwide campaign – and an internal campaign explaining the new rebrand to employees.

The new logotype became a strong symbol for the internal integration of the employees of three former express and logistics brands – Euro Express, Danzas and the old DHL. Everyone worked hard to contribute their part to the rebranding. So the rebranding guidelines helped create a lot of common sense.

The external replacement of the former brands was done quickly. DHL conducted a brand assessment survey in mid-2005 within Europe, and most consumers identified with the new DHL, rather than the brand's predecessors.

CHAPTER 08

THE FUTURE

INTRODUCTION

Leading business thinkers have said that the best way to predict the future is to create it. While brands may be here to stay, it can be difficult to establish where they're heading.

This chapter highlights some of the key aspects likely to play into the future of branding – a more human approach to branding, the global outlook, and brands as role models.

There is first a theoretical look at brand evolution and how brands survive.

The 'human factor' talks about how brands and individuals are now seeking to connect at a different level with more audience participation and truthful engagement. The 'international outlook' discusses the continuing driving force of globalisation and how this can help the emergence of local brands. 'The role model' looks at how brands are responding to wider global issues, like reducing poverty and global warming. What does all this mean for the graphic designer who works in branding? Read the chapter to find out.

The chapter closes with an interview with brand trends expert, Kristina Dryza, on the future of branding and our search for the truth.

Chapter 8 Contents:

THEORY CHAPTER 08 /

++

Brand Evolution: Where Next?

Throughout this book brands have been shown to be evolving from their earliest days as a promise of quality to their current almost social role of offering happiness and even a sense of identity.

In *The Brand Gap*, Marty Neumeier presents a timeline view of the evolution of brands that develops from the brand thinking about itself, to being about you, the consumer:

FEATURES	BENEFITS	EXPERIENCE	IDENTIFICATION
"WHAT IT HAS"	"WHAT IT DOES"	"WHAT YOU FEEL"	"WHO YOU ARE"
1900	1925	1950	2000

"The development of brands can be seen as a memetic one, and the people who create and develop them are 'memetic engineers'"

This evolution has been driven by the brands' need to survive and compete. In his book, *The Selfish Gene,* the biologist Richard Dawkins coins the word 'meme'. Whereas the gene is one of the building blocks of life, a meme is a building block of culture and can take the form of an idea, a design, a tune,
a slogan or even a social value. Like a gene, a meme is carried from generation to generation, but in order for it to do so it has to mutate, often quite slowly, and it has to survive like a virus with one person 'infecting' another with a meme they find interesting, useful or just funny (a joke can be a meme, as can a rumour).

The development of brands can be seen as a memetic one, and the people who create and develop them are 'memetic engineers'. The survival of brands and the techniques discussed in this book – such as repositioning, audience segmentation, spin-offs, mergers and takeovers, even self-sacrifice – are all traits of memes.

Brands do not exist for altruistic, selfless reasons (in other words, to 'make our lives better'); they make our lives better in order that they can exist. And just as we become immune to viruses as we are exposed to them, so we may be becoming immune to brands and the tactics they use, which explains their constant evolution.

All of which leads to an important question: what will brands do next to survive? How will they evolve so that they become more infectious?

It is impossible to predict the eventual development that brands will make, but three routes are possible. Perhaps as we reach information overload brands will start to disappear as a few big names dominate to "make our lives simpler". Already we can see big corporations excusing their existence by subverting the word 'choice'. Microsoft, for example, uses the term when describing its monopoly in certain areas such as media formats.

Or, the messages the brands send us will become simpler, returning to the straightforward "what it does". The iPod example used throughout this book points the way, perhaps, as its simple "carry 10,000 songs in your pocket" is allied to images of uninhibited behaviour - "what it does" and "how it will make you feel" presented together without any of the complex technical information that usually accompanies electronic gadgetry.

Or perhaps, as many critics of branding hope, we will finally become entirely immune to the influence of brands. The *Adbusters* and *No Logo* generation is the one currently studying design, and there has been a noticeable shift in recent years among students towards scepticism of the world view that supports our reliance on brands and the methods they use to survive. In science, genes are altered by injecting new material, not by attacking them from the outside. Perhaps the same is true of memetics? If this new, politically-aware generation of designers, rather than rejecting branding advertising and campaigning in protest against their influence, instead embraces and exerts their own influence on branding decisions, change may well happen from within. If, indeed, that is what we want.

"The impact and effects of globalisation will continue to dominate and play into the future of branding"

WHAT NEXT FOR BRANDS?

It is difficult to predict the future of branding when so many influences and influencers play a part in the brand creation process.

Yet despite a complex branding environment there are some strong trends and characteristics that are likely to affect the future of branding. A major influence is that of the individual and his or her demand of brands: that brands be more authentic and truthful in their engagement with us, and that life be simpler than it currently is.

The impact and effects of globalisation will continue to dominate and play into the future of branding. Already there is an increasing expectation that brands should engage with society and take some responsibility for the global issues that we face. Ongoing globalisation will play out in other ways – from the growth of brands in new markets, to the growing strength of local brands, to more common standards of responsibility, transparency and accountability.

Yet while the boundaries are changing for brands, they are also becoming more blurred. The way we perceive brands is changing; the positioning of a brand can be multifaceted, both competing and partnering with other brands; the scope of a brand and its product range is flexible; and the brand structures within companies are never the same. This means that the graphic designer's role can also vary.

Despite all the theory, one major event or new product can have a huge influence on the future of branding. While it is impossible to predict what these significant forces will be, the future of branding really lies in the response of the individual.

1

1–3: 'THE DAILY AFRICAN' CAMPAIGN BY DIESEL

Brands reflect the society we live in. A look at advertising in your own environment can give you an idea of trends, influences and issues in society. Some are subtle – such as advertising that tries to connect with the consumer through using words like 'love' and 'your'– other advertising, like that of clothing brand Diesel, is deliberately provocative on current social and global issues.

Diesel's 'Daily African Advertising series', run in 2004, put the world in a different context by using images that showed Europe and the USA as the poor recipient nations of wealthy African donor countries. Headlines included 'Africa agrees on financial aid to America' and 'European developing countries targeted by African tobacco industry'.

THE HUMAN FACTOR

One of the major shifts in branding and business that the experts talk about is the 'emotionalisation' of branding (see also p.74). We have entered a humanitarian stage of brand evolution, moving from the 'experience' phase (what you'll feel) to that of 'identification' (who you are)[1]. This evolutionary shift has affected the way we perceive brands. The relationship between the brand and the consumer is becoming closer as people seek more authenticity in their contact with brands – the brand audience wants truth. This means wanting brands to acknowledge their parameters and to be relevant. Consequently, the kind of brand development that happened in the closing decades of the twentieth century, where the audience was more remote from the brand, may increasingly alienate consumers today. Brands need to be more accessible than before and the consumer will play a more active role in creating the brands they want.

As more human values and identities come to the forefront, the value of a brand will be measured on its engagement with the audience. This means that audiences will actively participate in the evolution and development of emerging brand identities. People are more involved and excited when they play a part in creating a brand (such as voting for the next big popstar on TV) even if these brands are transient – emerging rapidly and disappearing just as quickly. This engagement with an audience extends beyond customer awareness and interaction – it includes involving employees and other stakeholders in decision-making about the direction of the brand and the company. It also means that brands need to respond to audience engagement – if they seek the opinions of stakeholders, they must act on the outcomes. While some brands do this already, listening and responding will become a necessity for all brands if they wish to be sustainable and to retain customers and employees. The management of these brands works on a model of consensual engagement, including this methodology within traditional brand management will be a challenge for the coming decade. Does the audience really know what it wants or are they as surprised as marketeers when new brand styles and product trends take hold in the minds of consumers? Attempts to exploit apparent audience engagement without delivering on the promise will be viewed as inauthentic. Yet there is a balance point to be found where the brand objective and audience empathy exists in equilibrium.

There is also strong evidence of the emergence of the 'identification' age (who you are) as more people turn towards spirituality and religion. People are seeking more meaning and purpose in their lives. Many seek meaning from their careers and want to feel more connected with the companies they work for. However, there is a limit to what brands can deliver. Brands cannot pretend that they can serve individual tastes or needs with bespoke tailoring, or that the brand belongs to each of us, especially if the underlying product or service is increasingly commoditised. The brand needs to behave in line with its values and be relevant to its audience – it must act with integrity, be consistent in its actions, and deliver on the promise. This includes honesty in the degree of audience engagement that is permitted. Only then will it connect at a deeper, intangible level. This comes back to the notion of 'truth' – that the brand must be believable if it is to gain credibility and trust.

Until brands make a connection between what is said and what is done, from the board level through to the on-the-ground operations, by creating workforces that are involved and whose opinions matter, those caught in a love/hate relationship with their audience will not move beyond that. This is not only applicable to the big corporations but to any brand that achieves success and grows.

"We have entered a humanitarian stage of brand evolution, moving from the 'experience' phase (what you'll feel) to 'identification' (who you are)"

1

1: BRANDS WANT TO TOUCH YOU EMOTIONALLY

We are currently in a phase of emotionalisation in branding. Brands
are attempting to engage with us through emotional connections – to
establish a closeness and understanding between the audience and
the brand. A lot of brand campaigns use words like 'love' to catch our
attention and, seemingly, our hearts. But the age of emotionalisation
is more complex than this. Empathy with a brand or brand loyalty
requires there to be an alignment between what the brand says and
how we experience it.

THEORY   PAGE / 218
See 'Brand Evolution: Where Next'

1 Marty Neumeier, The Brand Gap, New Riders,
UK, 2003

"The home-grown brand can play on the stereotypes and traditions which create a natural affinity – even if they are inaccurate"

THE INTERNATIONAL OUTLOOK

The globalised world has changed the landscape of brands. Some branding experts believe that brands must have a global view and reach if they are to compete and survive. On the other hand, there is a trend towards regionalisation, with an increase in popularity among brands that project a local or national identity. Achieving a neighbourhood feel from a national or international brand takes more than adding 'local' to a supermarket chain brand name or a claim to use local ingredients and raw materials, or even reflecting the ethnicity of the community. It needs engagement and perhaps a little imperfection in execution.

Meanwhile, the international picture is changing. A new middle-class with deep pockets are emerging in other nations, and the speed of growth means that these 'BRIC' nations (Brazil, Russia, India, China) are likely to outgrow spending in some of the current G8 nations. As brands look for new markets and investments, the BRIC nations – China, in particular – offer huge opportunities: it is predicted that by 2009, the annual increase in total dollar spending in the BRICs could be greater than that in the G8. By 2025, spending could be increasing twice as fast in the BRICs. In future, there may be a shift in brand spending from the current Western nations to emerging countries.

Within this global framework, different countries and cultures perceive brands in a different light. The audience's relationship to brands varies according to their exposure, ranging from scepticism at one end to a ready acceptance at the other. Newer markets, with more recent exposure to international brands, tend to associate brands with wealth and status, while holding on to traditions may be viewed as a sign of backwardness and lack of progress. Yet in the over-exposed brand cultures of the West, there is a sense that we need to return to simplicity and truth – or, at the other extreme, become 'unbranded'. This, according to some brand experts, has led to a surge in support for heritage brands (brands with a history). It also creates more room for the rise of the home-grown brand with a strong domestic identity. Historically, the increase in wealth within emerging economies has led to a homogeneous style and spending pattern in the new wealthy classes, as success is demontsrated through the association with traditional perceptions of wealth. Even this is changing as the BRIC nations form their own wealth indicators and success identities. Western wealth brands may or may not find a place within these new BRIC economies in the coming decade.

While global brands may dominate in size and wealth, there is evidence that the 'home-grown' brand may be on the increase. Firstly, buying home-grown brands offer an alternative to global brands – US footwear brand FUBU, which stands for For Us, By Us, was created as an alternative to the large sportswear brands, like Nike and Adidas. Secondly, the emergence of local brands and new ideas are a natural outcome of globalisation as people work and travel more, are exposed to other cultures and ideas, and use their experiences to create business opportunities back home.

There is equity in local brands and their development should be encouraged and supported. Domestic brands, which are not measured by their international impact, encourage innovation and can help boost local economies and growth. The home-grown brand can play on the stereotypes and traditions which create a natural affinity – even if they are inaccurate. Many brands have successfully used national identity and traits as promotional tools: there's surf-wear from Australia (Mambo and Quiksilver); technology from Japan; quality gentlemen's tailoring from London (Thomas Pink); perfume from France; bagels and doughnuts from the US (Krispy Kremes) and quality wool from New Zealand (Merino).

Playing on the theme of local identity can also help differentiate a brand internationally. The representation of the local culture can play on perceptions of that country: New Zealand is not considered a vodka-producing nation, yet it is exporting a home-grown brand, 42 Below, which uses the country's perception of purity and its location to promote the brand. Lager brands have often used the notion of national identity to differentiate themselves against similar products: Fosters promotes the Australian way of life; American beer, Budweiser, successfully played on American slang with its 'whassup' ad; Stella Artois has always used its Belgian roots to promote its beer; while Heineken prides itself on its Dutch family-owned history.

While home-grown brands may be on the increase, the challenge lies in competing with the large multinationals which can successfully undercut in price and quantity and limit competitor access to market. However, it is realistic for strong local brands to co-exist in harmony with strong global brands. A growing middle-class and increasing numbers of upper-class earners means people can afford choice: someone may choose to buy their cheese from the local farmers' market, their bread from the supermarket and a foreign car, but then use their national airline. Whether playing on an international or local field, brands need to be aware of the cultural differences and nuances in their markets, simply because of their global reach. The multinational business challenge is to provide the best of these local experiences while using the traditional buying power and resources of a large corporate body – to think globally but act locally.

"The multinational business challenge is to provide the best of these local experiences while using the traditional buying power and resources of a large corporate body – to think globally but act locally"

1: THE DISPARITY OF BRANDING GLOBALLY

Globalisation has led to brand ubiquity. Yet in every nation, and for each different culture, there is a different response to the brands and often a different way in which the brand markets itself. Brands like IKEA are proving hugely popular across the globe – from the UK, to the Middle East, to China – despite the disparity in the wealth and culture among these nations. In the over-branded West, there is now increasing popularity for the traditional brands which play on the past.

"Brand reputation is closely linked to how brands behave regarding the environment, labour and human rights "

THE ROLE MODEL

Until the late twentieth century brands tended to avoid playing politics. Most did not want to be seen as siding with a world-view or policy regarding issues relating to international affairs, the environment, labour practices or human rights. All this is changing.

There is an acknowledgement by many corporations behind the brands that they have a duty to society, to the future of the planet and the people in it. The motive may sound altruistic, but it is simply sound business sense. The world's future, according to environment experts and international organisations, is not looking too rosy: the global population increases at an alarming rate; there are huge divides between rich and poor; and climate change and poverty pose huge risks which could impede human progress. Not only this, but brands are responding to their audiences and their desire for brands to demonstrate responsible behaviour.

Global brands are obviously affected by the domestic issues in the countries in which they operate. The world's developing nations are often great sources of products and the world's natural resources will not last forever. These populations also offer an attractive market for brands, particularly when some products may have reached market saturation point in Western markets. While developing nations are often the most vulnerable, the risks affect everyone, and brand reputation is closely linked to how brands behave regarding the environment, labour and human rights.

Corporations have been actively encouraged by international organisations, like the United Nations, to form partnerships and alliances to tackle global issues such as poverty reduction, AIDS, and water shortages. The UN Global Compact was set up in 1999 by United Nations Secretary-General Kofi Annan, to encourage corporate participation in the areas of human rights, labour and the environment. Mary Robinson, the former UN High Commissioner for Human Rights, actively works with multinational corporations to get them to adhere to human rights principles in their working practices. Many familiar brand names were present at the international World Summit on Sustainable Development while many others participate in sector-based consortiums and initiatives to address specific issues that impact their industries: 12 multinationals from the oil and automobile industries have developed goals towards reaching 'sustainable mobility' by 2030, for the World Business Council for Sustainable Development (WBCSD). While these positive tactics also have their detractors (there are often insufficient reporting mechanisms and many view the tactics as public relations exercises without any substance), it is, at least, a positive tactic in encouraging action and best practice for brand behaviour.

It is highly likely that, in the near future, brands will increase their participation in global initiatives and these initiatives will extend to the smaller brand players. The international organisations, such as the United Nations and World Health Organization, have very little money and want to work with brands, and collaboration with these organisations can boost a brand's reputation, particularly within their own companies. It is also likely that, in future, corporations will be legally obliged to adhere to Corporate Social Responsibility (CSR) principles under international law, so many are now taking steps to report and regulate their own practices internally. The collapse and mis-management of Enron has led to regulations, like Sarbanes-Oxley, and laws being enforced in financial institutions. It is feasible that the environmental impact of brand development may well come under the same scrutiny from governmental monitoring agencies as sound fiscal management does now.

Tackling humanitarian and environmental issues can also open up business opportunities – renewable energy, clean fuels and hybrid cars are just some of the products that address environmental concerns.

1: THE LITERATURE OF BRANDING DESIGN

Branding is unavoidable. It is now no longer limited to products and commodities but to people and ideas. What was once viewed as an intangible, nebulous concept is now a real science. The extensive literature on every aspect of branding proves that it is a lucrative business, is fundamental to companies and fundamental to global and national economies.

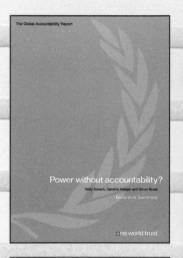

2: CORPORATE RESPONSIBILITY REPORTS

Responsible business is becoming integral to doing business. Many companies now release an annual Corporate Responsibility report which describes how companies respond to issues such as the environment and human rights as well as the company's involvement in its local communities. These reports are aimed at consumers as much as investors. At present, there is no regulation that demands that these reports are published and there is no consistency in reporting style, although there are external metrics that measure the impact of elements of corporate social responsibility. However, corporate responsibility is now a huge growth area and is becoming a necessary part of doing business.

THE FUTURE ROLE OF THE GRAPHIC DESIGNER

The expression of the brand through graphic design is one of its most powerful forms of communication. Graphic design makes the brand tangible and this makes the graphic designer's role a fundamentally important part of branding. It is the graphic designer who ensures that what is presented to the brand's audience is a genuine expression and communication of the brand. And the visual expression of the brand is a powerful means of communication.

Because of the importance of design to branding, the graphic designer should be involved and informed of the branding process from the outset: they need to understand the bigger picture of the branding process; they need to play a key role in defining the direction of the brand; they should, ideally, be involved in the brand development from conceptual ideas to tangible execution. This will make them a key decision maker in the creation of the brand.

The current trend towards the emotionalisation of branding offers huge opportunities for the graphic designer. It is the designer that can make emotions tangible through creating the style, tone and 'voice' for the brand. Brands also have to connect with a number of different audiences at a number of different levels. It is the designer who has the power to engage these audiences – and this is what so many brand-related campaigns often lack. While the brand audience will often drive the direction of brands, it is the graphic designer who, in the end, will bring the brand to life.

The reality is that it is marketing people with business backgrounds that currently dominate the senior positions in branding, particularly within the corporations. This may change over time if designers move into these roles, but it is more likely that designers will be working as part of a collaborative process, as branding is now becoming a discipline requiring a range of talent and skills. The graphic designer need not become a marketer; instead they are the creative expertise and talent that need to be working with the brand team on an equal footing. The changing of business structures to more fluid, collaborative structures offers designers a change to work in broader areas and apply their talent in different media and areas of work.

While branding is still about working within these structures, it is essentially driven by relevant, new ideas. Those ideas are brought to life by the creative process and a graphic designer is the lynchpin of that process.

THE FUTURE

"**People who decide the future talk about ideas. It is the graduate designers who will write the future**"

John Williamson, Wolff Olins

interview

Kristina Dryza, Trends Consultant: the future of branding

How do you see brands changing in the future?

In the West, brands will become less relevant as we find other means for self-expression. There'll be a focus on other 'organisations' that give us an identity, like our family and volunteering groups. Brands will become a means to an end – no longer will they be an end in themselves. There's a realisation that brands give little 'life' satisfaction – that is what people do.

What will be the relationship between the customer and the brand?

As more people begin to define their personal value systems, and live their lives according to those beliefs, it'll be easier for us as consumers to choose, relate and buy brands that serve our quest for a meaningful and purposeful existence. We know what brands fit into our world view, and those that don't.

Basically consumers are getting cleverer – we know most brands won't give us a sense of contentment or purpose. We won't expect a brand to give us that emotional fulfilment. We'll look elsewhere for it.

Do you believe that people are seeking authenticity and meaning from brands?

We're seeking authenticity and meaning from brands as we've yet to learn how to find it in ourselves. Losing our ego in the West is a difficult thing to do, but we're starting to shift our focus to personal assets, like family, friends and experiences, rather than material possessions. Branded goods don't show you love, or help you build your character. There's been a reinterpretation of authenticity to something deeper, and that is 'truth'.

How will this express itself in reality?

I think occasion branding will become more important in the coming years as it's all about truth. Occasions are expressions of time, energy and space; whether they're formal like a wedding or informal, say, meeting a girlfriend for a coffee. Brands that are connected to occasions – like food, music, stationery and linen brands – will become more relevant to consumers' lives as they'll be where laughter and love occur. We'll turn to brands that help us celebrate the rituals of life.

How does a brand address this search for truth? What does it mean for those working in branding?

Brands obviously need to be truthful themselves. At some point they'll have to go back to the essence of themselves – what it is that they stand for and why the brand exists.

But brands that act truthfully will be those that increase our enjoyment of life. They'll help us live simply, get us back to nature and help us to develop our character and potential. People are turning to those rare few brands that have a human component.

The brand marketers need to understand that people are craving freedom from social pressures and conformity. They need to try to understand an individual's varying definitions of happiness and introduce more sensitivity into the brand's communications. But they should not expect the brands to be the ultimate source of love for people.

"Brands will become a means to an end – no longer will they be an end in themselves. There's a realisation that brands give little 'life' satisfaction – that is what people do"

APPENDIX

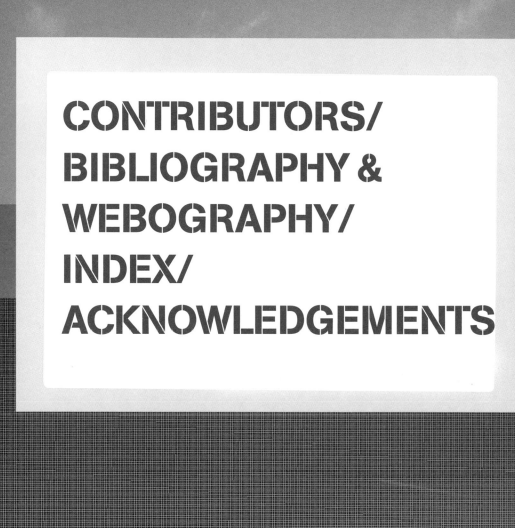

CONTRIBUTORS/
BIBLIOGRAPHY &
WEBOGRAPHY/
INDEX/
ACKNOWLEDGEMENTS

CONTRIBUTORS

Ralph Ardill

Ralph Ardill was Marketing and Strategic Planning Director of Imagination and the driving force behind the strategic development of Europe's No. 1 design and communication agency (est. 1978).

Following spells in the fashion, music and corporate identity industries, Ralph joined Imagination in 1993 and was quickly appointed to the board in 1995 having developed Imagination's (as then) new and pioneering Brand Experience offer.

On a day-to-day basis he is responsible for both the general marketing and strategic development of Imagination along with overseeing strategic planning and development work for key accounts including Guinness, Coca-Cola, Warner Brothers and the Ford Motor Company.

Ralph is also a recognised pioneer of experiential branding, design and communication. Having written and lectured extensively on these subjects around the world, he is proud to have led the development of the highly successful and critically acclaimed Guinness Storehouse brand experience in Dublin.

Simon Anholt

Simon Anholt is regarded as one of the world's leading specialists in the theory and practice of creating brand strategies for countries, cities and regions.

Anholt is currently the British Government's advisor on Public Diplomacy, and has advised the governments of several other countries, states and cities including Croatia, the Netherlands, Jamaica, Tanzania, Sweden, Botswana, Egypt, Ecuador, New Zealand, Switzerland, the Czech Republic and Slovenia, as well as the British Tourist Authority, the British Council, the Goethe Institute, the World Travel and Tourism Council, the World Bank, the United Nations, the World Intellectual Property Office, UNCTAD/WTO's International Trade Centre, the World Association of Investment Promotion Agencies, the World Technology Network and many other bodies and organisations worldwide. He is a Parliamentarian of the European Cultural Parliament and an internationally reputed public speaker. He is the founder and author of the Anholt-GMI Nation Brands Index.

Anholt is the author of the best-selling marketing book, *Another One Bites The Grass*, and Editor of the quarterly journal, *Place Branding*. He also guest-edited a Special Issue of the *Journal of Brand Management* in 2004, on the subject of Nation as Brand. His book on the role of brands in economic development, *Brand New Justice*, was published in 2003 and is now in its second edition. He is also a co-author of *Beyond Branding* (Kogan Page, 2003), *Brands and Branding* (*The Economist*, 2003), *Heritage and Identity – Shaping the Nations of the North* (Donhead, 2002), *Destination Marketing* (Butterworth Heinemann 2001/2003), *Brand America* (Cyan Books, 2004) and *Place Branding* (Kogan Page, 2005). His next book will be *Brand China*.

Shari Swan

Shari Swan is founder of Streative Branding, an Amsterdam-based international agency that helps multinationals connect more authentically with consumers, by adapting trend research to business strategy.

One of Shari's key concepts at Streative is called Project Mole – an underground network of global trend influencers and creators who provide commentary on the latest new products, marketing strategies and cultural shifts within their community. From this network of Moles, Streative produces customised trend reports for clients in a variety of engaging formats. The most popular format is the Molezine – a trends publication that presents multi-layered field and desk research and strategic brand recommendations.

Shari's current clients include Coca-Cola, Nike, drinks brand Bacardi, and telecoms companies O_2 and UPC.

Before Streative, Shari worked for over 14 years in branding, marketing, product development and trend research for multinationals including Reebok and fashion brand, Mexx. While at Reebok, Shari focused on the global 18–24 year old influencer market – an audience that is now key to consumer brands. She also lectured at the Amsterdam Fashion Institute.

As founder of Streative, Shari travels the world lecturing on trends and brand strategy, conducting innovation workshops, creating limited edition 'special reports' for clients, and consulting on brand and product development.

Iain Ellwood

Iain Ellwood is a Director of Strategy at Interbrand. He has 15 years of international experience, living and working in Japan, Hong Kong, the Netherlands and the United States as a marketing strategist for blue-chip companies. As a consultant he has led highly effective engagements for clients including Mitsubishi, BT, Guinness World Records, Swiss Airlines, J.P. Morgan, EDF Energy and Tesco.

Previously, Iain worked at Prophet Management Consultancy, where he led worldwide engagements for BP, Philips and UBS – covering a range of issues including customer proposition development, brand operationalisation and marketing strategy.

Iain's focus is on driving higher margins and profits through putting the customer at the heart of the organisation. This is achieved through effective and inspirational marketing strategy, brand operationalisation and touchpoint development. Working with CEOs, his extensive expertise and knowledge have shaped corporate strategy and customer-focused propositions as well as internal brand campaigns that motivate and educate employees.

He is the author of *The Essential Brand Book* (Kogan Page, 2001), which was translated into several languages, and a regular press commentator on marketing and branding issues for *The Economist*, The BBC, *Sky News* and numerous business magazines. Iain is a frequent international speaker on branding, innovation and communications. He also occasionally lectures on the MBA courses at London Business School (LBS).

Iain is a Member of the Chartered Institute of Marketing (MCIM); a Member of the Marketing Society and a Fellow of the Royal Society of Arts (FRSA).

He holds a Masters degree in Social Psychology from the University of London.

Tom Geismar

Tom Geismar is a founding principal of Chermayeff & Geismar Inc. and widely considered a pioneer of American corporate graphic design. During the past four decades he has designed more than a hundred corporate identity programmes.

His designs for Xerox, Chase Manhattan Bank, Best Products, Gemini Consulting, PBS, Univision, Rockefeller Center and, most notably, Mobil Oil have received worldwide acclaim.

Tom has also been responsible for many of the firm's exhibition designs and world's fair pavilions. Burlington Industries' 'The Mill' was a major NYC tourist attraction for 10 years, as today are the Ellis Island Immigration Museum, the Statue of Liberty Museum, and the recently opened Truman Presidential Library.

He has received all the major awards in the field, including one of the first Presidential Design Awards for helping to establish a national system of standardised transportation symbols.

Kristina Dryza

Kristina Dryza is a trend specialist, a freelance strategist and is currently the Contributing Consumer Insight Editor for Breaking Trends, a research consortium sponsored by Microsoft, BT, Virgin and J. Walter Thompson.

Kristina travels the world interviewing experts and innovators in their field (as well as the ordinary person on the street) to gain an insight into emerging social, cultural and consumer trends. She then interprets and translates these trends into commercial propositions.

Michael Hockney

In June 2003, Michael Hockney was appointed Chief Executive of D&AD. The D&AD is an international professional association and educational charity for commercial design and advertising.

Michael has an extensive career in advertising that began in 1972 at J. Walter Thompson. He later joined advertising agency, BMP, and became a member of the Executive Board in 1981. In 1987, Michael founded the BDDH Group, was Group Managing Director and chaired the group board until 1993.

For ten years he chaired the IPA Advertising Effectiveness Awards and in 1993 he joined the auction house, Christie's, as a member of the International Management Board with responsibility for marketing and strategy. He also worked as an adviser to the Ministry of Defence on a variety of non-operational issues concerning the British Army.

In 1999 Michael was appointed an Executive Director at the Institute of Chartered Accountants in England and Wales for two years. He later became an adviser to an international company on post-acquisition strategy before his appointment to the D&AD.

Michael holds fellowships from three professional institutions and has lectured on business management, strategy development and communications at universities, business schools and at the Police Staff College. He is also a Fellow of the Royal Society of Arts. He has a number of appointments outside of his professional work, including as a trustee of the Army Benevolent Fund and Christian Aid, a governor of the Army Foundation College and a board member of the English Chamber Orchestra.

CONTRIBUTORS

Dr Stefano L. Marzano

Stefano Marzano is Chief Executive Officer and Chief Creative Director of Philips Design. He was born in 1950 in Italy. He holds a doctorate in Architecture from the Milan Polytechnic Institute.

During the early part of his career, he worked on a wide range of assignments for several design firms. In 1978, he joined Philips Design in the Netherlands, as Design Leader for Data Systems and Telecommunication products.

He returned to Italy in 1982 to direct the Philips-Ire Design Centre (Major Domestic Appliances), becoming Vice President of Corporate Industrial Design for Whirlpool International (a joint venture of Whirlpool and Philips) in 1989.

In 1991, he took up his present post in the Netherlands. He is involved in a number of professional affiliations and regularly participates as a juror on international design competitions and speaks at conferences worldwide.

Ingelise Nielsen

Ingelise Nielsen is Head of Marketing Communications for IDEO in London and Munich. She studied at Copenhagen University and joined the company in its early days. She has been responsible for European press strategy since 1989. She creates materials and events for clients, and has coordinated the publication of two IDEO books: *Masters of Innovation* (both editions with Jeremy Myerson), and *Extra Spatial*.

IDEO is an international design and innovation company located in Europe and the USA. IDEO creates visible and tangible strategies for innovation and executes all aspects of design and development from conception through production. Clients include Procter & Gamble, BBC, Braun, GAP and Prada.

John Williamson

John Williamson is a Board Director at Wolff Olins. A brand expert with more than 25 years of experience in the industry, John has helped clients tackle many brand challenges in business contexts such as new market entry, pressure of commoditisation and increased competition, M&As (Mergers and Acquisitions), rationalisation of business portfolio, strategic refocus and business transformation.

His clients are some of the world's leading organisations including Akzo-Nobel, Athens 2004 Olympic Committee, Audi, Boehringer Ingelheim, ENI, E.ON, Lufthansa, Panasonic, Q8, Repsol, Saab, Shell, Unilever and Volkswagen.

John is frequently invited to comment in the media and his thinking is extensively quoted.

TV engagements include participation in the BBC's *Money Programme* and *Newsnight, Channel 4 News, Sky News*, CNBC's *Power Lunch* and *Europe Tonight* and various programmes on ZDF (Germany).

John comments frequently in the international press and has been invited to write for the *Financial Times* and leading trade magazines including Mergermarket.com, *The Daily Deal* and *Petroleum Economist*.

John is also experienced in addressing diverse groups, formats and nationalities. He has spoken at the 1999 World Economic Forum in Davos, events and conferences organised by Dow Jones, Dresdner Kleinwort Wasserstein, Gartner, the US Association of National Advertisers, Euromoney, Infoma and the Financial Times.

With thanks also to Karen Rice Gardiner, Frank Heemsoth, Jonathan Ive, Mike Tiedy and everyone else who contributed their expertise.

BIBLIOGRAPHY & WEBOGRAPHY

David A. Aaker, *Building Strong Brands*, Simon & Schuster, UK, 2002

David A. Aaker, *Brand Leadership*, Free Press, UK, 2002

Joel Bakan, *The Corporation: The Pathological Pursuit of Profit and Power*, Constable and Robinson, UK, 2004

John Berger, *Ways of Seeing*, Penguin Books Ltd., UK, 1990

Alain de Botton, *Status Anxiety*, Penguin Books Ltd., UK, 2005

Stuart Crainer and Des Dearlove, *The Ultimate Book of Business Brands*, Capstone Publishing Ltd., UK, 1999

The Economist, Rita Clifton and John Simmons, *Brands and Branding*, Economist Books, UK, 2003

Richard Florida, *The Rise of the Creative Class*, Basic Books, UK, 2004

Malcolm Gladwell, *The Tipping Point*, Abacus, UK, 2002

Nicholas Ind (Ed.), *Beyond Branding*, Kogan Page, UK, 2005

Naomi Klein, *No Logo*, Flamingo, UK, 2001

Felicity Lawrence, *Not on the Label*, Penguin Books Ltd., UK, 2004

Wally Olins, *On Brand*, Thames & Hudson Ltd., UK, 2004

Alissa Quart, *Branded*, Arrow, 2003

Kevin Roberts, *Lovemarks: The Future Beyond Brands*, PowerHouse Cultural Entertainment Books, USA, 2004

John Simmons, *The Invisible Grail*, Texere Publishing, USA, 2003

Mary Spillane, *Branding Yourself*, Pan Books, UK, 2000

Helen Vaid, *Branding (Design Directories Series)*, Cassell Illustrated, UK, 2003

Alina Wheeler, *Designing Brand Identity*, John Wiley & Sons Inc., UK, 2003

Brand Management (Harvard Business Review paperback series), Harvard Business School Press, USA, 1999

----

www.brandchannel.com (produced by Interbrand)

www.economist.com

www.guardian.co.uk

www.hbr.com (Harvard Business Review online)

www.mckinseyquarterly.com

www.news.bbc.co.uk

www.trendwatching.com

INDEX

There are many people who have contributed to the creation of this book and deserve a massive thanks. These include those who helped provide images and interviews, including the press and legal people. I especially want to thank my friends and professional contacts who helped out with brand observations around the world, contacts and writing advice: Kristina Dryza, Catherine Somers, Maryam Teschke, Paul White, Emma Moloney, Kym McConnell, Suzanne Smith, Karin Tang, Laura Boutwell, David Hope-Johnstone, Paul van Berkel and Vanessa Markwell, to name a few.

Many thanks to all the people from companies and brand agencies who took time out to be interviewed and offer sage words for the book. Britt Iverson, Kristen Davis, Stephen Cheliotis, Iain Ellwood, Sally Crabb, Stuart Jane, Ralph Ardill, Jonathan Ive, John Williamson, Mike Tiedy, Tom Geismar, Karen Rice Gardiner, Charlie Graves, Guy Slattery, Ingelise Nielsen, Michael Hockney, Shari Swan, Stefano Marzano, Frank Heemsoth, Christoph Baumgarten, Simon Anholt, John Blyth, Duncan Blake, Dan Germain, Adam Scott, Ben Whittman, Sameera Hassan, Jo Farrelly, Stephanie Fletcher, Reinier Evers, Patsy Youngstein, Jeroen Bruins Slot, Martyn Allen, Chris Sauve and Jennifer Goldfinch.

On the image side, thanks to Sarah Jameson and Natalie Hunt who had the tough task of helping to source images, permissions and approvals. Particular thanks to Chloe Couchman, Kerry Olsen, Federico Banos-Lindner, Tom Trinkle, Carmen Marrero, Luke Disney, Anya Calcott, David Hill, Linda Nylind, Ivon Mersmans and Pim Buissant who went beyond the call of duty to provide great images.

And finally, my deepest gratitude to Steve Everhard, a former Apple client, who provided valuable insight, support and input into the book. Thanks also go to Jonathan Baldwin who wrote the strategic overview pages and a special thanks to the Editors at AVA Publishing who made this book possible – Natalia Price-Cabrera, Caroline Walmsley, Renee Last and Kate Shanahan – and to the Publisher, Brian Morris.